British Discovery Literature and the Rise of Global
Commerce

British Discovery Literature and the Rise of Global Commerce

Anna Neill

First published 2002 by
PALGRAVE
Houndmills, Basingstoke, Hampshire RG21 6XS and
175 Fifth Avenue, New York, N.Y. 10010
Companies and representatives throughout the world

PALGRAVE is the new global academic imprint of
St. Martin's Press LLC Scholarly and Reference Division and
Palgrave Publishers Ltd (formerly Macmillan Press Ltd).

ISBN 0–333–97374–7

This book is printed on paper suitable for recycling and
made from fully managed and sustained forest sources.

A catalogue record for this book is available
from the British Library.

Library of Congress Cataloging-in-Publication Data
Neill, Anna, 1965–
  British discovery literature and the rise of global commerce/Anna Neill.
    p. cm
  Includes bibliographical references and index.
  ISBN 0-333-97374-7
  1. Great Britain – Commerce – History. 2. Merchant marine – Great Britain –
History. 3. Merchants – Great Britain – History. 4. Explorers – Great Britain –
History. 5. International trade – History. 6. Travelers' writings, English. I. Title.
HF3505.2 .N45 2002
382'.094–dc21

10 9 8 7 6 5 4 3 2 1   2001056126
11 10 09 08 07 06 05 04 03 02

Printed and bound in Great Britain by
Antony Rowe Ltd, Chippenham, Wiltshire

Contents

v

List of Illustrations

Acknowledgements

Thanks go to all the friends and colleagues without whom this book could not have been written. I owe a special debt to those good friends who tirelessly read and re-read chapters of the manuscript, and who allowed me to believe it would all come together in the end: Giselle Anatol, Katie Conrad, Byron Caminero-Santangelo, Dorice Elliott, Joe Harrington, and most of all, Gil Harris. I am also extremely grateful for the generous guidance of David Bergeron, Laura Brown, Rod Edmond, Richard Hardin, Jocelyn Harris, Jim Hartman, Jonathan Lamb, Peter Mancall, Michael Neill, Felicity Nussbaum, Bridget Orr, Neil Saccamano, Janet Sharastanian, Marjorie Swann and the anonymous readers both at Palgrave and at Oxford University Press.

Portions of the book were researched at the British, Newberry, Huntington, Kenneth Spencer Research, and William Andrews Clark Memorial Libraries. At all of these institutions, the bibliographical and curatorial staff helped me to track down books and manuscripts for which I sometimes only had half references. I am especially grateful to Jim Akerman and Robert Karrow at the Newberry, Jennifer Schaffner at the Clark, Stephen Tabor at the Huntington, and Richard Clement, James Helyar, Karen Cook and Rob Melton at the Spencer. Thanks too to Ross Wilson and to Barbara McCorkle, who generously gave me access to her private collection of special geographies.

Earlier versions of portions of this book appeared in other publications and I wish to thank the editors for permission to reproduce material from the following articles. The first is 'South Seas Trade and the Character of Captains,' forthcoming in Nussbaum, Felicity A. (ed.), *The Global Eighteenth Century* (The Johns Hopkins University Press, Fall 2002). This material is reprinted by permission of The Johns Hopkins University Press. The second, 'Buccaneer Ethnography: Nature, Culture and Nation in the Journals of William Dampier' appeared in *Eighteenth-Century Studies*, vol. 33, no. 2 (1999–2000), pp. 165–80. The third, 'Crusoe's Farther Adventures: Discovery, Trade, and the Law of Nations' appeared in *The Eighteenth Century: Theory and Interpretation*, vol. 38, no. 3 (Fall 1997), pp. 213–30. I also wish to thank the Newberry and Spencer Research Libraries for permission to reproduce images from volumes in their collections, and the British Library for permission to quote from ms. 3236 in the Sloane Collection.

This book would have been much harder to write without the fellowship assistance I received from the Newberry Library, the University of California, Los Angeles, and from both the Hall Center for the Humanities and the General Research Fund at the University of Kansas. Along with research time, several of the fellowships also provided me with invaluable administrative support. The staff at the Center for Seventeenth- and Eighteenth-Century Studies at the University of California, Los Angeles, and at the Hall Center were very generous with their time and helped me with every kind of problem.

I also want to acknowledge my debt to those people in my life who, although they were not readers of the manuscript, saw me through the various hurdles that accompanied the central and closing stages of the project. They all, in different ways, made it possible to keep going. Kirk Branch, Marta Caminero-Santangelo, Jill Cassid, Elizabeth Duffy, Tracy Floreani, Stu Olsen, Cotten Seiler, Lee Skinner and my brother, Luke Worner were all closer to the project than they probably know. Finally, I thank the members of my family in New Zealand – Michael, Tuataroa, Te Ao Huri, Priscilla and Dermot Neill – who are an enduring source of support and inspiration for each new endeavour, however far away from home it takes me. This book is dedicated to them.

ANNA NEILL

1
Introduction: Commerce, Society and the Sea Voyage

Eighteenth-century British travellers have been much talked about in recent decades. The journal records of, among others, merchants, explorers, pirates, ordinary seamen, press-gang victims, slaves, slave dealers, passengers, indentured servants and convicts have provided a rich archive for investigating the discursive character of colonial relationships and of imperial expansion in the period of Britain's rise to global commercial pre-eminence.[1] Many of these studies have shown how metropolitan identities are shaped by exchanges, observations, misperceptions or acts of resistance that take place in 'peripheral' regions of the globe. They have argued that imperialism has not simply been a matter of a powerful culture exploiting, eradicating or transforming a less powerful one, but rather that cultural and political transformations take place on both sides of the colonial equation. Travellers – those who literally stand between cultures and places – can therefore be seen either as agents of or as antagonists to the technologies of imperialism. Sometimes they assist and sometimes they confound the commercial aspirations of colonizing states. They can belong to what Paul Gilroy, following Deleuze and Guattari, has identified as a 'rhizomorphous' transnational community, as they form subterranean lines of connection and modes of collective organization that defy the social hierarchies determined both by states and by the world economy.[2] On the other hand, they can be loyal representatives of imperial nations, seeking out new markets and new territories for plantation and settlement. Sometimes they can function as sites of rhetorical excess where the transmission of colonial ideology between core and periphery breaks down; at other times they can act as communicators of cultural value across time and space or as agents of an 'anti-conquest'[3] in which science takes the place of direct coercion in assisting the global ambitions of powerful commercial states.

This recognition that the traveller may be either friend or foe to commercial imperialism is not, however, new. The curious double status of the traveller, the unpredictable nature of the sea voyage which may turn civilized men into savages or renegades into civilized men, is in part the creation of seventeenth- and eighteenth-century histories of sociability in which civilization and commercial modernity were closely linked to fixed geographical location. These philosophical histories married a new scientific emphasis on the observable diversity of natural and cultural phenomena across the world (and the probable influence of environment on human behaviour) with a jurisprudence that considered certain aspects of human nature to be governed by universal laws. Influenced by the methodologies of new scientific investigation, they tried to combine the representation of a diverse body of particulars assembled through observation and experiment with general, conjectural ideas about the nature and history of human societies. The European traveller is doubly implicated in this endeavour. By gathering data about remote countries and peoples, he (less often she) enables the universalizing abstractions that make it possible to rank societies on a scale that runs from savage and nomadic to civilized and settled yet, at the same time, at an enormous distance from home and hence subject to the affecting influences of the strange and the barbaric, he might easily turn his back on the civilized world. On the one hand, travellers provide the scientific community with essential data about non-European peoples and customs, and thus the raw evidence that 'better' societies are more settled and more capable of a regular commerce. On the other hand, lacking any fixed location, and gradually less and less attached to their country of origin, they may also threaten to reproduce the behavioural characteristics of members of nomadic societies and to abandon the moral and civil codes of the communities into which they were born. They are at once agents and objects of scientific speculation, and they are just as likely to become enemies as servants of a 'civilized' commercial state.

Peter Linebaugh and Marcus Rediker have already shown that the accumulation of merchant capital in the early modern period also stimulated the formation of a radical proletariat in the maritime community. The ship, they argue, 'became both an engine of capitalism in the wake of the bourgeois revolution in England *and* a setting of resistance'.[4] This book will examine how such historical links between acts of nomadic resistance on the one hand, and the accretion of imperial wealth on the other, presented a problem for theories of social order and social development. Travel narratives, it will argue, may at once illustrate the powerful reach and increasing sophistication of nascent global capitalism and the 'civilized' world, and at the same time animate a certain kind of countermodernity; one in which the very experience of increased mobility and exposure to the non-European world creates new social identities and forms of behaviour that are anathematic to commercial imperialism.

In a new edition of *Anthropology as Cultural Critique*, George Marcus and Michael Fischer describe the transformation of anthropology in the late twentieth century from the investigation of 'other' discrete societies to the exploration of cultural interstices and spaces of negotiation that are created by newly global and infinitely complex networks of communication and overlapping spheres of interest or skill. Such spheres, they point out, are not defined by the boundaries of the nation state or traditional communities.[5] Although my study focuses on a period in which the concepts of both national identity and state sovereignty were becoming increasingly useful for western Europeans trying to understand their relationship to other peoples, I suggest that globalization also played a part in these much earlier definitions of self and other. The pressures exerted on, in particular, maritime travellers by the demands of commercial states created modes of allegiance with, and forms of reflection about, other communities that chafed against the classificatory schemes of natural and political philosophy. While some travellers were able to use their experiences and observations for national commercial interests and thereby reconfirm their loyalty to their own country, others left records that situated them, as James Clifford phrases it, 'between ... the boundaries of civilizations, cultures, classes [and] races'.[6] In an era when civility was defined to a significant degree through the achievement of statehood, such fluid identities and modes of intercultural exchange signified a return to primitive, violent and unproductive ways of life.

The paradox of travel in what is properly the first era of global commerce[7] is that it at once demonstrates how easily social beings can become, according to the definitions of the time, de-socialized, and yet at the same time enables the modernization of cultures. This modernization takes place through the increase of capital in the metropolitan regions of the world and through the spread of 'civilized' manners in the 'peripheral' regions. In this latter capacity, travel, as Eric Leed has put it, itself 'creates socialities.'[8] It is travel that makes possible the communication between and the mapping and identification of territories, things and peoples. Only through the experience of passage does it become possible to develop 'a sense of distance between an observing self and a world of objects'[9] and, accordingly, the distinction between members and non-members of a given group and between 'civilized' and 'savage', commercial and pre-commercial peoples. Such distinctions in turn make it possible, through contact and education, to 'rescue' isolated peoples from their supposedly brutal and savage lives. Travel is therefore a condition of deracination and cultural disorientation, a source of identity based on itinerary rather than bounded location,[10] that perversely also makes it possible to chart the material progress of human societies. The sailing voyage, in particular, because it frequently involved a journey of enormous distance and because during the seventeenth and eighteenth centuries it was invariably an expedition of discovery (even if its immediate goals were commercial or military), combined the promise of a better-mapped and ultimately more civilized world of countries and cultures with the threat of sailors' recalcitrance. Weary, hungry and alienated members of a crew might mutiny or desert. 'Lost' sailors might go native or turn into pirates.

Travel, science and the state

This threat of errancy – of turning one's back forever on home and on duty to family and country – is particularly charged, I am arguing, in an early imperialist and mercantilist era in which commerce is formally joined to the national interest. Such ties, it should be said, are in evidence well before the period I investigate in this book. England's efforts to secure a foothold in the Iberian-dominated, developing world economy of the sixteenth century (which linked the Americas to Asia and Europe) involved centralizing the economy according to the principles of a balance of trade, or the accumulation of wealth from trade at the expense of other nations. Combined with a centralization of *power* in the state after the Reformation, this emphasis on the accumulation of the nation's treasure elevated commerce from a local to a national concern.[11] For its part, the state guaranteed royal charters to trading companies such as the Merchant Adventurers of England (which was involved in seeking out a North East or North West passage to Asia and the Pacific) and the East India Company, and supported (sometimes informally or covertly) the expeditions of discovery and attempts at illicit trade and reprisals against the Spanish made by John Hawkins and Francis Drake. Elizabeth I also awarded letters patent to adventurers such as Humphry Gilbert and Walter Ralegh to search out territories in America that had not yet been claimed by any European prince. She did so largely in response to the advocacy of those such as John Dee, Richard Hakluyt and Ralegh himself, who saw colonization and the expansion of trade as the solution to England's economic difficulties in the second half of the century.

Compiled in these twin contexts of nascent imperialism and an emerging national commerce, Richard Hakluyt's *The Principal Navigations, Voyages, Traffiques and Discoveries of the English Nation* hero-icized those travellers whose 'high courage and singular activitie' had enabled 'the search and discoverie of the most unknown quarters of the world'.[12] But it also suggests that the grandeur the nation soon to accrue from these discoveries can be attributed not just to acts of discovery but also to the operations of commerce. *The Principal Navigations* includes acts of corporation, records of money, weights and measures used in different countries, documentation of the places where particular commodities can be found, and letters patent. Hakluyt, as Richard Helgerson has shown, recognized English merchants as the heroes of national strength and economic growth.[13] In the Epistle Dedicatory to the second edition, Hakluyt emphasizes the economic imperative of 'find[ing] ample vent of our woollen cloth, the natural commoditie of this our realme' (1:lxxii) and points out the advantage of Virginia for absorbing the superfluity of English labour and, in the preface to this edition, he highlights how English travellers have helped to expand trade. The collection, he suggests, makes legible the national coherence and imperial potential of England as, with the help of geography and 'chronologie', the 'torn and scattered limbs of our ancient and late navigation by sea, our voyages by land and traffiques of merchandise by both' are 'drawn into due time and place' (1:xxxix). For Samuel Purchas in 1625, the collection of voyages presents an even more expanded potential as it enables its royal dedicatee to see 'the merchant coasting more shores and islands for commerce than his progenitors have heard of ... [and shows] the mariner making other seas a ferry and the widest ocean a strait to his discovering attempts'.[14] Purchas, like Hakluyt, recognizes the national service performed by travellers who witness and report on the enormous diversity of commodities and cultures in the world 'dispose[d] by Providence' (1:xxxix).

The characterization of travellers as loyal subjects who risk life and limb for the sake of national (and Protestant) glory – and for commer-cial advantage as much as for personal gain – comes self-consciously to life in the career of Sir Walter Ralegh, whose expedition to Guiana he hoped would restore him to royal favour. In *The Discoverie of the large and bewtiful Empire of Guiana* [1596], he endeavors to 'seek the profit and honour of her Maiesty and the English nation'[15]and secure the 'great good, and rich trade which England maie be possessed of'.[16] Taking advantage of a well-established political rhetoric that linked the security of the nation and its imperial future to the Queen's virgin body, he remarks that Guiana is a country that, never sacked, 'hath yet her maydenhead' (73), and that it is therefore rich in commodities, including gold. Once it becomes colonial territory, however, its virtues will accrue to the English nation and neighbouring countries will 'heare the name of a virgin, which is not only able to defend her owne territories and her neighbors, but also to inuade and conquere so great Empyres and so farre remoued' (76). His adventures are unequivocally linked to England's imperial might and her consequent winning of a favourable balance of power.

The balance of power, however, was inextricably tied to the balance of trade as the account of Virginia written by Ralegh's servant, Thomas Harriot, infers. In his report, dedication 'to the honour and benefit of our nation'[17] takes the form of describing in detail the region and the character of its inhabitants in order to encourage settlement and plantation in England's first colony. The careful cataloguing of Virginia's 'merchantable commodities' (and of the native people who inhabit it) in *A briefe and true Report* contributes to what Purchas was later to describe with the empiricist emphasis of reformed scientific methodology as 'natural and universall knowledge in the diversified varieties which the various seas and lands in the world produce, seeming as exceptions to general rules' (1:xliii). In his attention to the diverse particulars of the natural and human environment, Harriot provides taxonomic documentation of this environment, rather than a narrative of his adventures. He offers his countrymen detailed information about the region that, like John White's 'ethnographic' illustrations of the native culture (which accompanied Harriot's text in Theodore de Bry's *America*), promoted further development of the colony.[18]

As the nation emerged as an imperial entity, then, science was yoked to commercial enterprise. Institutionally, this yoking began at Gresham College in London, which emphasized the value of new scientific ideas and empirical method, and which challenged the classical curriculums at Oxford and Cambridge. The fact that Gresham and other London locations for scientific learning served more than a learned elite (classes were conducted in English rather than Latin and were accessible to anyone who could read) had everything to do with these institutions' relationship with the merchant community. Gresham was founded by a merchant and financier and built on revenue from the Royal Exchange. It was erected in the spirit of mathematicians and astronomers such as John Dee, Robert Recorde and Thomas Digges, whose work provided practical and theoretical knowledge for middle-class merchants and artisans.[19] The connections that the Gresham community forged between science and commercial activity provided the foundation for Bacon's projects for the advancement of learning among men in general: a learning that promised to forge connections between scientific knowledge and those who were directly involved in mercantile enterprises, from merchants to craftsmen. Bacon's cosmopolitan emphasis on the creation of universal sciences and the cooperation of those involved in them across national borders was thus able to sit comfortably with an economic nationalism that recognized the future glory of the nation in its commerce.

In this intellectual climate, reliable travel narratives and the information about places and people that they provided became increasingly valuable. This idea of the traveller as a collector of data from remote parts was formalized in seventeenth-century accounts of the methods and ends of scientific observation. Travellers, Bacon suggested, provide information about 'many things in nature ... which may let in new light upon philosophy', and the expansion of the material globe that they make possible, he argued, needs to be matched by an extension of the boundaries of the intellectual globe.[20] In Thomas Sprat's *The History of the Royal Society*, the scientific discoveries rooted in observation are shown to be the profit of a division of labour according to which 'some must gather, some must bring, some separate [and] some examine'.[21] Philosophers, historians and natural scientists depend upon the information brought to them by those who visit different parts of the globe, for

> whoever shall soberly profess to be willing to put their shoulders under the burden of so great an enterprise so as to represent to mankind the whole fabrick, the parts, the causes, the effects of nature: ought to have their eyes in all parts, and to receive information from every quarter of the earth: they ought to have a constant universal intelligence: all discoveries should be brought to them.[22]

In this formulation, travellers perform the key labours of 'gathering' and 'bringing'. Knowledge is produced in the accumulation of data and at the same time in the generation of abstractions out of deracinated particulars: the two forms of labour that belong to what Mary Poovey has identified as the creation of the modern fact.[23] It is also worth noticing that facts are generated as a *whole world* is opened up to the eye of the philosopher. Science can only create general truths out of a variety of particulars by investigating the entire physical globe. Travellers thus acquire their increasingly respectable status from the role that they play in the newly global outlook of science.

Yet as a character in narratives of social improvement, the traveller is not so honored. In accounts of the progress of manners and the rise of social institutions, the roving life often appears as the lowest stage in human civilization. Such accounts inevitably put a great deal of emphasis on the historical moment at which a people abandons its nomadic way of life and forms settled communities and laws. For Samuel Pufendorf in 1672, human lives become properly structured, and property becomes secure at the point that people begin to 'bear some settled relations to one another' and thus are able to govern their actions by a fixed moral method.[24] Actions driven by 'a wild and wandering impulse' (117) violate natural law, the providential juris-prudence that aligns the history of human civilizations with the ratio-nal, and for Pufendorf, social nature of man.[25] Such actions mimic the 'vagabond life' that humans lived 'like the brutes about them' before natural order was institutionalized in the civil state (457). One hundred years later, Lord Kames identified patriotism as the artefact of settled life. Like other historians of the Scottish Enlightenment, includ-ing Adam Smith, he divided human communities into the 'four stages' of hunter-gatherer, pastoral, agricultural and commercial.[26] Feeling for those who share the same national territory, he argued, is an affection that arises when people are intimately connected by shared economic activity. Hence 'the sense of a patria begins to unfold itself when a people leaves off wandering to settle upon a territory which the com-munity can call its own'.[27] Smith concurs that the natural self-interest which drives humans to exchange goods also encourages them to look beyond the mere self-sufficiency of the nomadic hunter's life and to consider the more efficient production of surplus through the division of labour which is more successfully accomplished in a settled com-munity.[28] In each case, nomadism represents the poorest and most miserable of the social states.

Although most maritime travellers in the long eighteenth century were tied to foreign trade in some fashion, whether as merchants, mer-chant seamen, naval officers or seamen serving in commercial wars, or explorers sponsored by the state to investigate new territories and markets, the very *act* of heading out to sea represented a form of sever-ance from the communities of family and nation that uncomfortably resembled a return to the pre-civil, 'vagabond' state. Jonathan Lamb has recently argued that the traveller-eyewitness in eighteenth-century discovery literature was looked upon with suspicion by a public that had begun to link tales of encounter with the alluring fictions behind disastrous capitalist experiments such as the South Sea Bubble. He proposes that the dependence of experimental science on the authenticating eyewitness rendered it vulnerable to the Hobbesian objection that, removed from the restraints of civil society, the travelling 'ethnographer' would be imaginatively subject only to the sensible pressure which objects exerted on him, and would thus become a less-than-reliable authority.[29] The chapters that follow investigate a range of narratives in which travellers venture so far from home that they become not just unreliable but dangerous, threatening the integrity of the state even as they play their part in the accumulation of wealth and knowledge that this state has sponsored. Whether outlaw adventurers who journey 'beyond the line', independent entrepreneurs who fail to bring home the riches they accumulate, or maritime workers whose affection for their country becomes dangerously weakened under the influence of foreign customs and climates, these travellers all in different ways threaten to reverse the progressive history that has brought about security and opulence.

This disturbingly antisocial behaviour among sea travellers is at one level disciplined directly by the state in its prosecution of piracy and mutiny. At another level, however, the reform of maritime errancy takes place discursively as renegade travellers begin to assert their own scientific authority, representing themselves not merely as accidental observers of foreign countries and customs, but also as social or economic analysts of the data they have compiled. Among the texts I examine in the following chapters, the journals of William Dampier, pirate-turned-ethnographer, illustrate precisely this kind of transformation. So, too, do Daniel Defoe's discovery narratives, each of which parallels the spiritual reform of the criminal or irresponsible hero with his capacity to make social and economic calculations about the people and places he has explored. Another example is to be found in the journal of James Morrison, one of the mutineers on board His Majesty's Ship *Bounty* who was captured in Tahiti and returned to England for court martial. Following his account of the injustices the crew suffered at the hands of their captain, he provided a detailed account of the (he suggests) technologically backward culture of the Tahitians. This account, much more persuasively than his defence, demonstrated his loyalty to the state by positioning him as an apologist for British intervention in the Tahitian economy. Together, these show how the development of a field of investigation – ethnography or political economy – belongs as much to what Michel Foucault calls a 'discursive formation' as it does to the accumulation of knowledge about a particular set of phenomena. Observable facts about places and peoples can only be assembled as a body of information about a particular subject, Foucault argues, through 'the interplay of the rules that make possible the appearance of objects during a given period of time'.[30] In the seventeenth and eighteenth centuries, the needs of a more centralized state to acquire influence over distant geographies and to control the actions of subjects who explored them constituted one such set of rules and state patronage of the sciences another. The facts that travellers collect from around the world are therefore combined into a body of knowledge at the same moment that their 'authors' are transformed from maritime renegades into loyal subjects and men of science.

This transformation therefore depended upon the uniform quality of the evidence gathered about human communities in far-flung corners of the globe. The reform of the traveller had to coincide with the creation of a single readable history in which human communities could be assessed and ranked on a single scale of development. Efforts to achieve such uniformity might be seen to have their origins in the earliest imperial literature about the Americas. Stephen Greenblatt has argued that what Columbus observed about the Indians' nomadic habits enabled him to assert the radical differences between primitive self and civilized other. Columbus's account of the Indies represented a cultural-imperialist departure from the less stable discursive mode of *Mandeville's Travels*, he argues, since the latter described a bewildering medley of marvellous objects that forced the traveller into a relativistic understanding of the world. The effect in Mandeville's text, Greenblatt suggests, was to uproot the traveller permanently from his home and to deprive him of an original point of origin by means of which he could assert his difference from the strange and the primitive. Columbus, on the other hand, used wonder as a rhetorical instrument of possession that appropriates objects of astonishment to an imperial gaze. For Columbus, wonder becomes an experience not of sublime confusion, but of renaming and cultural re-mapping, thus making it possible to take possession of territories that are legally already those of another people.[31]

Greenblatt's distinction between relativistic and possessive wonder suggests that the discovery and possession of the new world is coterminous with a scientific globalism that can make sense of strange peoples and customs according to a hierarchical and universalizing conception of nature and human societies. This is what Lorraine Daston and Katharine Park have called 'a new epistemology of facts'.[32] In the seventeenth century, Daston and Park show, marvels ceased to be understood as anomalous or preternatural phenomena retrieved from the margins of the world and instead became objects of systematic inquiry. Bacon's reform of natural philosophy transformed curious objects into observable particulars which, through a painstaking method of ordering, could be included as evidence in the formation of axioms or universals. Later, during the Enlightenment, under the regime of the 'anti-marvellous', wonders were ghettoized as the products of the superstitious minds of enthusiasts, primitive peoples and the ignorant.[33] In this sceptical spirit, travellers tales were viewed with suspicion as unreliable and prone to exaggeration; guilty, many complained, of fabulous and romantic inventions or distorted representations of the natural and human phenomena they encountered. Widely considered as the inventions of traveller-narrators, for example, the natives of Patagonia continued to be described through the eighteenth century as giants, up to ten feet in height; and traveller-cartographers such as the Baron Lahontan who charted new regions of the Mississippi were exposed as frauds.[34] Such scepticism then motivated fictional voyage narratives like Swift's *Gulliver's Travels* which used the improbable, the marvellous or the singular to highlight the limits of scientific methodology and imperial perception.

In the effort to reduce the epistemological impact of the fantastic and the marvellous, eighteenth-century philosophy emphasized that individual traveller's tales only acquired scientific value once they were combined with other evidence so as to form general principles. In the transformation of diverse particulars into general laws, Hume argues in *An Enquiry Concerning Human Understanding*, 'the constant and universal principles of human nature [made] by showing men in all varieties of circumstances' become the means by which 'we may form our observations and become acquainted with the regular springs of human action and behavior.'[35] This argument is confirmed by John Millar who, in *The Distinction of Ranks*, argued that particulars recorded by maritime travellers may provide the material necessary to reach such general conclusions about the nature of society and government. While some travellers may not possess the 'character and situation in life' to make them reliable sources of evidence for the stage of civilization that human beings have achieved in different parts of the world, he suggests, the number and variety of their narratives confers on them a kind of collective authority 'upon which we may depend with security'.[36] He then invites historians and philosophers to study information about the manners of different nations with the premise that 'man is everywhere the same', and by so doing to calculate 'those institutions and modes of government which appear most worthy of being adopted'.[37] Dugald Stewart explored the interplay between observation and reasoning in his suggestion that the 'detached facts' provided by travellers 'may frequently serve as landmarks to our speculations', and even that 'sometimes our conclusions a priori may tend to confirm the credibility of facts, which on a superficial view appeared to be doubtful or incredible'.[38] The detachment both of the traveller and the facts that he brings back from the 'most remote and unconnected quarters of the globe' is therefore corrected by 'a philosophical commentary on the history of law and manners' (lv). The labour of extracting universalizing abstractions from unreliable and unconnected particulars is first and foremost political, Stewart argues, because it enables philosophers to determine 'general principles which ought to run through and be the foundation of the laws of all nations' (lxxxiv).

However, where travellers took on several tasks in the division of scientific labour, becoming natural historians or conjectural philosophers as well as observer-recorders, they were also involved in the excavation of general principles of rule. Any sustained analysis of the material and moral culture of foreign peoples therefore renews the traveller's loyalty to the state by investing both the subject and the object of investigation in the evolution of settled society and secure forms of government. In the process of reinventing himself as a national subject, the traveller's investigation of savage societies confirms the arguments made by historians of sociability: namely, that improvements in the mode and efficiency of production (as well as the invention of property) are intimately connected to the emergence and consolidation of state authority. Such observations put this kind of traveller in the company of philosophers such as Hugo Grotius, Pufendorf and John Locke, all of whom argued that, according to the laws of nature, human beings will form settled communities, cultivate land, create private property, and contract to obey laws and governments in order to protect that property.[39] Whether as 'gatherers and bringers' or as 'separators and examiners' (in Sprat's formulation), travellers often find themselves at the centre of philosophical debate about both the origins and progress of society and the conditions of such knowledge. Voyage narratives often address questions about the relationship between modes of subsistence, forms of government and degrees of social happiness even as they illustrate the complex problem of how to combine observed particulars into general and reliable rules.

Government, manners and the social knowledge of travellers

The body of knowledge to which travellers contributed about the evolution of civil communities was particularly valuable to seventeenth- and eighteenth-century theories of the state and society. With more emphasis on the power of government to *create,* rather than simply to protect, social relationships, Hobbes argued that a society where rela- tionships with one's fellows are mediated by property ownership and complex forms of exchange with others requires the protection of the peace-making, judicial and military power of a sovereign.[40] In *The Spirit of the Laws,* Montesquieu argued that 'the spirit of commerce produces in men a certain feeling for exact justice'.[41] Among the Scots, even the anticontractualist David Hume linked the evolution of material culture to the emergence of political society and the regular administration of justice.[42] Lord Kames, John Millar and Adam Smith all made equations between the recognition of property in more advanced societies and the evolution of complex and settled forms of government.[43] The state and the laws that it enforces, in other words, are, for all of these writers, designed to address the social needs of subjects or potential subjects.

As Hannah Arendt has shown, this formulation of general principles of law and government via a history of manners represented a shift in emphasis in political thought from the life devoted to public matters to the arena of the social. In the social realm, civic character, which belongs to the province of the political and which embodies principles of duty and governance, is reconfigured as social behaviour and citizens are replaced by rights-bearing subjects.[44] With the ascendance of the social, law or right, as J.G.A. Pocock has put it, 'was pitted against virtue, things against persons, the empire against the repub- lic'.[45] Political activity, in the modern age of the social, can be under- stood as merely one form of behavioural interaction in a whole network of relationships of which perhaps the most central is econ- omic: all relationships are mediated by property – by the ownership of *things* and hence by labour and exchange – rather than by civic princi- ples. Social relationships are thus by their very nature commercial. By comparing human behaviour across time and space, not only the history of human society in general but also the form of the administra- tive state best suited to a given society at a given stage becomes legible. The modern state thus acts as manager of an evolved social body rather than as the expression of a public will. And the alibi of this state is to be found in the methodologies of social-scientific knowledge.

In his praise of the ability of Adam Smith's political theory to 'investigate those universal principles of justice and of expediency which ought ... to regulate the social order' (lxxxii), Stewart argues that government should be concerned with the administration of social needs more than the expression of civic ideals. The happiness of mankind depends, he emphasizes, 'not on the share which the people possess, directly or indirectly, in the enactment of laws, but on the equity and expediency of the laws that are enacted' (lxxxiii). This transformation of civic beings into social, and ultimately commercial, creatures is of course a focus of concern for the revived republicanism of the second half of the eighteenth century. Rousseau's identification of the corruption of moral life with commercial society in the *Discourse on Inequality* famously reconfigures the antisocial 'savage' as a creature with a commercial sensibility. In his contributions to Abbé Raynal's revised *Histoire philosophique et politique des établissements et du commerce des Européens dans les deux Indes*, Diderot argues that the corruption of manners to which travellers are susceptible represents a falling away from civil and commercial society rather than a realization of the antisocial tendencies that are already alive in it. He suggests that in modern European nations the substitution of imperial greed for republican duty and of commerce for virtue has created a new breed of itinerant and 'anomalous savages':

> those men who traverse so many countries, and who in the end belong to none ... those amphibious creatures, who live upon the surface of the waters; who come on shore only for a moment; to whom every habitable latitude is equal; who have, in reality, neither fathers, mothers, children, brothers, relations, friends, nor fellow-citizens; in whom the most pleasing and the most sacred ties are extinct; who quit their country without regret; who never return to it without being impatient of going out again; and to whom the habit of living upon a dreadful element gives a character of ferociousness. Their probity is not proof against crossing of the line; and they acquire riches in exchange for their virtue and their health.[46]

In Diderot's formulation, the correcting view of science will not bring travelling men home. Travellers are 'anomalous' not because they are somehow identified with the distorted truths and unreliable facts that they deal in, but because they belong nowhere. They are the creatures of an imperial culture that reduces the particularities of place to homogeneous commercial space: every 'habitable latitude' is equal to every other. The lack of attachment and placelessness created by colonial and commercial ambition reflects a moral as well as a physical itinerancy that is a characteristic of advanced social life rather than an aberration. The question as to whether commerce has a benevolent and progressive or a malevolent and degenerating influence on the societies it finds and transforms is here answered in the behaviour of the European traveller as much as in the manners of the peoples he encounters. If the detached and solitary traveller were, like any of Defoe's narrators, to embrace the family and country-fellows he formerly abandoned; if in crossing and re-crossing the line he were to recognize 'backwardness' and to facilitate communication between civilized metropolis and savage periphery, the expansion and integration of the commercial world might be seen to improve human sociability and happiness. But if his behaviour becomes barbarous, if he is motivated by greed rather than genuine feeling for his fellow creatures, then this shrinking and homogenizing of the globe represents the attenuation of social feeling in modern commercial life.

The corruption of civic culture in commercial nations – a corruption that is visible in the greedy indifference and narrow-mindedness of the traveller – is also the theme of Adam Ferguson's *An Essay on the History of Civil Society*. For Ferguson, commerce creates human beings who act only with a view to personal profit, sacrificing political spirit to appetite. The division of labour, he argues, has produced a country of tradesmen who, although they contribute by their industry to the preservation and enlargement of their nation, are ignorant of all matters beyond the orbit of their own interest and are therefore, contrary to what Kames argued, entirely lacking in patriotic feeling. Propertied men are more concerned about securing and enjoying what belongs to them than about the wellbeing and liberty of the nation as a whole. The 'boasted improvements of civil society', Ferguson complains, 'chain up the active virtues more than the restless disorders of men'.[47] And as nations become wealthier and increase in size, the common ties of society are no longer visible to their members, who become languid and unfeeling. It is therefore in the commercial, rather than the rude, state that 'man is sometimes found a detached and solitary being' for whom 'the bands of affection [are] broken' (17). Refinements in material culture reverse, rather than advance, social solidarity and patriotism. In a chapter on the manners of polished and commercial nations, Ferguson illustrates how misleading a progressive reading of history can be with the hypothetical example of a modern traveller, such 'as we sometimes send abroad to inspect the manners of mankind' (195), exploring ancient Greece. This traveller 'vie[s] with the celebrated author of the voyage to Lilliput' in recording the uncivilized customs of an aggressive, unrefined people who indulge in violent sports and exercises, who allow their rulers little state, and who have few genteel accomplishments. What he is incapable of recognizing is how ancient Greek society rewarded personal valour over property and rank, how it valued equality, how it made no distinction (as modern nations do) between state and subjects, and how the violence of its members' animosities was complemented by the strength of their affections. He fails to recognize these things precisely because the manners of his own time and country are characterized by an atomizing spirit of luxury and self-interest.

For Ferguson, however, evidence that social feeling can decline rather than grow with the progress of material culture does not compromise the intellectual's ability to compose the materials of history into a cohesive whole. Although the historian of manners may be 'embarrassed with a multiplicity of particulars and apparent inconsistencies' (16), he can navigate his way through these with the help of two fundamentals of social life: the 'principle of union' and the 'principle of dissension'. The first drives men into a state of war, and the second encourages them to unite under the influence either of affection or fear. This foundational theory of human nature then enables a 'general and comprehensive knowledge of the whole [of human social history]': the knowledge that can 'overlook many particulars and singularities, ... [by which we] fix our attention on certain points, in which many agree; and thereby establish a few general heads, under which the subject may be distinctly considered' (65).

This kind of confidence in the power of generalities to generate an even representation of historical progress of course makes epistemological assertions as imperious as the historical claim that human sociability finds its fullest expression in commercial nations. It ignores what Hume warns against in philosophical accounts of the progress of the arts and sciences, a tendency to reduce 'what is merely contingent to stable and universal principles'.[48] History is in fact, he argues, governed as much by chance or 'secret and unknown causes' as by discernable general rules. Philosophers, he cautioned, take less account of the diversity than the uniformity of natural phenomena and operations, and in their haste to extend a favourite principle 'over the whole creation' they 'reduce ... it to every phaenomenon, though by the most violent and absurd reasoning'.[49]

True generalities are therefore much more difficult to perceive than social-scientific learning claims they are. Ferguson's modern, Gulliver-like traveller is a bit like the critic in Hume's essay, 'Of the Standard of Taste', who deals in false generalities. Failing to transcend his particular circumstances and become 'a man in general', he 'obstinately maintains his natural position' and is unable to make a proper judgement about the beauty of an object or a performance addressed to those who belong to a different age or nation from his own. 'Full of the manners of his own age and country', he 'rashly condemns what seemed admirable in the eyes of those for whom alone the discourse was calculated'.[50] While principles of taste do have a universal standard, few are able to express it since the human organs of sensation are usually defective or so disordered that they do not fully respond to general principles. Hume's rash critic behaves like the imprudent sovereign, who presumes to be able to single-handedly establish a large state or society on general laws, a 'work of so great difficulty' that it requires the experience of many over time to complete it.[51] Neither is capable of seeing the whole or of discerning the relationship of the particular to the general, as he believes he is. The hubris of judgement in each case assumes that differences in customs and habits created over time can be overcome merely by imposing what masquerade as universal principles, whether of taste or of government.

Like Ferguson's republicanism, Hume's scepticism recognizes the possibility of errors of judgement and acts of epistemological violence at the heart of social knowledge. Yet elsewhere he argues that both the science of politics and the progress and effects of commerce are reducible to general rules because the passions upon which they depend are universal. The first position turns the philosopher loose in a Swiftian landscape in which generalities become nonsensical, and in which one set of social circumstances in one particular place can only be mapped with another set in another place by sheer force, creating epistemological distortions. The second position argues that one region of the world can be opened up to another through the abstractions or universal principles that show how fundamental needs and desires are shared by all humankind. These shared passions are thus what make commercial relationships possible. Where voyage narratives often remake travellers as philosophers, Hume's philosophers here become two different kinds of travellers: one journeys through a world of monstrous particulars which in the end confuse and alienate him from the body of knowledge that he thought could make sense of the strange and the foreign; the other deals confidently in generalities and experiences each country and culture he visits with the detached eye of a cosmopolitan.

Mercantilism and global commerce

Under the guidance and patronage of the Royal Society the spirit of scientific inquiry was supposed to transcend national interests. In his *History*, Sprat emphasized that the Society 'freely admitted men of different religions, countries and professions of life ... [who] openly profess not to lay the foundation of an English, Scotch, Irish, Popish or Protestant philosophy, but a philosophy of mankind' (63). The intellectual community that it fostered included 'inquisitive strangers of all countries [in] its number' (65), and it transcended the interests of individuals and nations with 'the universal light of modern times' (81). Yet the work of generating universal rules out of the evidence about a fantastically diverse human world also performed an enormous service to commercially advanced nations that needed to expand their markets. Leaving the question of travel aside for the moment, I want to look briefly at how theories of how nations accumulate wealth did or did not intersect with the cosmopolitan, scientific vision of a world of translatable differences. This will be to some extent to break down the traditional opposition between protectionist 'mercantilism' and liberal 'political economy'. Both, I will suggest, are invested in forms of globalism that make remote, 'backward' regions of the world accessible to 'advanced' European commercial nations.

   Since the term 'mercantilism' was coined by Adam Smith, it would only be anachronistic to try and describe its meaning for seventeenth- and eighteenth-century commentators on the science of wealth. According to Smith, the mercantile system was concentrated on two related 'fruitless care[s]' (*The Wealth of Nations*, 1:464). The first was the effort on the part of European nations to accumulate gold and silver. Mistaking these for real wealth, governments took various measures to limit the export of bullion. Under the influence of merchant objections to such prohibitions, however, bullionists eventually came to recognize that the only means of preserving or increasing the volume of gold and silver in a nation was through a balance of trade, maintaining the quantity of exports over imports by restraining the importation of foreign goods that could be produced at home. Smith shows that both arguments against the free exportation of bullion and advocacy for a favourable balance of trade emphasized the role of government in augmenting the quantity of precious metals in the nation. As such, both failed to recognize that money makes up only a small part of the national capital compared with what is produced from land and labour. The discovery of America, he argues, did not enrich European nations by cheapening gold and silver, but rather by opening new markets to European goods and, in so doing, determining 'new divisions of labour and improvements of art, which, in the narrow circle of the ancient commerce, could never have taken place for want of a market to take off the greater part of their produce' (1:470). Similarly, the trade with the East Indies, which some mercantilists decried because it involved the exportation of such a great quantity of silver, in fact opened new markets to European commodities and so increased the productive power of labour and hence the real wealth of European nations.

Despite Smith's support for protecting British naval interests through the Acts of Navigation, *The Wealth of Nations* has been seen as the founding text for the free trade principles of *laissez-faire*, replacing the narrow-minded economic nationalism of mercantilist doctrine. According-ing to most commentators in the nineteenth and early twentieth centuries, mercantilism represented either the mistaken conflation of money with wealth or the principle of a strongly state-centred economy. More recently, however, the notion of mercantilism as a coherent body of economic theory or a consistent political practice has come under scrutiny. Forms of economic liberalism, Terence Hutchison and Lars Magnusson have shown, were expressed in writings about wealth as early as the 1620s, and of the writers who are grouped together as mercantilists, some are more avidly defensive of protective policies than others.[52] Richard Wiles has challenged economic histor-ians, such as Eli Heckscher, who identify mercantilism with a static conception of wealth (the assumption, in other words, that there is a fixed quantity of resources in the world), by showing that many of the eighteenth-century 'mercantilist' writers, including Davenant, Defoe, Malachy Postlethwayt and Josiah Tucker, recognized that wealth was the effect of an expansive rather than a jealous commerce.[53]

The label 'mercantilist' is used to cover such an enormous range of writers that their differences as a group from Adam Smith are sometimes less considerable than those between themselves. Edward Misselden argued that the East India Company drained the nation of money;[54] Thomas Mun defended it by showing how imported goods from the East Indies are re-exported at a profit.[55] Mun and Misselden's analysis of the balance of trade saw the laws of the market, rather than the influence of the state, determining price; Gerard de Malynes argued that the only means of maintaining a favourable balance was by prohibiting the expor-tation of bullion.[56] With a very different emphasis, Josiah Child recog-nized national wealth in production as well as in foreign trade and consequently advocated the relief and employment of the poor.[57]

Charles Davenant emphasized the importance of land, population, low wages and increased manufacture over foreign trade, but warned that the intrusion of political faction and corruption on the liberties of the people would eventually affect the prosperity of the nation.[58] John Locke, on the other hand, reiterated the balance of trade theory, arguing that the loss of national riches could be attributed to 'the overbalancing of trade between us and our neighbours'.[59] Barely 'mercantilist,' in Smith's formulation, William Petty's political arithmetic calculated the nation's wealth through 'lands, people, buildings, husbandry, manufacture, commerce, fishery', as well as through the influence of policy, rather than through the quantity of bullion that remained in the country.[60]

Mercantilists were also divided among those who advocated loyalty to the principle of corporate welfare, or the responsibility of the state for the good of the whole public body; and those who emphasized the responsibility government owed to property-owning individuals. Such conflicting positions, as William Appleman Williams has shown, are most strikingly represented in the differences between the Earl of Shaftesbury and his pupil, Locke. Shaftesbury's involvement in the framing of the Navigation Acts, in the regulation of the treasury, in developing an equitable tax system, in the creation of political parties, and in the expansion of colonial trade was presented in the rhetoric of the public interest: preventing political corruption and improving national wealth through imperial commerce. Locke agreed that wealth would be created through imperial growth, but he identified this wealth as the creation of the natural laws of property and labour rather than of effective state policy, and hence argued that political respect for the rights of property owners was the fundamental principle behind good government and broad social wellbeing.[61]

Economic theory in the eighteenth century inherited these sometimes contradictory prescriptions for wealth and social happiness. On the one hand, this took the form of a condemnation of foreign luxuries which both create an unfavourable balance and cause an attenuation in the moral health of the nation, particularly given Britain's imperial growth and the historical lesson of the decline of the Roman empire.[62] On the other hand, the same authors often acknowledged that, while a balance should be procured, the riches of a people were inherent in the means of production (land, industry, labour and so on) rather than in money *per se*.[63] In an assertion of state-centred, 'mercantilist' principles, Josiah Tucker identified the advantage the French held through their political illiberalism by protecting the common people against the influence of luxuries and keeping them subordinated and

therefore more industrious.[64] Yet under Tucker's influence, Hume came
to the view that trade could expand infinitely and criticized those
writers who were preoccupied with the increase of the supply of
money, pointing out that money is nothing but the representation of
labour and commodities. Hume also refuted the balance of trade
theory by observing that a nation grew richer not at the expense of her
neighbours but with their improvement, since the latter stimulates
trade. Yet he warned that a decreased money supply would nonetheless
weaken the nation.[65] Arguments for economic liberalism became well
established during the 1750s and 1760s, well before the publication of
The Wealth of Nations. They were also being challenged by arguments
such as that of James Steuart's *Inquiry into the Principles of Political
Economy*, which argued that self-interest must be overseen by government or it will create enough social ills to risk destabilizing the state.[66]
Proponents of *laissez-faire* and 'corporate welfare' principles, however,
continued to agree on the importance of empire and trading
supremacy to the health of the economy. All in all, it makes less sense
to collapse these many different positions into the single category of
mercantilism than to acknowledge that economic liberalism, rather
than 'succeeding' mercantilism, coexisted with older, state-centred
conceptions of how the economy should be run. This is also to recognize that Adam Smith's conception of how nations accumulate wealth
did not come out of thin air.

This is important because in suggesting that the economic emphasis
on production (with its confidence that wealth is generated in a freer
market) could coexist with balance-of-trade arguments, it also becomes
possible to see how mercantilism could be at once another name for
economic nationalism and at the same time celebrate the 'natural' and
beneficent force of global commerce that brings together all the useful
things in the world to create opulence and happiness. At one level, of
course, this is simply a justification for the acquisition of colonies in
which raw materials are shipped to the mother country in exchange
for the 'gifts of civilization', yet there is more than imperial hypocrisy
at work in this odd combination of economic nationalism and cosmopolitan good will. The goods of which there is an abundance in
some parts of the world and a deficit in others are happily re-distrib-
uted by commerce. However, nations continue to be threatened from
without by foreign rivals and from within by the atomization of
society into competing private interests. While, as Ferguson put it, 'the
great work of forming a society ... must be carried out with a view to
the advantages which mankind derive from commerce and mutual

support' (1966, 16), commerce itself, he shows, has a divisive influence, and it is the 'rivalship of nations' that gives civil society 'object and form' (24). Commerce disaggregates human beings even as it brings them closer together. In the 'mercantilist' system, the state corrects this disaggregation either by Hobbesian discipline or by over-seeing, as Bernard Mandeville argued, with 'dextrous management' the transformation of private vices and private losses into public benefits.[67]

Heckscher's history of mercantilism, which puts unification and the nationalization of trade at the centre of economic history from the Middle Ages on, emphasizes the regulation of economic activity by the state. He argues that however much mercantilist writers such as Mun, de Malynes, Petty and Mandeville might have tried to reconcile the liberty of private interests with the restrictions of public regulation, all these writers finally concurred that the free trade must be overseen by government. In this way they privileged the concentration of power in the state over the accumulation of wealth. For this reason, Heckscher sug-gests, mercantilism and *laissez-faire* systems, while they may share roots in the theory of natural rights and the notion of man as a social animal, are fundamentally different: one sees state interference in society as the expression of natural laws; the other believes in the inherently rational nature of social systems and hence in the power of an 'invisible hand' to improve the arts and augment the wealth of a society.[68] Yet, as we have seen, the relationship between liberal and conservative components of economic theory are quite complicated in this period, and one cannot neatly line up protectionists against free traders, or starkly contrast a 'static' bullionism with the dynamism of a conception of wealth based on production. The transformation of private into public interests, for the Adam Smith of *The Theory of Moral Sentiments* as well as for Mandeville, is overseen by a statesman-like spectator. The role of the state is thus neither necessarily overbearing in mercantilist systems nor invisible in *laissez-faire* ones. In both cases, forms of governance, whether moral or political or both, are important to the workings of commercial culture. One of the things this book will explore is how mechanisms of economic and moral 'correction' by the state or its agents operate even within a discourse of deregulation and expansion of markets.

Outline of the argument

The chapters that follow do not attempt to draw any definitive connec-tions between mercantilist and *laissez-faire* economics on the one hand, and particular models of social theory on the other. Instead they

show more generally how representations of culture and cultural difference, drawn from the history of manners, are bound up with the
expansion of economic interests into further and remoter corners of
the globe. These interests are expressed through 'statist' economic
nationalism, as well as through liberal and cosmopolitan arguments
about how commerce creates the worldwide increase of wealth, the
universal improvement of manners through civilized exchange
between different nations, and ultimately, therefore, an increase in
human happiness. All of the texts I examine here include episodes of
errancy and efforts at 'correcting' errancy that take place during journeys to peripheral colonial or uncharted regions of the globe. The
transformation of these travellers from vagrant outlaws into civil subjects, or from subjects into outlaws, takes place against the political-
economic backdrop of commercial expansion and the integration of
small isolated societies into a world economy. In some cases the transformation is the occasion for this integration; in other cases it
unhinges the 'improving' relationship between parent nation and
colony or between civilized metropole and remote, 'savage' societies.

In the journals of William Dampier and in Defoe's maritime adventure narratives, the nomadic traveller, however individually enterprising
he might be, is identified as an antagonist to global commerce as well as
to the state. Dampier's 1681 journal manuscript, which recorded his
journeys with a crew of buccaneers across the Isthmus of Darien
(Panama), around the Spanish American coast and across the Pacific,
depicts him as a bold maritime adventurer: at worst a pirate, plundering
Spanish ships and sacking Spanish towns and settlements for personal
gain rather than national advantage; at best a privateer, exercising semi-
authorized violence against his country's enemy. In the published
version of his journal, however, he downplays the violent circumstances
of his encounters with members of other nations in order to make room
for elaborate descriptions of peoples, plants and animals in the countries
that he visits. This reinvention of himself, this transformation from
buccaneer to man of science, coincides with the state's increasing
concern in the late seventeenth century to maintain direct control over
foreign trade and to prevent errant subjects from provoking unnecessary
conflict with foreign powers. In this respect, his change can be seen as
an opportunistic defence against the charge of piracy, and the scientific
data that he gathers as the profit of state discipline. Yet in Dampier's
reform we can observe more than a newly invigorated state hegemony.
His connections to, and patronage from, members of the Royal Society
position him at the interface of natural science and state power where

the study of the manners and institutions of 'primitive' peoples provides data important to the history, and therefore the legitimation, of government. Where the manuscript records only the bare bones of encounters with indigenous peoples, emphasizing where and how such peoples acted as enemies or as allies and guides, the published journal emphasizes the cultural distance between European visitor and native and dwells on the observable differences between civil, industrious, trading nations, and those who have little commercial success owing to their primitive or tyrannical form of government.

Defoe's vagrant travellers follow the trajectory established by Dampier, abandoning their roving lives to become respectable merchants and English subjects, although they are motivated to do so, of course, by the pressure of a spiritual crisis. In Chapter 3, mercantilism is understood as the accumulation of wealth under the directorship of the state. Read together, *Robinson Crusoe*, *The Farther Adventures of Robinson Crusoe* and *Captain Singleton* can be seen to document emerging ties between merchant capital and state authority. I take issue with a tradition in Defoe criticism stretching from Karl Marx to Michael McKeon that identifies entrepreneur figures – such as Crusoe – as self-created individuals. I suggest instead that *Robinson Crusoe* is indebted to Locke's *Second Treatise of Government*, less because Locke identifies private property as the basis of civil identity than because he highlights the political problem of the orphan, or improperly educated 'savage.' Defoe's novel shows how the accumulation and protection of wealth requires a strong, paternalistic government, and the lessons that Crusoe learns about God's authority are tied up with a recognition that profit should be reconciled with power.

In *The Farther Adventures* and *Captain Singleton*, this recognition assumes a particularly mercantilist emphasis as Crusoe and Singleton both renounce their independence and attempt to reinvent themselves as subjects of a British state. Where Crusoe's first story is concerned with managing political subjects at the colonial periphery, disciplining the violent ambitions of rival colonists and mutineers as well as indigenous peoples, his second story emphasizes that the island should be managed as a colonial satellite of Britain, not as a private kingdom. Having made this realization, Crusoe goes on to consider that his proper vocation is not as an absolute ruler of a Caribbean island but rather as a defender of British markets against the protective jealousies of isolated and uncivilized peoples. *Captain Singleton* dramatizes the same relationship of commercial isolation to violent unsociability. Here the pirate crew is as savage as the peoples that Singleton encounters in his journey across Africa, and the seas which should be the medium of exchange and enlightenment are instead as metaphorically barren as the treeless, unproductive wasteland of the central African desert. Singleton, unmoored from both family and nation, finds himself in the awkward circumstance of having a 'subsistence but no residence', the price of which is wastefulness, excess and indulgence. His drive to acquire more and more without any means of learning how to spend wisely gives his acquisitiveness the character of a kind of purposeless desire. This is what Defoe endeavours to correct in the second half of the novel where Singleton is struck by the signs of God's wrath and finds himself longing for a means to retire to England and find an honest life. The identity crisis that he suffers at the end of his story and the fact that he cannot both return and enjoy the fruits of his criminal labour is as much a feature of the allegory of economic nationalism as of that of spiritual reformation.

Gulliver's Travels of course also ends with an identity crisis. In Swift's story, however, mercantilist globalism and economic nationalism are the cause of, rather than the remedy to, a disordered sense of self. Gulliver's reactions to the extraordinary cultures he encounters are at first mediated by national pride and by a confidence in the capacity of geographical science to organize all countries, oceans and peoples into a comparative study of different parts of the world. I begin this chapter by looking at a range of geographical studies from the early eighteenth century, including those of Herman Moll (who is explicitly mentioned in *Gulliver's Travels*), John Senex, Thomas Salmon and Patrick Gordon. Maps, atlases and geographical treatises in this period not only make aggressive nationalist assertions about territorial sovereignty, but they also naturalize the production of global space: space that is in fact organized by the needs of merchant capital. Geography's 'transparent' global space in fact works to interconnect different parts of the world, showing how the commercial and cultural properties of one country can be made measurable and quantifiable in terms of those of another country. Those societies that remain too remote, too savage and too unsettled for trading visitors are figured as the dangerous, uncharted regions of global space. *Gulliver's Travels* struggles against this triumphant colonizing of global space by merchant capital. Swift turns Gulliver loose into a series of alien landscapes in which his body shape and size is so hopelessly mismatched with those of his hosts that his many efforts to measure objects in impossibly large or impossibly small spaces, and to use those measurements to orient his encounters with other kinds of people, becomes patently absurd. The obscenely 'embodied' moments in Gulliver's journal (the scatological episodes of

Book one, the grotesque voyeurism of Book two, and the racism of Book four) have the effect of detaching him more and more from his English identity even as his insistence on the virtues of global commerce become increasingly inappropriate to his circumstances. Through Gulliver's transformation from curious, detached observer into brooding misanthropist, Swift produces a dystopic critique of the spatial logic of British commercial imperialism.

For two commentators on the impact of commerce on social life later in the century, it is aberrations in the moral, rather than the physical, condition of the traveller that reveal the corrupting influence of commerce. The phrase 'current[s] of fancy', which forms part of the title for Chapter 5, is taken from Samuel Johnson's remarks in *The Rambler* on the morally destructive realism of picaresque narratives which fail to demonstrate the fixed principles of virtue but whose characters and circumstances correspond closely enough to contemporary experience that they cannot be dismissed as romance. Smollett's *Roderick Random*, I argue, uses the figure of the picaro – the morally itinerant traveller – to dramatize a connection between the expanding commercial world and the moral depredation caused by 'worldliness', or the ruthless pursuit of wealth and advantage at the expense of one's fellow creatures. 'Currents of fancy' therefore invokes at once the moral arbitrariness of the picaresque and the transportation of goods, particularly luxury goods, from one part of the world to another.

Johnson concurs with Smollett that the commercial ambitions of European powers and the appetite for luxuries that characterize commercial nations cause all kinds of moral ruptures in the body politic, including faction, rebellion, self-interested war-mongering masked as patriotism, and sloth. He also sees them creating an increasingly inhumane state that supports colonial abuses such as the slave trade and the treatment of native peoples in colonial territories. In place of the morally unreliable picaro he tries to create a traveller with a detached, cosmopolitan point of view. This traveller can see beyond the rage of party faction, or jealous patriotism, or the influence of appetite to appreciate the enormous variety of people, places and things in the world, to marvel at the providential wisdom that allows commodities to be exchanged and transported from one place to another so as to prevent both want and superfluity, and to recognize that in civilized commercial exchange lies the promise of greater sociability and greater humanity. Yet he finds that his sophisticated traveller is no more assured of locating moral order than Smollett's picaro-rogue is of demonstrating it. The epistemological conundrum that concludes

Rasselas – whether to continue to seek to know the world in its entirety and then to act to improve it, or simply to float along life's stream, hoping for the best – is emblematic of the vexed condition of knowledge in the commercial age. This accounts for much of the melancholy which infects Johnson's writing. The further abroad one looks, the harder it becomes to calculate whether commercial culture has improved or corrupted social life, or whether bringing distant countries into what, in *The World Displayed*, he calls a 'general view' is a correction to or an aggravation of the ills which attend a world integrated by 'fancy'. Like Smollett's Random then, his travellers are unable to assign either a moral or an epistemological value to fancy.

Despite Johnson's claim that the impact is incalculable, the journal records of British voyages into the Pacific in the last quarter of the eighteenth century do attempt to assess the influence of commerce on the lives of peoples and travellers in remote regions of the world. In these enormously long voyages, the likelihood that seamen would become rogues becomes a factor in calculating and directing the relationship between commerce and sociability. Captains thus took on the role of moderators of the unrestrained passions that European sailors might succumb to at an enormous distance from home. In the commemorative literature that appeared after his death as much as in his own journals, James Cook becomes both arbiter of civil behaviour in acts of exchange between natives and Europeans and agent of a *doux commerce* that brings together people from distant parts of the world for their mutual advantage. Questions about the negative impact of the European presence in the South Seas, raised in particular by the naturalists Johann and Georg Forster, are neutralized by the idea of the captain as a sympathetic spectator, an impartial judge of the kind Adam Smith proposed in *The Theory of Moral Sentiments*. This spectator, whose humanity is more extensive that that of ordinary, passion-driven human beings, is capable of entering into the feelings of others and yet at the same time moderating their immediate passions so as to transform potentially antisocial impulses into more tempered, social feelings. In his restrained observations on instances of South Seas savagery and in the careful discipline that he exerts over the members of his crew who would otherwise trade with native peoples according to the unpredictable dictates of 'fancy', I suggest, he endeavours to exercise the normative agency of Smith's impartial spectator. However, at crucial moments the mechanisms of sympathetic government fail and he is forced to take violent measures to secure his ship, his goods, and the safety of his crew.

If Cook's task is to socialize the Pacific in the process of opening it up to trade, William Bligh's instructions are more overtly tied to colonial profit. His assignment, to transport breadfruit from Tahiti to the West Indies in order to supply food for plantation slaves, did, however, carry the secondary 'humanitarian' charge of furthering Cook's project to deliver botanical and agricultural knowledge to 'backward' regions of the globe. In his reconstruction of the events surrounding the mutiny on HMS *Bounty*, Bligh identifies the rejection of his authority as a symptom of his sailors' unreflective admiration for the Tahitian lifestyle and their dwindling connections to home. He defends himself and the loss of his ship by arguing that he demonstrated the character, foresight and careful discipline worthy of an officer who formerly served under Cook. No captain, he insists, could have had the necessary moral agency or sympathetic authority to have foreseen or to have reversed the violent sequence of events brought about by the sailors succumbing so entirely to fancy. The events that took place on the *Bounty*, Bligh implicitly recognizes, show how the expansion of commerce can only ever be imperfectly united with Enlightenment principles of sociability and sympathy.

This group of texts is in a great deal of dialogue. Cook's journals and *Gulliver's Travels* both refer directly to Dampier's discoveries in Australia. Defoe's protagonists are vagrants who have gone 'beyond the line' in one way or another and who attempt to repatriate and 're-civilize' themselves, as Dampier does. The thematization in *Roderick Random* and *Rasselas* of moral and civil incalculability in a world whose diverse parts are connected by fancy is, in a sense, brought to non-fictional life in the journals of Cook and Bligh, both of whom recognize that the success or failure of their expeditions depend upon the ability of the captain to make moral calculations about the impact of commercial enterprise on seamen and natives. Together, these narratives show how tenuous the relationship between commerce and civility becomes in the age of global expansion. Even as commercial ties are expanding sociability, they are also shrinking it. The de-civilized vagrant travellers, who help to open up enclaved regions of the globe to the improving influence of trade and European manners, are also paralysed by persistent failures of communication, by private greed, and by the sheer distance from home that perpetuates the condition of savage nomadism.

* * *

It remains to say something about the combination and selection of narratives used in this study. This book is not an exploration of exclusively literary representations of the world economy, and neither does it aim to provide an exhaustive account of how travel narratives in general respond to economic and social theory in the eighteenth century. The choice of texts is, in fact, deliberately selective, as I focus on a group of popular maritime narratives from the period that is coming to represent something like a 'canon' in studies of eighteenth-century British discovery literature. My contribution to the existing scholarship on these writers, some of which is very extensive indeed, is in the particular emphasis that I put on the status of the traveller in what might be called the pre-history of globalization, rather than in the investigation of lesser-known travellers' tales.[69] I do not suggest that non-fictional texts offer a more reliable account of the parts of the world which they represent than fictional ones; neither do I argue that imaginative literature offers a more critical or detached account of its subject matter than 'mere' documentary records. In fact, I concur with Pierre Bourdieu that what we treat as works of art cannot be read independently of their social conditions of production, and in particular of the institutions that make them available as objects of study.[70] Another way of putting this is to identify the literary in Raymond Williams's sense, as part of a 'whole way of life'. Along with non-fictional journal records, imaginative literature is part of the web of meanings and values produced in the lived experience of ordinary social exchanges.[71] This means, of course, that neither type of writing is simply 'reflective' of the social world in which it is produced; it is also an actor in it. The legal, administrative and discursive work that went into preventing and correcting acts of maritime errancy is proof enough of the potentially transformational agency that belonged to the stories told by long-distance travellers.

One of the things that this book aims to show is that the expansion of a world economy depended upon disciplining passions in the peripheral parts of the globe, even while commercial expansion required that appetites be stimulated in the metropolitan regions. It is not difficult to make the leap from the eighteenth to the twenty-first century; from a globalism which was already dividing up the world according to the needs of commerce and manufacture to a fully-fledged globalization in which goods are produced in the South mainly for consumption in the North at enormous human cost for the inhabitants of poorer countries, whether or not they are directly employed in that production. Yet I have focused on the traveller here – the figure who belongs to both ends of history ('savage' life and commercial modernity), in order to explore how such vicious inequalities are exposed as well as concealed in the literature that deals most directly with the creation of an economically integrated world in the eighteenth century. In all of these voyage tales, global space is homogenized and cultural differences are overcome by the common denominator of shared human passions. But the transformations in moral, spiritual and national identity which sea-travellers undergo in these narratives reveal the violence and disaffection in the social relations that make the flow of goods from one place to another possible. And they remind us that, however unfixed global capital has become, it still depends upon fixed populations of producers and consumers, and so upon nation states to organize, 'civilize' and settle unruly or itinerant subjects.

2
Buccaneer Ethnography: Nature, Culture and State in the Journals of William Dampier

Science and statecraft

Both a piratical adventurer and a man of science and letters, at once a lawless adventurer and an observer of plants, animals, peoples, winds and tides, William Dampier was, over the course of his life, both an agent and an enemy of English commercial interests. Like many of his fellow buccaneers, he sometimes excused himself from the charge of piracy by claiming that he pillaged by commission. Yet he also fashioned himself in the journals as a Baconian eyewitness of non-European peoples and a natural world that both late seventeenth-century science and English merchants were interested in knowing better. In one sense, the fact that he could be so apparently untroubled by the contradictions in his career suggests the existence of loose constellations of power and wealth, wherein the boundaries between subject and outlaw and between high-seas criminal and merchant-capitalist remain quite fluid: the existence, that is to say, of a tolerant state that made a certain kind of free primitive accumulation possible. Yet his reformation also seems to reflect an intensification of state authority as the latter was able to reach farther into the widening world to discipline unruly subjects. As privateering became an increasingly less legitimate means of securing advantage over rival states and as piracy became less and less tolerated, the erratic identity and independent agency that buccaneers expressed in their double roles as renegade outlaws and national heroes hardened into circumstantial proof of their crimes. Dampier's journals can be seen to document his response to such discipline, revealing the changing focus of his observations and reflections as his text transforms him from a roving outlaw into a respectable English captain whose task is unequivocally to identify where and how England's national commercial interests can be expanded.

This refashioning takes place between the manuscript and (very different) printed versions of his journal. In the published account of his voyages, which bears the mark of his association with several members of the Royal Society, he downplays the swashbuckling adventures of the buccaneers and adds a great deal of documentary material about the characters of remote nations and peoples, including their manners, forms of government and commercial activity. In so doing, he provides ethnographic evidence for the natural-jurisprudential principle that successful commercial activity is linked to the evolution of a strong civil authority. Moreover, he not only supplies raw data about the material cultures and manners of the societies with which he has come into contact, but also assesses the degree of civilization they have attained and draws connections between degrees of commercial sophistication and forms of government. He is therefore able to reinvent himself as a kind of spokesperson for the natural law principle that humans form societies and create civil governments in order to combat their own asocial tendencies, thus aligning himself with several major seventeenth-century arguments about the relationship between government and material culture. According to Pufendorf, this principle accords with the will of God, who 'would not that men should pass their life like beasts, without culture and without rule, but that they and their actions should be moderated by settled maxims and principles'.[1] Without these laws, human beings are under no form of restraint and are directed only by their 'wandering inclinations' (74). For Pufendorf, such laws are not imposed from above, but are the expression of a fundamentally social disposition and one that has also made it possible for men to agree upon having a fixed property in things. For Hobbes, on the other hand, the diverse passions of men can never be organized into harmonious relationships with others except through the authority of an absolute ruler. Yet whether it is giving coherent form to already existing social passions or managing a collection of appetite-driven men who would otherwise be perpetually at war, the state which Dampier implicitly addresses is designed to overcome the kind of social disaggregation and 'savagery' that piracy represents. In other words, his abjuration of the life of wandering is expressed in his endorsement of the theory of social evolution that puts the needs and appetites of men – the qualities that both inspire them to seek commercial relationships with one another and put them in violent competition with their neighbours – under the jurisdiction of the state.

This philosophical context matters because it shows how not only his testimonies of loyalty, but also the investigative features of his narrative, are integral to the question of his status as an English subject. The character of his writing shifts, I will be arguing here, from an account of erratic encounters with members of other nations and cultures in which identities and epistemologies shift and change, to a more stable zone of scientific exploration in which the boundaries between the ethnographic observer and the object of his study are firmly drawn. In the first model of contact, events and actions are shaped not by what science has identified as the natural disposition of a people, but by the interactive circumstances of the encounter itself.[2] This form of contact is often a feature of the kind of fragmented colonialism wherein private merchants, pirates, and other independent entrepreneurs pursue their fortunes in 'new' regions of the globe separately from the direct interests of the state. The mode of colonial encounter documented 'ethnographically', on the other hand – the one that takes care to differentiate between degrees of technological sophistication and civilized behaviour in different societies – represents a more direct and engaged interest on the part of the state. This interest stems at once from the modern state's growing concern with the management of foreign commerce and from the questions about human society that have become so central to principles of sovereignty. What stands to be gained from such study is not a recognition of how cultures mutate reciprocally in response to contact with one another (this would be to remain in the zone of fluid identity, or 'between civilizations' in Clifford's terms[3]); instead, societies are compared and ranked. An understanding of how cultural change and commercial progress belong to the province of natural jurisprudence then supplies the legal basis for the power of princes.

In many ways, of course, a journal of buccaneer adventures could not be more ill-suited to this ethnographic task. By the very violence of their actions, this society of maritime outlaws based in the Caribbean in the seventeenth century had confounded the distinction between civilized colonizer and savage colonized. Yet, as we shall see, the increasingly direct interest of the state in scientific discovery in the last third of the seventeenth century had the effect of bringing them more closely into the fold of civilized statehood, either as objects of its disciplinary control or as reformed sovereign subjects and men of science. The domestication of the buccaneers, then, has everything to do with *both* the technologies of colonization and merchant capital as they are developing in this period *and* with the relationship between state and subject in England as it is newly mediated by the science of western exploration. Hence the study of an 'uncivil' culture has, in cultural-political terms, little or nothing to do with the practical consequences and contingencies of the encounter itself. As a condition of their acceptance by the state, the buccaneers must learn that 'savage' peoples are objects of scientific knowledge before they are friends or enemies, guides or captors.

* * *

By the beginning of the eighteenth century enough privateer and buccaneer journals and memoirs had been published to mark them as a distinct genre. Exquemelin's *Buccaneers of America* (1678) appeared in numerous editions and languages with the first English edition becoming available in 1684. Of the Caribbean adventures alone a whole series of 'English' buccaneer travelogues were published: Basil Ringrose's supplementary chapter to an edition of Exquemelin in 1685, Dampier's *New Voyage Round the World* in 1697, Lionel Wafer's *A New Voyage and Description of the Isthmus of America* in 1699, and Bartholomew Sharpe's *A Collection of Original Voyages* in 1699. Dampier's book went through five editions before 1706, then was published with a second volume as *Voyages and Descriptions* in 1699, and with a third volume, *A Voyage to New Holland* in 1703. William Funnell's *A Voyage Round the World* appeared in 1707. In 1712 Woodes Rogers published *A Cruising Voyage Round the World*, which contained the famous account of the marooning of Alexander Selkirk on the island of Juan Fernandez that inspired Defoe's *Robinson Crusoe*. George Shelvocke's *A Voyage Round the World by Way of the Great South Sea* followed in 1726. These texts in turn provided the raw material for imaginative travel literature well into the nineteenth century. They were also important contemporary resources for merchants of London and Bristol who were keen for information about commercial opportunities in Spanish America and the Dutch East Indies. At the same time the information about distant countries included in the buccaneer journals appealed to those in scientific and official circles who saw that, along with opportunities for raw products and new markets, such information offered a significant contribution to the national geographical archive. The tastes of this more 'disinterested' readership might be seen to express an important facet of later seventeenth-century English political culture: the increasingly strong institutional links between scientific discovery and state practice.

In *Leviathan*, Hobbes recommended that 'he who is to govern a whole nation' should expand his knowledge not of particular (individual) men

but of mankind as a whole.[4] In so doing he put a specifically anthropo-
logical emphasis on Bacon's counsel that the sovereign should have
knowledge of 'the natures and dispositions of the people, [and] their
conditions and necessities'.[5] Such grounding of state power in the study
of human desires and needs sets at least part of the scene for Stuart
patronage of science in the later seventeenth century.[6] In 1660, an
organization made up of a group of men from Oxford and London who
shared an interest in natural phenomena and experimental philosophy
was established to institutionalize the advancement of learning. In
1662, it was granted a royal charter of incorporation by Charles II 'out
of', as Sprat put it, 'our princely affection to all kinds of learning and
more particular favour to philosophical studies, especially those which
endeavour by solid experiments either to reform or improve philosophy' (*The History of the Royal Society of London*, 134). Now English imperial spirit was formally linked to state investment in scientific discovery
and the improvement of natural knowledge. In his account of the
history of the Royal Society, Thomas Sprat emphasized the importance
of scientific discovery to proper state practice, arguing that 'to make a
man prudent in the affairs of state, it is not enough to be well vers'd in
all the conclusions which all the politicians in the world have devised
... or [to rely] on ... universal precepts ... but there must be a sagacity of
judgment in particular things' (17). This Baconian emphasis on the
observation, compiling, and analysis of particulars is tied to Hobbes's
advice concerning the usefulness of information about primitive societies such as those found in America to the understanding of how to
govern passion-driven, self-interested, always potentially 'savage' men.[7]
The state, Sprat added, should be especially invested in travel and
exploration since those rulers who will know nature in all its particular-
ity will have 'their eyes on all parts, and [will] receive information from
every quarter of the earth' (20). The 'search into knowledge', he then
went on to argue, makes men of science 'serviceable to their country'
(26) since, even as they teach kings better government, they also open
up channels for the transmission of both scientific data and merchant
capital back to the metropolis: 'in a short time there will scarce a ship
come up the Thames that does not make some return of experiments, as
well as of merchandise' (86).

It is difficult not to see such arguments intersecting with seventeenth-century mercantilism and the state's role in the management of
trade.[8] At the legislative level this took the form of a series of
Navigation Acts granting England exclusive trading rights with its
colonies and restricting the use of foreign ships in order to maintain a

strong merchant marine. Less directly, the state became implicated in commercial initiatives through the public debt. Between 1688 and 1720 this debt was transferred to major joint-stock companies – the East India Company, the Bank of England, and most spectacularly the South Sea Company – which in return were granted privileges of monopoly and incorporation. Since these companies then had to raise further capital to support their operations, and since they were considerably advantaged by these privileges, the state indirectly encouraged their expansion in the form of foreign trade and colonization.[9] In what follows, I will look first at how the state began to subject the buccaneers more often to the rule of law in the later seventeenth century, suggesting that such severity is a feature of the tightening of the mercantilist reins. Moving focus from the overt to the circuitous exercise of state power, I will then explore how Dampier's journals are committed to English commercial interests, and how his shift of allegiance from the buccaneer fraternity to his fellow Englishmen unfolds in a study of manners.

Beyond the line: stateless outlaws or English subjects?

The transformation of the sea-raider into man of science must therefore be understood first in terms of the way that state power is immediately exercised over errant subjects. The growing extent to which maritime violence came to be managed by state and legal apparatus during the course of the seventeenth century points not only to the need to maintain control over those subjects who have strayed beyond the reach of the state (or 'beyond the line') but, in so doing, to reincorporate them into the national body; to assert, that is to say, the authority of the state over and above any independent sovereignty exercised either by merchant adventurers or maritime outlaws. During this period privateering, a form of maritime plundering that was formally authorized by the state, came under much closer scrutiny, while piracy (which carried no such authorization) was gradually more firmly disciplined. Colonial governors were instructed to prosecute privateers who sought commissions from foreign princes or who simply took to unlicensed plundering 'as pirate[s] and English subject[s]'.[9] In the second half of the century, such measures were repeatedly taken against the 'English' buccaneers whose national and legal status was particularly ambiguous: at times they served the colonial administrations of the Caribbean and at other times teamed up with buccaneer gangs of other national origins. Although its attitude towards the buccaneer communities often wavered, the state became less and less tolerant of their waywardness and, in an effort to limit their independent mobility in the area, it began to identify them as subjects of English law and government.[10]

However, both state and merchant commissioning of privateers did continue to be a regular practice during these decades. The peripheral colonial economies of the Caribbean had difficulty resisting the extra revenue that the buccaneers brought to the colony. Here the buccaneers were regularly preying on Spanish ships and hence were perceived by the Jamaican colonists (whose recent arrival and perilous proximity to the Spanish empire made them anxious for their safety) as invaluable allies. After 1655 the buccaneers often sailed under commission from the governors of Jamaica. Although, following the Treaty of Madrid in 1670, buccaneering was more carefully policed in the Caribbean, the arrest and return to London of both buccaneer Henry Morgan (for the sacking of Panama) and Jamaican Governor Thomas Modyford (for commissioning him) was transparently a gesture to appease the Spanish. Morgan was treated like a hero in London and eventually returned to Jamaica as Deputy Governor, and Modyford was imprisoned for only two years after which time he too was able to go back to Jamaica and assume the post of Chief Justice.[11] In 1669 Modyford defended the need to grant commissions against the Spanish by pointing out that the buccaneers know 'all the ports, bays and creeks ... [and] every path [in these islands.]'[12] In a petition to the King in 1670, he argued that trade and plantation would be discouraged in Jamaica if privateering was reduced.[13]

Yet England did genuinely endeavour to honour the Treaty of Madrid and to restrain buccaneering, both licensed and unlicensed, in the Caribbean and around the coasts of Spanish America after 1670, in which effort the state increasingly found support in commercial circles and amongst colonists. Concern that buccaneer aggression against the Spanish was seriously disrupting the *assiento* (the Spanish contract with foreign nations to supply African slaves) and preventing the efficient administration of plantation trade at the end of the century contributed to a growing sense that buccaneering was bad for English business.[14] In 1680 Henry Morgan (now well and truly re-nationalized as Deputy Governor of Jamaica) turned on his former brethren and insisted that buccaneering should be stamped out in the interests of protecting England's trade with Spain.[15] Already in 1670 the King had instructed the new Governor of Jamaica, Thomas Lynch, to pardon privateers for any and all offences committed since 1660 (on condition that they cease all hostilities) and to encourage them to take up planting. In 1672 Lynch reported that the privateers had been so reduced to obedience 'that there now is not one English pirate'.[16] Concerns about their effect on trade then precipitated an assault on the independent sovereignty of the buccaneer societies: the 1683 Jamaica Act attacked the federation of buccaneer colonies (English, French and Dutch) by making it a felony for any British subject in the West Indies to serve under a foreign prince. Even as the buccaneers came under the firmer disciplinary hand of the state, they were also being interpolated as English subjects.

The state's more general concern to present itself as the central actor in the international arena and to assert its authority over wayward subjects by drawing aggressive distinctions between privateer and pirate is reflected in the juridical rhetoric of the period. In the proceedings before the Lords of the Council concerning the trials of John Golding and others for piracy in 1693, the viability of the charge of piracy rested on whether the former King James had the authority to issue commissions to these men. The prosecutor ordered by the Admiralty to proceed against them as pirates refused to do so on the grounds that pirates 'are common enemies of all mankind, having no legal authority for what they do ... and ha[ve] thereby lost [their] right in the Law of Nations'.[17] As subjects of even a deposed King, he argued, privateers, unlike pirates, are legitimate actors in the global civil arena. Similarly, in the trial of Joseph Dawson and others in 1696, the Judge of the Admiralty reminded the court that pirates operate beyond the civil line as he argued that 'the King of England hath not only an empire and sovereignty over the British seas, but also an undoubted jurisdiction and power in concurrency with other princes and states for the punishment of all piracies and robberies at sea, in the most remote parts of the world'.[18] This identification of pirates as the enemies of global commercial and civil order also figured them, by the logic of natural law, as degenerates and barbarians. In the later trial of Major Stede Bonnet (1718), Attorney General Richard Allen declared that pirates are worse than beasts of prey for the latter 'eat only to satisfy their hunger ... [and] are never found to prey upon creatures of the same species as themselves ... [whereas] pirates prey upon all mankind, their own species and fellow creatures, without distinction of nations or religions'.[19] The suggestion that those who operate outside of the international legal community are not merely uncivil but also, because they prey on their own kind, cannibalistic, featured also in Judge Forbes' representation of piracy in the trial of Thomas Green in 1705:

> A pirate is in perpetual war with every individual and every state, Christian or infidel. Pirates properly have no country, but by the

nature of their guilt, separate themselves, and renounce on the matter, the benefit of all lawful societies. They are worse than ravenous beasts, in as far as their fatal reason gives them a greater faculty and skill to do evil: And whereas such creatures follow the bent of their natures, and that promiscuously, pirates extinguish humanity in themselves, and prey upon men only, especially upon traders, who are the most innocent. The crime of piracy ... is made up of oppression, robbery and murder committed in places far remote and solitary.[20]

In each of these cases it is the rootlessness of pirates, their wilful renunciation of all national ties, that constitutes the primary offence against the law of nature. Pirates, according to these prosecutors, are the stuff of Lockean nightmare: self-created savages who prey on civilized men of commerce. The act of claiming independent sovereignty, 'renounc[ing] ... the benefit of all lawful societies' means turning back the clock of nature to Hobbes's state of war where, unrestrained by government, men have no sense of civil responsibility towards one another or respect for the compact which creates social cohesion, civil stability, and, with security, greater prosperity.

The history of the buccaneers of America made them especially vulnerable to the accusation of nationless barbarism. The buccaneer associations of the Caribbean in the seventeenth century consisted of a mixture of originally English, French or Dutch bands of 'masterless men': deserters, dissenters, crews of wrecked vessels, or chance marooners; masterless, because, according to sailors' law, having passed the tropic they had left behind all their former obligations to the state, as well as to their families.[21] On the northern shore of Hispaniola they first banded together as a group of cattle hunters, acquiring the name 'buccaneer' from their habit of curing strips of beef (a practice which they learnt from the Caribs, who called this meat 'boucan'.) They governed themselves by what they called 'the customs of the coast': a code which, however violent, stressed the egalitarian character of their communities. In an effort to rid the island of the buccaneers, the Spanish destroyed the wild herds of cattle on which the former lived, but in so doing only drove them to prey on passing merchant ships, and eventually to attack Spanish coastal vessels and fortified towns. Until the middle of the seventeenth century they constituted a kind of independent republic, a transnational federation of exiles, known for their extraordinary brutality and, in the case of L'Olonnais, reputed cannibalism.[22]

Official condemnation of the buccaneers after 1670 often presented them as pirates, *hostis humanis generis* (enemies of all mankind), by

pointing to their lack of national character. Living beyond the reach of
the state they were represented as both un-English and uncivilized. In
1681, for example, Governor Lynch accused those privateers who held
commissions from the Spanish of barbaric indifference to the laws which
stand between civil community and a brutal state of nature. In so doing
he associated their violent behaviour with ethnic heterogeneity: they
have committed barbarous cruelties and injustices, and better cannot be
expected, for they are Corsicans, Slavonians, Greeks, mulattos, a mongrel
parcel of thieves and rogues that rob and murder all that come into their
power without the least respect to humanity or common justice.'[23]

This linking of unlicensed, non-state violence with both ethnic
mixing and the rejection of national ties is precisely what Dampier is
responding to as a travel writer in the 1690s.[24] In his efforts to reas-
sume English identity and to distance himself from the pirate fraterni-
ties that Lynch describes, he emphasizes his cultural and, in at least
one instance, racial difference from the 'semi-civilized' peoples he
encounters. He also directly links this cultural difference and distance
in relation to the commercial potential of the places he visits and to
the capacity of the societies he studies to resist the ambition of trading
nations that rival England. In his journals, ethnographic detachment
begins to overtake looser descriptions of the strategic significance of
contact with native peoples. Correspondingly, the authority of the
buccaneer shifts from legal documents in the form of letters of marque
(which enabled privateers to attack legally any enemy vessels as acts of
reprisal) to natural scientific and ethnographic narrative, as what
becomes valuable about his account is the accuracy of his descriptions
of plants, animals, climate and peoples in the places he visits. To the
extent that these are also regions where English commerce needs to
take a firmer hold, he also opens up trading spaces beyond the line.

Piracy and ethnography

Dampier took part in the buccaneer crossing by foot of the Isthmus of
Darien (Panama) from the Caribbean into the Pacific in 1680. The expedition was led by John Coxon and Bartholomew Sharpe and was intended
to lead to the sacking of Panama and raiding of Spanish gold mines in the
interior of Darien. However, as the Spanish were warned in advance that
pirates were headed for the South Seas, the attempt on Panama was
unsuccessful. Subsequent quarrels over leadership encouraged Dampier
and 43 others to break off and return across the Darien. On the return
journey, exhausted and depleted in numbers, the buccaneers depended

even more than they had a year earlier on Mosquito and Cuna allies as guides and informants about Spanish activity in the area. In 1681 Dampier took part in a third crossing of the Isthmus, a trek this time of over 100 miles. A later journey took him around Cape Horn and eventually across the Pacific. The manuscript of his journal, which he carried with him across the Isthmus in a bamboo holder sealed with wax, was published by James Knapton in 1697 as *A New Voyage Round the World*.

One of the most striking things about Dampier's record of his journey is the way in which he was able to fashion it into both a natural-scientific and a maritime resource in the published version. *A New Voyage Round the World* offered detailed meteorological, botanical and ethnographic accounts of hitherto unexplored parts of the Spanish American coast, and the most thorough English navigation of the Pacific to that date.[25] His wind maps may have provided the prototype for the depiction of trade winds in eighteenth-century cartography, and his accounts of the behaviour of tropical storms and of tides and currents remained authorities for English sea travel throughout the following century.[26] Dampier himself claimed that his journey was motivated by a scientifically disinterested intention 'to indulge [his] curiosity [rather] than to get wealth'.[27] The scientific community was convinced: while other members of the buccaneer party were defending themselves against charges of piracy, Charles Montague, president of the Royal Society, had introduced Dampier to the First Lord of the Admiralty, who then commissioned him to explore the coast of New Holland. Sir Robert Southwell, President of the Royal Society between 1690 and 1695, and Sir Hans Sloane, a member and later president, were also Dampier's patrons. In the portrait that Sloane commissioned Thomas Murray to paint, Dampier is described as both a 'pirate and hydrographer', yet in his right hand he is holding not a musket but a volume of his *Voyages*.

In his dedication to Montague, Dampier professes to have abandoned his buccaneering past and to have assumed the responsibilities of an English explorer as he begs the Earl 'in perusing these papers by your goodness [to] distinguish the experience of the author from his faults and to judge him capable of serving his country'(*Voyages*, 1:18). This is less of a plea for clemency, in fact, than it is a claim that the value of scientific journalism is more important than the possibly criminal circumstances in which such data were collected. He will, he says, satisfy the Society's 'zeal for the advancement of knowledge, and anything that may … tend to my country's advantage' and in so doing present some 'things in them new even to [the President]; and some possibly, not altogether unuseful to the publick' (1:17). In his tribute to the reader he remarks on the contribution that this data will make to the scientific archives, humbling himself before a community of informed readers in whose company he will then be able to assume the status of a man of science:

> In the description of places, their produce, &c. I have endeavoured to give what satisfaction I could to my country-men; tho' possibly to the describing several things that may have been much better accounted for by others: choosing to be more particular than might be needful, with respect to the intelligent reader, rather than to omit what I thought might tend to the information of persons no less sensible and inquisitive, tho' not so learned or experienced. For which reason, my chief care hath been to be as particular as was consistent with my intended brevity, in setting down such observables as I met with. (1:19)

Scientific authority here is located both in eyewitness experience and in a society of not only 'sensible' and 'inquisitive', but also 'learned' persons. His two kinds of readers – one the intelligent and inquisitive 'countryman', the other an informed man of science – together validate his English identity and initiate him into scientific circles. His accurate representation of the phenomena he encounters, while it is the authentic product of his first-hand experience, is of scientific value only once it has been made available to a circle of enlightened readers and fellow Englishmen.

It is in this same spirit of enlightened observation and respect for the principles of the Royal Society that Dampier distances himself from the accounts of earlier travellers, explaining that he has not 'confined [him]self to such names as are given by learned authors, or so much as enquired after many of them', because he 'write[s] for [his] countrymen' and 'shall leave to those of more leisure and opportunity the trouble of comparing these with those which other authors have assigned' (1:20–1). Yet if his text takes its authority from what he finds in the natural world, he is nonetheless the compiler and organizer of the data he has collected, shaping and editing his raw material in such a way as to make it most accessible to its readers. What he originally intended as a lengthy appendix including a 'chorographical description of all the south sea coast of America' is left off because 'such detail would have swelled [the book] too unreasonably' (1:21). Rewritten and revised, carefully organized so that they will maintain the interest and patronage of an informed readership, Dampier's eye-witness observations are not without mediation. His concern not to 'prejudice the truth and sincerity of [his] relation ... by omissions' (1:20) is challenged by his subsequent reflection that in some places he may not 'have express'd [him]self as [he] ought' (1:23), and by his submission to the 'judgment and candour' of his readers in accordance with whose wisdom, rather than with the raw truth of his observations and experiences, he will compose later accounts. Moreover, his design in publishing the journal, he insists in the dedication to Montague, is to produce the kind of document that will qualify for the Royal Society's 'general magazine of the knowledge of foreign parts' (1:18).

Such narrative shaping and the commitment to the scientific community that it reflects is strikingly represented in the differences between the manuscript and the printed editions of the journal.[28] In the manuscript, 'serv[ice to] my native country' does generate 'a desire ... to travell to the South Seas',[29] yet at this stage such 'service' has less to do with botanical and ethnographic discovery than with informing his countrymen of 'the riches which may be gotten out of the mines in America' (Sloane MS, f.29v.). He befriends the Darien Indians because they know the whereabouts of the mines and because they are useful allies in conflicts with the Spanish, and he explains why the party did not explore certain regions of the northern coast by remarking that their business was not to find places to settle in but only convenient harbours in which to careen. The service to the public which his narrative might offer is, he confesses, beyond the direct compass of his text, since as a mere eyewitness he leaves any consideration of the value of his discoveries to 'the ingenious publick spirits of the age' (MS, f.30r.). Not only does he make little effort to identify with this public in the manuscript text, but he is also less anxious to excuse himself from the charge of piracy. Instead he points out that his journal aspires to nothing more than a record of his piratical adventures: 'If it is objected that the point of right was not soe well studyed in these adventures as it ought to have been I can only say that the Politicall rights [,] alliances, and Engagements betweene Empires and states are too high for me to discuss' (MS, f.30r). Where the modesty of the preface to the printed journal, as we have seen, is intended to link Dampier with a community of polite, scientifically educated readers, here his humility takes the form of a professed ignorance of the law of nations and, given his not-so-subtle disrespect for the 'point of right', of natural law as well.

It is therefore no surprise that his emphasis on the cultural habits of the peoples with whom he comes into contact is much more pronounced in the printed edition of the journal. His descriptions of the inhabitants of Guam and Mindanao are much sketchier in the manuscript than they are in *A New Voyage*.[30] In the latter, more elaborate accounts of their manners are explicitly tied to their form of government and capacity for trade. In the manuscript, the fullest ethnographic description is of the Darien Indians. However, this account, he tells us, is in the words of the surgeon, Lionel Wafer, who was forced to rely on the assistance of the Darien people when he received a gunpowder wound during the crossing and was left behind by the rest of the buccaneer crew. Dampier's own account of contact with the Indians is restricted to narrative detail: he describes how the Indians received, fed, and helped to guide the buccaneers to their ports of prey; how the latter tried to win the trust of their Indian guides by offering them beads, money or hatchets; and, where these commodities had no effect (as in the case of the Indian at Garachina), how 'one of our men tooke out of his bagg a sky coloured Pettycoate and putt it on his wife whoe was soe much pleased with the present that shee immediately begun to chatter to her husband and soe brought him into a better humour' (MS, f.6v.). The journal's elaborate description of the survival of the Mosquito Indian on the Isle of John Fernandez (which supplied one of the sources for Defoe's *Robinson Crusoe*) is anticipated in the manuscript only by the brief observation that 'his cloaths were all woren out and he had only a piece of Goate skin ab.t his waste' (MS, f.32v.). Dampier questions, at one point, whether 'we ever had gott [across the Darien] without [the Indians'] assistance because they brought us from time to time to their plantations where wee allways got provisions which we should have wanted'. He then remarks that 'I shall always owne it to be much better to be friends with the Indians' (MS, f.13r.). The elaborate digression on the appearance, social organization, hunting practices, fishing, marriage, war, and plantations of the Mosquito Indians which concludes the first chapter of the printed edition is only matched in the manuscript by a marginal note where he comments that 'the muskito Indians allways have armes and are ... courted by all privateers ... they strike fish[,] turtle, and manatee [which help to] maintaine the ship's company' (MS, f.1r. [marginal note B]).

   What is represented here is a mode of contact in which the need to secure alliances with, and practical assistance from, the Indians shapes the cultural logic of the encounter. Even the culturally marked spectacle of the woman discovering the petticoat is framed by the exigencies of the moment and the need to secure her husband's assistance as a guide. In the printed journal, however, Dampier highlights the cultural distance between Indians and Europeans not only through the wealth of descriptive detail about Indian ways of life, but also by suggesting that the objects of his study have not progressed far enough to be capable of independent sovereignty. Having emphasized what accomplished mimics of the English the Mosquitoes are, he concludes his description by remarking that '[t]hey have no form of government among them, but acknowledge the King of England for their soveraign' (*Journal*, 1:42). As they become richer objects of ethnographic study they also take their place in the theatre of colonial rivalry that European powers are playing out in the Americas. This projection of English commercial ambition on to the desires and character of a people (whose own strategic reasons for courting the English remain invisible) will adapt itself to different trading environments: in the East Indies, as his later writings show, Dampier often emphasizes how keen a particular people are for the English to set up a factory on their territory and to break up the Dutch monopoly on the spice trade.

The work of distinguishing Englishman from Indian is also carried out through race difference. Describing the party which returned across the Darien, Dampier's manuscript identifies the group as consisting of 45 white men, two Mosquito Indians and five slaves. In a marginal note he clarifies that 'by white men I meant all that bore armes for we had a Spanish Indian [who afterwards] stayed among the Indians in Darien' (MS, f.1r.). The printed journal assimilates the information from the footnote into the body of the text by eliminating the racial ambiguity of the original description: 'We were', he says in this version, 'in number forty-four white men who bore armes, a Spanish Indian who bore armes also; and two Mosquito Indians' (*Journal*, 1:33). Where 'white' comes to signify the cultural distance between European and Indian rather than, as it did in the manuscript, an ally bearing arms, then racial difference has become more important than an identification forged through strategic alliance. We might recall here how Lynch used the term 'mulatto' to describe the muddle of ethnic identities in the buccaneer communities, and how he linked such mixing to their violent disrespect for justice. Now, in this scene of encounter, Dampier and his crew become 'white' once loyalty to his own country becomes, retrospectively, more crucial than the need for guides and allies.

Discovery and trade in the East Indies and New Holland

Thicker ethnographic description in the published journals enables him to reflect not only on the 'historical' significance of ethnic differences but also on their importance for commercial relations between different peoples and states and ultimately for the wealth of his own nation. After cruising the southern coast for some months, Dampier joined Captain Swan in a gruelling voyage across the barely charted Pacific, hoping to find a profit in the East Indies. Since England's East India Company had been unable to compete with Holland's in the spice islands, English trade was restricted to India and to intra-Asian commerce in which it took advantage of the different values commodities held in a variety of Asian ports.[31] Swan's crew agreed to undertake the journey in the expectation that they would be able to make a profit from interloping on the East India trade. Dampier's journal, however, emphasizes his conversion to an honest way of life by pointing out additional commercial opportunities that England might take in the region. His representation of the character of the peoples he encounters is shaped by the degree of friendliness that they demonstrate towards English travellers and their willingness to trade with them.

Arriving at Mindanao in the Philippines, the crew was met with a welcome reception from the local inhabitants who hoped that an English settlement would protect them from both the Spanish and the Dutch. While he has considerable admiration for this people, observing that '[in] trading by sea with other nations, they are therefore the more civil' (1:332), he identifies flaws in their character that can be traced to a poor relationship between government and trade. Their unfortunate tendency to laziness, he suggests, does not 'proceed from their natural inclinations' (1:333), as he claims it does in most Indians, but from their system of government: their Sultan takes from them whatever they get by trade and in so doing dampens their spirit for industry. As a result they have developed a custom of begging from strangers. Yet their favouring of English traders over Dutch (who have oppressed peoples on neighbouring islands) and Spanish (by whom they were formerly colonized) suggests that they retain a spirit of liberty and hence an inclination towards open trade. Even as he implies that an English presence might emancipate these people into freer commerce, Dampier also reflects on the opportunity that staying on the island could have given him to turn to an honest and settled way of life. At the same time, he observes that this very reformation would provide England with a commercial foothold in a region where it has long since lost its hold:

> indeed upon mature thoughts I should think we could not have
> done better than to have complied with the desire they seemed to

have of our settling here; and to have taken up our quarters among them. For as thereby we might better have consulted our own profit and satisfaction than by the other loose roving way of life; so it might probably have proved of publick benefit to our nation, and been a means of introducing an English settlement and trade, not only here, but through several of the spice islands, which lie in its neighbourhood. (1:355)

From Mindanao, he goes on to argue, a lucrative trade could also be set up with other islands in the Philippine group. The transformation from 'loose rover' to honest settler, then, could model broader commercial initiatives in the area and break up the Dutch monopoly on the spice trade.

Throughout the journals he punctuates his own adventures with accounts of the conditions of different parts of the world and the customs, institutions and capacity for trade of the peoples who inhabit them. In the course of his first voyage to the East Indies he compares the 'bold and treacherous' Malayans with those who are fond of trade and therefore 'affable and courteous to merchants' (2:94). The Hottentots, he complains, are a lazy people who, although they live on fertile land, fail to take advantage of it and prefer instead to 'live as their fore-fathers, poor and miserable' (1:522). Worse still are the natives of New Holland, 'the miserablest people in the world' (1:453), whose poverty and ignorance are implicitly the consequence of their extreme isolation from other cultures: 'all the signs we could make were to no purpose for they stood like statues without motion but grinned like so many monkeys staring one upon another' (1:456). His opinion was confirmed on his return, ten years later in 1698, on the *Roebuck*, when he remarks that while it might be advantageous to a settlement to try to win the New Hollanders over to 'traffick and useful intercourse' (2:457), he has little confidence that it would be easy to do so.

The kind of commercial speculation that he makes about Mindanao in *A New Voyage* is undertaken at more length in *A Supplement to the Voyage Round the World*, published in the wake of the success of the first book and under the title of *Voyages and Discoveries* in 1699. This journal records in detail the manners of the inhabitants and the natural and manufactured products of the countries he visited while sailing with an East India Company merchant after he left the buccaneers in the Nicobar Islands. A detailed description of the physical form, customs and achievements of the natives of Tonquin (Northern Vietnam) introduces an account of their limited capacity for trade by sea, and their disadvantageous trade with Chinese, English, Dutch and other merchants (for whom they man-ufacture wrought silks and lacquer ware only as demand occasions). In his commentary on the journey that he made upriver to the capital of Cachao, he criticizes the chief of the English factory there for failing to pursue a trade with Japan 'much coveted by the Eastern people them-selves as well as Europeans' (2:32), adding that:

> where there is a prospect of profit, I think it not amiss for merchants to try for a trade, for if our ancestors had been as dull as we have been of late, 'tis possible we had never known the way so much as to the East-Indies, but must have been beholden to our neighbours for all the products of those Eastern nations. (2:33).

While at the English fort at Bencouli (on the west coast of Sumatra) he observed that a better correspondence should be kept between merchants and native inhabitants. His conclusion, following the descrip-tion of the people of Bangkali (on the eastern coast), that 'the more trade [a people has], the more civility; and on, the contrary, the less trade the more barbarity and incivility' (2:45) thus takes on a curiously self-reflexive quality as we are reminded of his own apparent transformation from roving pirate to self-appointed agent of British commercial inter-ests. Distancing himself still further from the kind of strategic relation-ships he and his fellow buccaneers established with the Darien Indians, he then observes that trade, and all the conveniences of life that it brings with it, might be introduced to 'even the poor American' (2:45).

In this turn to an interest in legitimate commerce, Dampier does not entirely abnegate his piratical past, remarking on one occasion that he 'had a great advantage above raw men that are sent out of England into these places, who proceed usually too cautiously, coldly and for-mally to compass any considerable design which experience better teaches than any rules whatsoever' (1:358). Yet in sublimating this taste for adventure into a spirit of mercantile enterprise he detaches himself from the violent behaviour of his companions. The 'wild, unruly men not subject to government' (2:44) that he encounters at Sumatra seem, by the end of *A New Voyage*, no more savage or unruly than the men with whom he travels. While cruising in the South Seas he had advised against attempting the straits of Magellan for 'our men being privateers and so more willful and less under command, would not be so ready to give a watchful attendance in a passage so little known' (1:108). During the crossing of the Pacific, he reports, the crew began to doubt they would find land before they exhausted their provisions, they planned to kill and eat Captain Swan, and after him anyone who supported his decision to undertake the voyage, including Dampier himself. In Mindanao they mutinied, leaving Swan ashore on the island and sailing southwards to prey on vessels engaged in the spice trade. Having tried without success to convince the men to pick up Swan on their return to Mindanao some months later, Dampier requested that he be left ashore in the Nicobar Islands.

Although no less daring than those he had undertaken as a privateer, the adventures which follow belong less ambiguously to the pursuit of legitimate commercial opportunities. Having briefly contemplated opening a trade in ambergris with the inhabitants of the Nicobar Islands, he then decided to sail by canoe to the English factory at Achin in Sumatra where he met and sailed to Tonquin with an East India Company crew under Captain Weldon. This journey was followed by one to the East India Company factory at Bencouli and his appointment as chief gunner at the fort. From there he travelled on another merchant vessel to the Cape of Good Hope and back to England, bringing with him the Meangian 'painted prince' Jeoly whom he had bought from a trader in the Philippines, and whom he intended to take back and display in London. Once he returned to England, he speculated, Jeoly would also be the means by which he could obtain a ship 'from the Merchants' to sail back to Meangis 'and by his favour and negotiation to establish a traffick for the spices and other products of those islands' (1:502). His plans for Jeoly, who in fact died shortly after arriving in England, highlight the way in which the journal continually weds ethnographic curiosity to merchant capital. Equally striking is his apparent lack of self-consciousness about switching his service on a privateering vessel to one of the Company's. Such easy erasure of his past also appears in his seemingly perverse complaints against the Dutch for obstructing the trade of other nations, as well as in his praise of those countries where merchants of different nations can trade openly. His adventures on the other side of the Pacific were only ever provisionally 'legal' in the context of war between England and Spain, and for the most part the expeditions in which he participated were nothing if not an encroachment on the free circulation of commodities from one part of the world to another.

The radical turns in his fortune are even more pronounced in *A Voyage to New Holland*. Based on his reputation as a navigator following the success of his book, Dampier was commissioned in 1698 by the Admiralty to explore the coasts of New Holland, New Guinea and the supposed 'Terra Australis'. As captain of the *Roebuck* he was empowered to punish mutinous members of his crew. Both his legitimacy and his authority, however, were challenged in the course of this voyage. The naval officers' suspicion of his buccaneer past caused some discipline problems to which Dampier responded first by beating and then expelling one of them (Lieutenant George Fisher) from the ship. This action led to a court martial on his return to England which, unfortunately for Dampier, was almost simultaneous with the execution of Captain Kidd for piracy.[32] In western Timor his past returned still more ironically to haunt him when the Dutch governor assumed that Dampier's crew were pirates and for some time refused to supply them with much-needed water. The emissary whom he sent ashore failed to convince the governor that this was an English ship, and the latter continued to believe for some time that the crew were 'of many nations (as is usual with pirate vessels)' (2:469).

As a consequence of these several challenges to his character, he is forced to defend himself all over again in *A Voyage to New Holland*, insisting upon his credentials as both a natural scientist and a friend of English commerce. He opens with the hope that the favourable reception his former volumes of voyages have already received will predispose 'candid and impartial readers' to a further account of the 'inhabitants, animals, plants, soil ... in those different countries which have either seldom or not at all been visited by any Europeans' (2:341). He then predicts that New Holland 'may afford rich commodities, and the natives may be easily brought to commerce' (2:345). For the first time the events of his earlier life seem to haunt his text as he is forced to defend himself 'against the objections that have been made to my former performances' (2:343). That he chooses to vindicate himself by pointing to the scientific and commercial value of his discoveries suggests that he is alert to an emerging syncretism between the history of manners and a commercially aggressive state no longer tolerant of private enterprise beyond the line.

There are moments in the journals when Dampier recognizes the human costs of integrating peripheral economies into the world market. His assumption that the poverty of the Tonquinese can be traced to their oppression by an arbitrary government is tempered by his subsequent account of the way in which trade in their country is managed by foreign merchants, while the native inhabitants themselves have no control over the export of the goods they produce. Having just declared that the civility of a people is proportional to the degree to which they have developed their trade, he then reflects of the people of Bangkali that perhaps with trade:

> they will be in danger of meeting with oppression: men not being content with a free traffick and a just and reasonable gain, especially

in these remote countries, but they must have the current run altogether in their own channel, though to the depriving the poor
natives they deal with, of their natural liberty. (2:45)

Such reservations temporarily drive a wedge between the ethnographic
dimensions of the journal and its apology for mercantilism. The transformation of social relations in these countries is suddenly the consequence of their peripheral status rather than the cause of their
supposed emancipation into systems of profitable exchange. Yet this
brief acknowledgement of the way that commercial imperialism works
– creating peripheral economies and colonial dependencies – is quickly
subsumed into an attack on the Dutch for obstructing the free trade of
other European nations in the East Indies. The first position is an
untenable one for Dampier because in his published writing, unlike his
manuscript, he *is* committed to the 'higher matters' of relationships
between states, a balance of trade, and state power. Since his career
depends on whether he can transform himself in the public eye from
roving outlaw to merchant capitalist, natural scientist and English
subject, the teleologies of natural law are built into the very framework
of his narrative. The journals dramatize the relationship of state to
social order even as they provide data essential to the expansion of
English commerce.

Most biographies of Dampier mention his influence on Defoe and
Swift, either because he introduced the South Seas and the inhabitants
of New Holland to the early eighteenth-century literary imagination or
because he provided the most recent English instance of circumnaviga-
tion.[33] Yet his relationship to the imaginative travel literature of the
early eighteenth century has to do with more than the exotic locations
and remote peoples that he provided information about. Both Defoe
and Swift explore, although to very different ends, the character of the
traveller as it is sutured into the fabric of the mercantilist state. In each
case what is examined is the relationship between the cultural and
biological diversity of an expanding world and the stability and power
of a commercial state. The peoples, colonized and peripheralized, who
are squeezed between that world and this state are more obviously
distressed in Swift's writing than they are in Defoe's. In both cases,
however, the vagrant character of the traveller who 'discovers' such
peoples comes under pressure both from state authority and merchant
capital as they try to find their way into hitherto unreachable and
enclaved regions of the globe.

3
International Trade and Individual Enterprise: Defoe's Maritime Adventurers

By dramatizing the reform of the vagrant subject who has strayed beyond the line, Dampier's journals in many ways provide the model for early eighteenth-century narratives of criminal adventure and economic endeavour. In Defoe's novels, the behaviour of the itinerant yet enterprising protagonists, whether pirates, merchant adventurers, prostitutes or thieves, raises the problem of how individual profit can be reconciled with duty to family, God and state. In the cases of Robinson Crusoe and Bob Singleton, such conflicts are concentrated in the way that these troubled heroes operate as free agents in an international arena, abandoning the ties to their homeland that would ensure the return of colonial profits to the metropolitan core. Thus, while Defoe's narratives look like allegories for both the primitive accumulation in which English economic power originates and the possessive individualism that such power makes possible, they are not really so economically 'modern'. The extraordinary initiative that their protagonists demonstrate under arduous circumstances must still be harnessed to the state. As a result, the relationship between individual enterprise and state sovereignty constitutes a kind of narrative undercurrent in each of these stories which surfaces in the consciences of the protagonists as they register the emotional and spiritual cost of accumulating wealth at an enormous distance from home. The transformation of Defoe's characters into repentant subjects of both providence and English government therefore has everything to do with harnessing wealth to power in the mode of early eighteenth-century mercantile capitalism.

It is obviously no accident that such transformational adventures take place in parts of the world where English commerce has a vested interest in investigating both peoples and resources. In the fictional histories of both Crusoe and Singleton, the relationship between the traveller and the state to which he at least once belonged is mediated by his encounter with non-European peoples: Crusoe travels to the Caribbean and through Asia; Singleton crosses Africa and cruises the Indian and Atlantic oceans. In these unfamiliar places, the protagonists comment upon the manners of the societies they encounter, the readiness for government that these societies demonstrate, their propensity for savagery, their degree of commercial sophistication, and whether they do or do not belong to a community of trading nations. The travellers then justify their own, often violent, behaviour towards such peoples according to the degree of 'civilization' in which they discover them. Yet because their own relationship to law, government and empire is so vexed, these characters' accounts of their actions and adventures are unstable and unreliable: what appears as a justifiable attack at one minute becomes an act of criminal abuse at another; an observation that seems in keeping with providential will in one part of the story is revealed as a hubristic falsehood in another part. The effect of these oscillations is not, however, to cast doubt on the validity of English colonial aggression. Instead the novels emphasize that such aggression must be directly tied to English economic interests, and they suggest that these interests should be overseen by the state. Thus, when Defoe's protagonists become stateless or semi-stateless nomads they sacrifice the basis upon which they can 'legitimately' accumulate wealth in the wider world.

Defoe belongs to the school of seventeenth-century English mercantilist thought represented in different ways by Mun, Child, Petty and Davenant. Like Mun, Defoe emphasized the primacy of foreign trade in building up the wealth of the nation 'wherein we must ever observe this rule: to sell more to strangers yearly than we consume of theirs in value'.[1] He was therefore generally in favour of imposing restrictions on a trade that promoted an unfavourable balance. He advocated, for instance, a prohibition on importing calicoes and silks, arguing that by sending too much wealth out of the country and by squeezing the market in English fabric, such trade enriched the East India Company at the expense of the nation.[2] He saw a favourable balance of trade as the basis of state power, insisting that governments 'are rich or poor as they have, or have not, a share of the whole commerce of the world'.[3] Yet he also argued that a thriving commerce depended on state encouragement, supporting (like Child) the Navigation Acts, which prohibited the colonies from trading most raw goods directly with any nation other than England and which restricted the use of foreign ships.

His economic nationalism was thus in harmony with what by the early eighteenth-century was considered to be a fairly conservative belief in a paternalistic state at the centre of the English commercial empire.[4] According to this belief, good government and a thriving trade are mutually beneficial. Before the English were united by trade, he argued in *A Plan of the English Commerce*, they blindly submitted to the will of their feudal lords, at whose command they would willingly rebel against their king.[5] Foreign trade is thus at the root not only of imperial power, but also of the unity of the nation itself and of its tolerant and reasonable government.[6] At the same time, trade *does* need the protection of the sovereign who, Davenant argued, 'take[s] a providential care of the whole'. [7] Such protectionism is readable in Defoe's arguments in *A Plan* that the wealth of a nation is as dependent on its navigational strength as on its manufacture (52) and that 'English men of trade ... received life from the powerful influences and paternal concern of their sagacious princes' (113). At the same time, he argues in the *Review*, 'subjects honestly labouring, honestly possessing, ought to be left quietly, enjoying what they are masters of; and this is the foundation of what we call law, liberty and property ... [and] the end of ... government'.[8] Together, liberty, trade, and protective government thus form a political-economic triad that is at the basis of national unity and prosperity.

At times, however, Defoe grants trade itself the role of principal protector, figuring it as the centre of the nation and the very means by which a people can form a settled community and an imaginative sense of belonging:

> Till trade brought you gold and silver and fetched away your manufactures, found vent for the produce and labour for your people, what was all your wealth? Your natives must have wandered abroad and been hirelings and mauls for Europe, as the Swiss are to this day .... *It is trade* has made your commons rich, your merchants numerous, your poor able to maintain themselves. *It is trade* has made you great, strong, terrible abroad and busy at home. *It is trade* has kept your people from wandering like vagabonds on the face of the earth.[9]

Here he is responding to an argument that the origin of wealth is in land, an argument that he finds as specious as the possibility that national wealth can be restored through credit. The circulation and consumption of goods, he points out, is the only means by which land can acquire value. In the process he demonstrates that such circulation is vital to the commonwealth, not only generating wealth and military strength but also creating settled society.

The recurring theme in Defoe's stories of maritime adventure is how to 'bring home' those who are possessed with an enterprising yet roving spirit, and who have severed their ties with their place of origin. Whether shipwrecked on the shores of a 'deserted' island or marauding in an ocean that is rightly the shared province of trading nations, these stateless or semi-stateless wanderers, we shall see, not only contribute nothing to the economic health of the countries from which they originally came, but they also interfere with the efficient exchange of goods and money between nations. I will begin here with the first part of *Robinson Crusoe*, since it is not only chronologically the first of the three texts I shall be discussing, but also (because it endorses the legitimacy of strong government) the first episode in a political-economic trilogy that examines how merchant and colonial capital can and should be overseen by the state. The second section will look at how Crusoe is transformed from colonizer-king to responsible English merchant, demonstrating that 'his' island will only become properly civil once it participates in the English Atlantic trade. The final section will look at the threat that the stateless, sea-roving protagonist presents to international commerce and thence to English interests. Read together, these three novels advocate a relationship between government and trade that respects the laws of nature and evolutionary history; laws that bring supposedly savage societies into civil community through the mechanisms of both state power and interstate commerce.

Crusoe's children: orphans, cannibals and colonial rule

The first part of *Robinson Crusoe* is in many ways the testing ground for questions about strong government and economic growth. In this capacity, its mode is allegory, since it uses the island as a location in which to explore more general philosophical concerns about the acquisition of property and the nature of legitimate government. The novel asks on what basis Crusoe is able to claim ownership on and off the island and how he then comes to exercise rule over the other human beings who inhabit it. However careful he is to examine the rightfulness of his claims to property and power, Crusoe remains a vagabond of sorts, even while he is king. Since he has abandoned both his family and his country, he is haunted by his orphan-like status and his resulting fear that he may be as capable of uncivil and violent behaviour as

the various 'savages' whom he eventually comes to rule. Allegory therefore gives way to history in the second of his adventures when Crusoe
recognizes that 'his' island needs to take its place in the wider commercial world, and that although planting and property may be an important feature in the evolution of colonial government, the laws of
nature determine that trade too is at the heart of what constitutes legitimate rule.

Many political-historical readings of *Robinson Crusoe* have identified
it as a parable of economic individualism and have represented Defoe
as the first major advocate of Locke's principles of property ownership
and political liberty. The novel offers, Isaac Kramnick has suggested 'an
articulate and lyrical rendering of Locke's ideas ... [whereby the] isolated individual is depicted free of society, history and tradition'.[10] Ian
Watt similarly argued that Defoe's protagonists are book-keepers and
entrepreneurs before they are members of a family or a nation and that
their first loyalties are to capital and profit. By this reckoning they are
self-created individuals, and the relationships that they establish with
others are more contractual than they are affective.[11] Of course, these
figures of political and economic modernity are nearly always subject
to the critical scrutiny of Defoe's more repentant narrators, who chas-
tise their over-materialistic younger selves for ignoring the ways in
which God's law resists or moderates human ambition. For Michael
McKeon, however, even this retrospective self-criticism has the effect
finally of sanctioning individual enterprise rather than of admonishing
it. He points out that, for Crusoe, economic individualism joins forces
with divine will once the voices of character and narrator are united
and episodes of 'self-invention' are retrospectively spiritualized. Thus
Crusoe's rights, not only to enjoy the fruits of his labour but also to
assume political dominion on the island, are morally secured by an
'internalization of God's society' that unites human ambition with
divine imperative.[12] Each of these approaches to the novel emphasizes
Defoe's recognition of the rights of the property-owning individual as
the cornerstone of good government.

Another reading of *Crusoe* that sees the island as a kind of economic
tabula rasa belongs to the history of political economy rather than literary criticism. Although in *Grundrisse* Marx is concerned to show that
natural man is an economic fiction of the eighteenth century, an 'ideal
... project[ed] onto the past',[13] in *Capital* he assigns Crusoe precisely
these mythic proportions. Alone on the island, Crusoe demonstrates,
for Marx, an instance of the 'pure' determination of the value of an

object before the relationship of labour to its product is obscured by the fantastic form of the commodity.[14] Marx posits an original man who is outside political history, one for whom the products of labour cannot assume a commodified form because while he is alone on the island they only ever have use value. Crusoe has no way of attaching value to a surplus as long as he is the island's only inhabitant, since there is neither occasion for exchange nor any need to build up and store supplies in case of an exigency such as war. The problem here, of course, is that the castaway is not, in fact, alone. The fences with which Crusoe secures his animals, Marx forgets, also protect him from 'wild beasts and men' and 'the fear of being swallowed up alive';[15] a 'fence' is also a 'fortress' (59). Following what is perhaps the most famous episode in the novel – the discovery of the footprint – Crusoe's concern for his own preservation 'take[s] off the edge of [his] invention for [his] own conveniences' (167). He concentrates instead on securing himself and his small enclosure against the violence of the savages whom he imagines will devour him and everything he owns. After he discovers the footprint, he considers tearing down his fences, turning his cattle loose and digging up his cornfields in order that he cannot be found. He is literally thrown back into the very wilderness out of which he had carved himself a civilized way of life.

Such readings, then, ignore the circumstances of contact that directly affect Crusoe's relationship to property as well as his productivity. Drawing attention to precisely this kind of interpretive ellipsis, Peter Hulme has shown how questions of both economic individualism and Protestant spiritualism are tied to the specifically colonial context in which the novel is set. Crusoe's sense of self, both as an industrious individual and as an English subject, he argues, evolves in the circumstances of Caribbean colonization. Crusoe's interactions with his physical and social environment stage the social-contractual power relations and international rivalries in play in a colonial economy based on slave labour.[16] On a related theme, I will consider how *Robinson Crusoe* reveals Defoe to be less an advocate of economic individualism than of mercantilism and a strong state. As other critics have argued, Crusoe's story can be seen to dramatize the consolidation of state power.[17] Sometimes in the form of absolute, sometimes of tolerant rule, Crusoe assumes a paternalistic sovereignty on the island, first over animals, then over indigenous peoples, and finally over Spanish sailors and English mutineers. He does so largely because his subjects are incapable either of governing themselves reasonably or (in the case of island 'savages' and English rebels) of paying due respect to property. While the episodes involving colonial trade are confined to the briefly described years in Brazil, Crusoe's account of his life on the island can nonetheless be seen to focus on the civil and political conditions under which commerce can flourish. My focus here will be on the way in which the model of government that Crusoe settles on takes advantage, through paternalistic rule, of the diverse products of nature that God has put in place for the welfare of human beings. In this respect the novel puts the natural laws of settlement and productivity that enable human beings to make the most of their environments – becoming, according to the time-line of such laws, first agricultural and then commercial – in the hands of a powerful prince. In so doing, I am suggesting, it prepares the ground for the more recognizably mercantilist agenda of the maritime adventure stories that succeed it.

Before it moves fully into political allegory, however, the first part of *Robinson Crusoe* focuses on the difference between a settled and a nomadic way of living.[18] The novel begins, famously, with Crusoe's rejection of his father's advice against adventuring or becoming 'famous in undertakings of a nature out of the common road' (4). Abandoning country, family and the comfortable 'middle station' of life he runs off to sea, surrendering to a 'meer wandering inclination' (4). His father, Kreutznaer (meaning wanderer) acquired 'an estate by merchandise' (3) and was a foreigner from Bremen; his ambitions for his son, we might conjecture, have to do with his recognition of the privileges of settled middle-class life and of being a native English subject. Throughout the rest of the novel, Crusoe is haunted by his father's words of warning which come to assume a providential character. Following the dream-vision in which he is sentenced to death for his lack of repentance and 'stupidity of soul' (88), he contrasts his years of 'seafaring wickedness' with the wisdom represented both by the 'good instruction of his father' and 'God in his deliverances' (88). His entire narrative is thus at one level organized around what becomes a *sin* of self-imposed exile from his country and his proper station in life.

Once he finds himself on the island, the contrast between a wandering and a settled life adapts itself to this new context. Here Crusoe experiences an oscillation between a Hobbesian state of nature characterized by fear and a more Lockean version of that state in which the goods of nature are transformed into products that satisfy primary human needs. This is also imaginatively, for Crusoe, an oscillation between the abject condition of the disobedient runaway – whose terror and confusion are the just consequences of disobedience to both his father and his middle-class calling – and the spiritually enlightened state of mind of the Protestant hero who recognizes what God has provided for him. Shortly after his arrival on the island, Crusoe draws up a balance sheet to describe his circumstances, 'stat[ing] impartially, like debtor and creditor' (65) the comforts and the miseries that he is exposed to. This list is divided into two columns. In the column listing evils he includes his banishment from society, his having 'no soul to speak to' and his being 'without any defence or means to resist any violence of man or beast' (66). In the column under 'good' he observes that he is alive, that he has some means of sustenance, that in a hot climate he has no need for clothes, that he sees no wild beasts to hurt him as he saw on the coast of Africa, and that the ship is wrecked close enough to shore that he can retrieve 'so many necessary things as will either supply my wants or enable me to supply my self even as long as I live' (66). The distinction in the first column, between violent and civilized men disappears in the second column where not only is he exposed to little danger but also the means of survival are supplied by nature or good fortune.

The disjunction between these two states of mind – one thrown in terror into the violent state of nature and the other in thankful contemplation of his deliverance – is what organizes the first half of the novel. Crusoe moves back and forth between resentment at the condition he has found himself in and gratitude to God for his escape from greater misfortune. Providence is at one moment his enemy, condemning him to first a solitary and then a dangerous life in a 'wild miserable place' (79) and at the next his benefactor, ensuring the fertility of the soil and his discovery of unspoilt grains of corn. In order to find his way more permanently into the latter condition and out of misery he needs to be able to see God's hand at work in everything he experiences, including his encounters (or likely encounters) with other people on the island. At that point, the organization of society becomes as much the product of providential design as the abundance and generosity of nature. In the second half of the novel this order will be achieved in the civil society that Crusoe sets up on the island.

Before moving closer in to the 'political' sections of the novel, however, I want to consider a likely debt that Defoe carries to Locke's *Second Treatise of Government*. This is not, however, the better known argument of Locke's that sees sovereignty residing in the propertied individual; rather, Defoe seems to echo the representation of paternal

authority that Locke's theory of civil society depends upon. The contractualism of the *Second Treatise* is introduced in Locke's dispute with
Robert Filmer, who argued that the origin of *political* power is to be
found in the authority of the father. The power of the magistrate or
king, Locke disagreed, is structurally different from the necessarily
much more absolute authority of a 'father over his children, a husband
over his wife, or a lord over his slave'.[19] Civil subjects (unlike children)
grant provisional sovereignty to the head of state on condition that the
latter does not abuse the rights of freeholding subjects. This is much
like the account of the evolution of political society that Defoe lays out
in *Jure Divino* (1706):

> First government was nat'ral all and free
> And fixt in patriarchal majesty
> From thence convey'd by right to property
> Where he bestows the soil and gives the land
> The right of that's the right of the command
> There can be no pretence of government
> Till they that have the property consent.[20]

Yet, more than an argument for limited government, what Defoe represents here is the evolution of a society into political maturity. The
genealogy of power that locates the consent of the property holders at
the origin of legitimate government, and that deliberately does *not*
identify paternal with political power, nevertheless originates in 'patriarchal majesty'. For Locke himself, the theory of government by contract is in some ways complicated by his idea that children must be
disciplined in the household if they are not to go out into the world as
savages. Hence, while the authority of the sovereign is limited by the
rights of the subjects as they are recognized in civil law, the power of
the father must be stronger: 'a child is free by his father's title, by his
father's understanding, which is to govern him till he hath it of his
own' (308). This brings Locke to the curious contradiction whereby the
child is born free but continues to be the subject of strict paternal rule
until such time as it is reasoning enough to be recognized as a member
of the civil community. Children must be disciplined in the household
if they are not to go out into the world as savages.

Locke's own pseudo-historical conjecture that 'in the beginning all
the world was America' (301) reconfigures the relationship between
father and subject child as one between the European who has made a

property of something by mixing his labour with it and the American who leaves the land to 'nature without any improvement, tillage or husbandry' (294). Property is created by appropriation for use. Since such property is at the origin of limited government, the indigenous inhabitants of America who live communally must be unable to rule themselves in this way. In the 'pre-civil' world, therefore, Locke's fundamental distinction between political and paternal authority must be suspended in order to deal with the figure of the 'savage', a subject who can only be effectively ruled by the strong hand of a 'father' who can educate him out of his barbaric habits. Locke's Americans are political children precisely because they have not yet advanced to the settled condition of an agricultural people who, in gradually making a property out of the land by cultivating it, are then ready for and in need of government and law.[21]

Crusoe's encounters with other visitors to the island, in particular the mainlander cannibals who, he deduces, regularly travel across in their canoes, follow the same racist logic as Locke's descriptions of America. His terror at the prospect of meeting what he assumes will be a barbaric people, confirmed when he discovers the remains of a cannibal feast, are concentrated around both the apparently visible threat to his person and the more hypothetical one to his property. At the same time, however, he has been busy setting himself up as 'governor' of this colony, and this magisterial charge becomes somewhat more convincing once he can add human beings to the collection of domesticated animals whom he identified earlier as his subjects and over whom alone he has hitherto exercised absolute dominion. Friday is of course the first and most tractable of these human subjects: having laid his head at Crusoe's feet, he is rewarded with the latter's protection as well as the gifts of clothing, the English language, and the correction of 'savage' habits such as cannibalism. In return for these, Friday offers not only faithful service but also filial love and obedience so that, as Crusoe puts it, 'his very affections were ty'd to me, like those of a child to a father' (209). This causes Crusoe to reflect that the people of whom he has had so much fear have in fact 'the same powers, the same reason, the same affections, the same sentiments of kindness and obligation ... and all the capacities of doing good and receiving good, that [God] has given to us' (209). With careful and sustained instruction in the spirit and laws of God they will be capable of the same, if not greater, capacity for good as Europeans. As Crusoe takes on the role of master, and ultimately (as he is to all his conquered subjects) ruler over Friday, he also becomes father and educator, instructing him in the 'knowledge of the true God' (216). The domesticated and infantilized 'savage' falls under the authority of paternal law (and becomes the beneficiary of paternal wisdom) even as he becomes a subject of Crusoe's government.

It is difficult, of course, to ignore the irony that Crusoe has discovered this new role of father-educator given that he has also recognized how his misfortunes are the consequence of own act of filial disobedience. The frequently vexed figure of the orphan in much of Defoe's work, at once the self-created Lockean woman or man of property and at the same time the improperly parented and untutored 'savage', in this novel splits into cannibal and rebellious younger son. Crusoe's wandering, a kind of willed self-orphaning, has reduced him to a condition that borders on the kind of incivility he considers the indigenous Americans to be guilty of. This is the case not only when, in his first panic, he considers destroying his plantations, but also later, when he recognizes that his fear of the cannibals has brought him 'to the murthering humour ... contriving how to circumvent and fall upon them' (184). Such action, he reflects, would have made him 'no less a murtherer than they were in being man-eaters; and perhaps much more so' (184).

The lessons of good government are thus as instructive to the colonizer as they are to the colonized. In an earlier commentary on colonial America, *Party Tyranny* (1705), Defoe represents the unstable political conditions of colonial life in an account both of the abused rights of the settlers and in the figures of good and bad political parenting. In this pamphlet he lists the grievances of the people of Carolina against the Lords Proprietors of the colony, and petitions the English Commons to protect the rights and liberties of freeholding colonists. These Lords Proprietors, the petition claims, have endangered the liberty and security of the English settlement by admitting non-freeholding voters into the electorate. The property-owning colonists should therefore legitimately be able to appeal over the heads of the Governor to the authority of English law, since 'the people ... by right of nature as well as by the constitution, revolves under the immediate direction and government of the English empire whose subjects they were before, and from whom their government was derived'.[22] A few pages later he adds, 'the king must be the father of his people, and ... there is a sort of patriarchal affection, as well as obligation between a king on the throne and the people he governs, which obliges [him] to treat them with gentleness' (13). The Lords Proprietors, on the other hand, are motivated not by affection, but by interest. They are 'step-fathers and strangers in the Government' (13).

This attack on bad political parenting is most effectively visualized in the preface to *Party Tyranny*, where Defoe describes the colony as a kind of unprotected infant. He does so in order to describe an error in Locke's constitution for Carolina. Locke, Defoe argues, established the foundations of independent government for a colony whose youthfulness really required that it remain under the protective control of the English crown:

> These constititutions I know have obtained upon the world, to be the contrivance of the old Earl of S—bury; but I think I have very good authority to assure the world Mr. Lock had the right of parentage to the former ... [he] handed the infant government into the world without leading-strings and turned it loose before it could stand alone; by which means like young *Romulus*, it has got a wolf to its nurse, and is like to be bred up a monster. (8)

And this, of course, is to accuse Locke of the very parental neglect that the latter warned against in the *Second Treatise of Government*:

> To turn [the child] loose to an unrestrained liberty before he has reason to guide him, is not allowing him the privilege of his nature to be free; but to thrust him out amongst brutes, and abandon him to a state as wretched, and as much beneath that of a man as theirs.[23]

Defoe is thus in a sense pointing to the conceptual limits of Locke's theory of social development. Although the latter's theory of property and government partly accounts for Crusoe's sovereignty on the island, it does not take account of how power must be exercised over those 'unsocialized' human beings who have little or no understanding of property and political obligation.

The check to Crusoe's sometimes violent authority on the island, therefore, comes not from his subjects but rather from the greater authority of providence. Observing that he has challenged the sovereignty of providence, he is also able to recognize that he has no right to make war on the cannibals and that he 'ought to leave them to the justice of God who is the governor of nations and knows how by national punishments to make a just retribution for national offences; and to bring publick judgments upon those who offend in a publick manner, by such ways as best please Him' (173). This reflection is in keeping, of course, with others he has made about the pattern of providence and the thankfulness he ought to hold out to God during his period of solitude on the island. Now, as he becomes first a defender of his territory against the threat of savage invaders and eventually a ruler over the various people who submit to his authority, he is able to reconcile both his actions and his power with providential design. The criminal acts of other people and of nations are punished by God, but by the end of the novel he has, in McKeon's words, internalized God's authority, coming to 'read the marks of God on his own mind'[24] and established himself as the legitimate ruler of the island. In the first half of the novel he learns of the gifts of nature which were provided for him and which signalled a greater design at work helping him to recognize his fear, loneliness and despair as nothing but contempt for God's work. He begins to recognize how nature, under God's direction, is providing for his needs. Astonished at the appearance of corn growing where he had in frustration tossed out some spoilt grains, he observes that perhaps 'God had miraculously caus'd this grain to grow without any help of seed sown, and that it was so directed purely for my sustenance on that wild miserable place' (78). In the second half he identifies providence as the dispenser of justice as well as nature's goods, but as the father-ruler of savage subjects who have no other means of learning civil behaviour he necessarily becomes the intermediary of this divine justice. It is by this means that he is able to become more than the rightful owner of the land that he has, in Locke's terms, mixed his labour with. By the time he leaves the island 'the whole country' is his property and, while he allows 'liberty of conscience' throughout this country, he is 'absolute lawgiver' over it, while his people are 'perfectly subjected' (241). This is no longer the hubris of the wild adventurer but rather the just rule of the father-king.

The island is thus governed more like a family than a modern, liberal state. Crusoe not only identifies Friday's affections for him as filial, but he describes the three men whom he has delivered from death and whom he recruits to help him fight the mutineers as his 'family': a family that must be supported by his own stock of corn and rice. His subjects, at this point, are the disenfranchised members of his household. In the second part of Crusoe's story, however, the political regime that he has put in place, and that he tries to return to having failed once more to settle down happily in England, will turn out not to be the political realization of providential will after all. The allegory of power, it will emerge in this sequel, needs to be adapted to fit the historical conditions of colonial trade, and Crusoe himself needs to be re-nationalized as an English merchant. I have argued that this recognition of providential design in the improvement of Crusoe's economy becomes the foundation of legitimate, paternalistic government in the first part of his story. In the second part, he recovers his proper status as a merchant and recognizes that a place might be found for his island colony in the arena of foreign trade. At this point the providential diversity of natural goods becomes more specifically tied to commerce than to agriculture. In order to find his way back into the progressive stream of history that God has ordained, Crusoe must reorient himself as a servant of an English state that both depends upon and, to a large extent, directs foreign commerce.

Crusoe's farther adventures: the nature of trade and the law of nations

Crusoe's return journey to the Caribbean and on into the Indian Ocean is one in which he discovers that the kind of rule he has hitherto enjoyed on the island is in conflict with the imperial and commercial ambitions of his own nation. In the course of these later adventures we learn that, in the colonized world, it is not so much violence as wilful isolation that most offends the natural laws regulating contact between different peoples. Crusoe is only fully able to abandon godless wandering and hubristic adventuring when he assumes the responsibilities of an English merchant. Although his claim to power on the island has been established in the first part of the story as an entirely legitimate one because it arises from his cultivating of land and enclosing of property, it is not appropriate once he is rescued from his solitary life on the island and delivered back into a modern commercial environment. Once there, his first responsibility must be to the foreign trade of his own nation. In this next part of Crusoe's story, the accumulation of national wealth, now based on trade, will take place in a global arena of exchange. Crusoe's recognition of this fundamental mercantilist fact will lead him to the concurrent realization that civil relations between states are as important as those between subjects. In keeping with Defoe's other writing on the destructive consequences of war,[25] the novel advocates peaceful interstate relations in which the national accumulation of wealth can proceed uninhibited by the protective jealousies of aggressive nations and isolated peoples.

In this respect the novels are responding not only to the seventeenth-century debate about contractualism, but also to that body of natural law theory which identifies the state itself as a subject of natural right and law. In Hugo Grotius's writing, the law of nations reproduces the distinction between child-savage and civil subject at the level of social organization, necessarily focusing on the differences between primitive and modern societies in order to determine which peoples are capable of membership in a civil community of nations. Outside this community are the pre-civil societies that have no concept of private property, much less of commercial relationships with other states. Although he doubts that any people so entirely uncivilized can be found anywhere, Grotius in principle denies that such a people could be the bearers of right:

> Neither moral nor religious virtue, nor any intellectual excellence is required to form a good title to property. Only where a race of men is so destitute of reason as to be incapable of exercising any act of ownership, they can hold no property, nor will the law of charity require that they should have more than the necessaries of life. For the rules of the law of nations can only be applied to those, who are capable of political or commercial intercourse, but not to a people destitute of reason.[26]

In *The Freedom of the Seas*, Grotius had argued that islands which have always 'had their own government, their own laws, and their own legal systems' cannot be subjected to the authority of a foreign sovereign, and that therefore their original inhabitants may allow the privilege of trade to any other nation they wish.[27] Yet at the same time, his argument that European powers have limited jurisdiction in foreign territories becomes tied up with a historicized account of the legal origins of political and commercial sovereignty. Grotius identifies two stages in the natural law as it is applied to the law of nations. The first is the primary or 'primitive' law, under which everything is acquired in common and held as a community of goods: 'fields [are] not delimited by boundary lines', and 'there [is] no commercial intercourse' (*Freedom of the Seas*, 23). Here no man has any particular right. A 'nation', by this primitive law, is simply understood as a collection of individuals who collectively own both the land that they occupy as a group and the objects that they have for their common use. The secondary law of nations involves the modern distinction of ownership, both as private property – that which is individually owned – and public property, or that which belongs to a nation. The concept of property, then, must be contemporary with the emergence of states. This marking out of boundaries, Grotius tells us, 'did not come violently, but gradually, nature herself pointing the way' (24), as the consumable properties of a thing – that which could be eaten or drunk, worn or used in any other way – made it by nature the property of the person who used it. This notion of property as the object of bodily needs then necessitated a theory of ownership by occupation. Public property is that which satisfies the needs of a whole nation. In its modern, positive sense, the nation must be recognized as that which has marked out territory as its own, some of which remains public (the private property of a nation), and some of which is the property of individuals.

As the institutions of public and private property emerge, Grotius argues, the law of nations establishes a distinction between natural objects that are available for appropriation, and those that are not. While rivers and inlets may be seen as part of the national territory, the sea can never belong to any particular nation since its natural properties prevent it from being seized or enclosed and any boundary established in it can only ever be an 'imaginary line' (39). This designation of ocean as the common property of all coincides with another positive (secondary) law of nature which recognizes that, although all things were originally given to all human beings in common, men living far apart from one another rely on commerce to provide them with many of the goods which they need or desire. He cites Aristotle in the assertion that 'the art of exchange is a completion of the independence which nature requires' (61), and Seneca that 'buying and selling is the law of nations' (63). This suggests that what remains under the jurisdiction of the primitive law of nations – that which is held in common by all men – is entirely encased in the secondary law, which seeks to protect commercial relations between both individuals and states. A people that is 'incapable of political or commercial intercourse' thus cannot become a bearer of right in the way that a commercial state can.

In *The Rights of War and Peace* Grotius insists that 'there can be no hesitation in pronouncing all wars to be just, that are made upon pirates, general robbers and enemies of the human race' (3:336). In the first part of *Robinson Crusoe*, Defoe seems to be questioning this right as he remarks that it is only God's charge as the 'governor of nations' to punish those who offend him. Yet by the end of that novel, as we have seen, Crusoe has more or less ceased to distinguish between God's authority and his own. In *The Farther Adventures*, this process is reversed: Crusoe returns to the island as the lawgiver that he was when he left it, but by the end of the novel he has assumed the more humble role of an English merchant. This change is motivated by the discovery that he has economic responsibilities to his own nation. Once it has taken place, he begins to think of 'savages' less as his natural subjects than as isolated peoples whose cannibal customs represent a more generally violent condition that prevents the development of commercial relationships with other nations. It is precisely this isolation, he comes to reflect, which deprives them of natural rights. Defoe's debt to Grotius, then, has less to do with the right to punish those who are guilty of unchristian behaviour than with the belief that rule and right are profoundly tied to commercial culture.

Such grounding of jurisprudence in manners puts the health of both commonwealth and empire in the hands of enterprising merchants (who are in turn answerable to the state) rather than in the hands of public-minded citizens. In *The Complete English Tradesman* (1738), Defoe argues explicitly that a tradesman cannot be a public figure. He who engages in party debate, joins clubs and studies politics will end up a bankrupt; a 'good patriot' is a 'bad shopkeeper'.[28] Yet although the tradesman must confine himself to his own sphere, he is nonetheless a man of reason who should be 'capable of making a general judgment of things' in order to defend himself against projectors (16), and know all the inland trade of England so as to be able to turn his hand to any aspect of manufacture in his country. In this respect he is the prototype of the merchant who ought to 'understand all the languages of trade within the circumference of his own country ... [just] as a merchant should understand at least the languages of those countries which he trades to, or corresponds with, and the customs and usages of those countries as to their commerce' (14). By pursuing his own interests, thoroughly and prudently, the tradesman and merchant contribute more than anyone else to England's wealth, helping it to become 'the greatest trading country in the world' (174). Despite its private character, 'trade is a public benefit' (304) since without it 'the lands must be laid down ... and left to bear no corn, or feed no cattle, because your produce is too great for your consumption' (301).

In his first set of adventures, Crusoe came to identify such wasting of the land with a lack of firm government. In the second part of his story when he returns to the island, he learns, like Defoe's tradesman, that the most efficient use of land depends on being able to trade what one cannot consume. This has a number of consequences for his narrative. On this later voyage he continues to reflect, as he did in the first part of *Robinson Crusoe,* on the imprudence of an adventurer's life. The difference here is that he interprets his misfortunes not so much as the just consequences of an original act of disobedience against his father, but as the result of his behaving like a reckless wanderer, journeying to places where he has 'no business', rather than acting like a responsible British merchant who might secure, plant, and settle new territories 'in the name of England' (216). As aimless explorer, as absolute ruler of the island, and as self-appointed prosecutor and judge of both his cannibal and his mutineer subjects, Crusoe presents himself as something more and less than a law-abiding citizen of his country and of the civilized world. *The Farther Adventures* begins where *Robinson Crusoe* left off, setting the relationship between patriarchal government and colonial settlement in the context of larger questions about commercial civility and the law of nations.

Unlike his father, Crusoe sets out from England each time not as a merchant, but as an adventurer, and hence his return home (between parts one and two of *Robinson Crusoe*) is not the happy reward of a life of industry, but rather a 'part' settlement (*Robinson Crusoe,* 305) which is inevitably disturbed by a restless desire to travel abroad again. At the beginning of *The Farther Adventures*, Crusoe confesses to a continuing 'propensity to rambling', despite his now having 'no fortune to make' and 'nothing to seek'.[29] His obsessive desire to see his plantation and the colony he had left on the island is only checked by his wife, whose distressed recognition of the way that this 'impulse of Providence' (4) works upon him brings to his mind the absurdity of wanting to exchange, in his declining years, an easy and settled life for one of hardship and suffering. He then satisfies himself for a time by moving with his family to a farm in Bedford, whose land he 'delight[s] in cultivating, managing, planting and improving' and, lest this should seem too reminiscent of his better days on the island, he remarks that 'being an inland country, I was remov'd from conversing among ships, sailors, and things relating to the remote parts of the world' (6). He believes that he has now achieved the middle stage of life that his father first recommended to him before he set out on his first voyage. On his wife's death, however, this comfortable life of retirement becomes suddenly so desolate that he is reminded of the days isolated on the island, when 'I suffered no more corn to grow, because I did not want it; and bred no more goats, because I had no more use for them; where the money lay in the drawer 'till it grew mouldy, and had scarce the favour to be look'd upon in 20 years' (9). Reversing the pattern of his father's life and career, Crusoe leaves a comfortable retirement to go back to sea, though once again not as a merchant but as a solitary adventurer.

Once he returns to the island we are reminded of how, in the first part of his story, the trials and successes of his solitary life were complicated by his encounter with the cannibals and consequently by questions of law and government. Cannibalism, for the older Crusoe as well as for the younger, signifies the absence of law. While he has been gone, hostilities have repeatedly broken out in the colony, both between the Spaniards and the English mutineers whom he settled there, and between all these and the neighbouring savages who have reportedly visited the island on cannibal raids. Although they repelled these attacks and managed to take a number of slaves, the Spaniards have not been able to educate these peoples out of their anthropophagous habits, and while faithful as slaves, none is quite as dependable as Friday who, Crusoe recalls in a peculiarly ghoulish metaphor, 'was as true to me as the very flesh upon my bones' (69). These slaves cannot be trusted with knowing anything of the plantations since they threaten to escape and bring their fellow invaders back to the island. This constant state of uncertainty is exacerbated by the lack of firm government on the island. Despite their having survived so many attacks, the Spaniards lack Crusoe's economic and political initiative: where he enclosed land, built up a store of goods, and established himself as sovereign ruler, they have remained hungry, dejected and in fear of their lives. All that is to be found on this island, they complain, are 'a few roots and herbs ... which ha[ve] no substance in them, and which the inhabitants g[i]ve them sparingly enough, and who could treat them no better, unless they would turn cannibals and eat mens flesh which was the great dainty of their country' (128). They are so dependent on the native peoples for their survival that not only are they are unable to assert authority over the latter, but they are haunted by the threat that they too might turn cannibal, finally and fully separating themselves from their civilized pasts.

This state of lawlessness is reversed with Crusoe's return. Several striking descriptions of encounters with cannibals in *The Farther Adventures* demonstrate how easily he once again assumes authority, both as governor of the island and as interpreter of what takes place on it. He reports the first of these encounters second-hand. The three renegade Englishmen whose crimes included destroying the Spanish plantations, attacking one of the Indian slaves, and intending to murder all the Spaniards in their sleep, he tells us, were permitted by the Spaniards to leave the island with several firearms and travel to the mainland. On what turned out not to be the mainland at all but an adjacent island, they met with a 'courteous and friendly' (83) people who supplied them with whatever they appeared to need, including 16 of the 200 prisoners taken in war who were being fattened for a coming feast. Crusoe, who is of course the third-hand narrator of this story (having been told it by the Spanish Governor who heard it from the Englishmen themselves), remarks that 'as brutish and barbarous as these fellows were at home, their stomachs turn'd at this sight ... [but] to refuse the prisoners would have been the highest affront to the savage gentry' (84). They decided therefore to accept the prisoners and to return to the island before they were expected to kill and devour their 'gift'. On the journey home they tried to communicate their good intentions to their captives, but every sign they made was interpreted by these as an indication that the Englishmen were about to murder them, and every offer of food as an attempt to fatten them up for the kill. Finally, with the help of Friday's father, they were brought to understand to their joy that they had fallen into the hands of Christians who abhorred the eating of human flesh, and that they were to be made into servants.

This incident is interesting because the fear of cannibalism is expressed on both sides, and also because its resolution takes the form of embracing of the new slaves into the 'family' (126) of colonists that Crusoe has rejoined as head. Although the encounters with the people of the cannibal island and their prisoners are only minimally comprehensible to the Englishmen, who interpret the meaning and feelings of the Indians through their gestures and expressions, their Christian disgust at the practices of this culture enables Crusoe to identify their civilized distance from the savages, and to represent them as fully aware of the misunderstandings of the latter, even as the savages read every movement of the foreigners as if they were no different from themselves.[30] Since the scene with the cannibals is presented retrospectively, the epistemological confusion that attended these earlier encounters with savages is repaired by informed cultural distance: Crusoe has already brought the Englishmen back into the Christian family fold, which they had wilfully left by destroying the plantations of the more industrious Europeans. Crusoe's description of the colony – Spaniards, English, and Indian slaves – is of the single family under his authority that the Spaniards in his absence were unable to establish. The colonists are only properly able to overcome their differences, that is to say, when, as sovereign, Crusoe returns, and finds of the subjects that meet him that 'it was impossible to guess what nation they were of' (43). Crusoe's patriarchal rule once again guarantees social order on the island where national differences would otherwise perpetuate violence and discord.

The most extreme form that such discord takes is of course cannibalism, and hence Crusoe makes no distinction between the ritualized
eating of enemies and human bodies as a source of nourishment. On
his journey to the island Crusoe rescues a ship from Bristol which has
lost its masts in a hurricane and whose crew and passengers have either
starved or nearly starved to death. Those who are still alive tell him of
their experience of extreme hunger which, Crusoe reflects, 'knows no
friend, no justice, no right, and therefore is remorseless, and capable of
no compassion' (236). The likelihood that hunger will overcome both
civil behaviour and natural affections is borne out when later in the
novel he learns of and reports the full story of the maid who faced star-
vation with her mistress. The maid is so 'ravenous and furious with
hunger' (201) that she imagines that had she had a child its life might
not have been safe with her. 'Had my mistress been dead', she considers,
'as much as I lov'd her, I am certain, I should have eaten a piece of her
flesh, with as much relish, and as unconcern'd, as ever I did the flesh of
any creature appointed for food; and once or twice I was going to bite
my own arm' (201–2). Crusoe rescues these people from their desperate
isolation just as he did Friday and the Spaniard from the cannibals, and
the captain from the mutineers. Had not his ship so providentially
found them, he reflects, 'a few days more would have ended all their
lives, unless they had prevented it by eating one another' (204). A merchant ship that has drifted beyond the boundaries of civil community,
according to Crusoe's observation, is no different from a 'savage' state
in which the weak stand to be profoundly violated by the strong.

It is Crusoe, however, who is, in the end, most severely judged by his
own ready association between isolation and uncivil behaviour. While
he is on the island he never doubts his civilizing mission, as he does in
the earlier part of his first story when he becomes aware of his own
resistance to the providential script. Only after he leaves the island
does he begin to reflect critically on the nature of his experiences. In a
striking change of mood, he then reproaches himself for pursuing an
adventure whose ambitions disobey the laws of nature and commerce:

> I had no more business to go to the East Indies than a man at full
> liberty, and having committed no crime, has to go to the turn-key at
> Newgate, and desire him to lock him up among the prisoners there,
> and starve him. Had I taken a small vessel from England, and went
> directly to the island; had I loaded her ... with all the necessaries for
> the plantation, and for my people took a patent from the govern-
> ment here, to have secur'd my property, in subjection only to that

of England; had I carried over cannon and ammunition, servants and people, to plant, and taking possession of the place, fortified and strengthen'd it in the name of England, and increas'd it with people ... had I then settle'd myself there, and sent the ship back, loaden with good rice ... and ordered my friends to fit her out again for our supply ... had I at least acted like a man of common sense; but I was possessed with a wandering spirit ... I pleased my self with being the patron of the people I placed there, and doing for them in a kind of haughty majestick way, like an old patriarchal monarch; providing for them as if I had been father of the whole family ... But I never so much as pretended to plant in the name of any government or nation, or to acknowledge any prince. (216–17)

In this passage the disturbing inclination to wander is tied to the arrogance of 'haughty majesty'. Crusoe leaves the island not to return to his native land, but to wander on through the east, having rather improperly re-established, he now seems to reflect, his patriarchal authority where he should, like a good merchant, have taken out a patent in the name of England and shipped goods back from the colony. Reversing the pattern of the first adventures, Crusoe's reflections become increasingly less authoritative, and his identity less secure. When, after assuming an authority on the ship that he does not have and exciting the hostility of both crew and captain, he is put ashore on the coast of Arabia, he reflects distressedly that he is 'alone in the remotest part of the world ... near three thousand leagues by sea farther off from England than I was at my island' (246). He must consider how to travel overland back to Britain, since, having no connection with the East India Company – either the ships' captains or the company's factors – he cannot get passage aboard an English ship. This sudden yearning for home almost turns him from explorer into merchant. An English merchant with whom he takes lodging suggests that they take a trading voyage to China together, and while Crusoe admits that trade is not his element, he confesses that after some debate with his companion he 'begin[s] to be a convert to the principles of merchandizing', and to 'conquer [his] backwardness' (252). Merchandising, 'a covetous desire of getting' on in the world, rather than a 'restless desire of seeing [it]' (250), is not only a modern achievement which makes Crusoe's kingdom look like a backwater, but it is also in keeping with the laws of providence that, rather than confirming his right to rule, humble his narrative before the greater plan of God: 'Let no wise man flatter himself with the strength of his own judgment ... Man is a shortsighted creature, sees but a very little way before him' (218).

Perhaps the most remarkable change of heart in Crusoe's narrative occurs towards the end of the novel when he is travelling back to Europe overland through Asia. Although this is primarily a journey home rather than a trading venture, Crusoe ends up travelling in the company of a great many merchants of several nations including Muscovites, Poles and Scots, and himself in fact procures in Peking a cargo of silks, tea, calicoes and 'three camel loads of nutmegs and cloves' (308). The Portuguese pilot who has been translating for him through the latter part of the Asian journey carries china silks to England, from where he intends to 'voyage back to Bengale, by the Company's ships' (306). When Crusoe learns of the caravan of merchants travelling from Peking to Muscovy, he is filled 'with a secret joy [which] spread itself over my whole soul' (306). His conversion to merchandizing is accompanied by a resurgent horror of 'wilderness'. The merchants are particularly fearful in the area beyond Northern China designated 'no man's land, being a part of Great Karakathie, or Grand Tartary, but that however it was all reckon'd to China; but that there was no care taken here, to preserve it from the inroads of thieves, and therefore it was reckon'd the worst desart in the whole world' (317). Crusoe identifies entirely with his merchant fellow travellers in his fear of this lawless wild over which no nation clearly has dominion. The Scottish merchant warns him about the Tartars, saying that they have no knowledge of letters or of any other language; that they live in a 'wretched ignorance' (332). They are subjected to the Czar of Muscovy's dominions and, lacking both sovereign identity and knowledge of other languages and customs, they are necessarily violent and brutish. Like Dampier, Crusoe is 'discovering' that some societies are less able to govern themselves and more inclined to violence than others, and that this degree of civilization is directly related to their capacity for trade.

Such distinctions then directly affect his treatment of the peoples he encounters. When he was abandoned by his nephew's ship on the coast of Arabia, his desire to return to England was accompanied by a righteous sense of how barbarously the crew had treated the natives whom they encountered at Madagascar. In revenge for the murder of one of their number who raped a native woman, the men of the ship set fire to the village and murdered as many of its inhabitants as they could find. Crusoe described this as a 'rage altogether barbarous' and a 'fury, something beyond what was human' (234). Several natives who ran into Crusoe and pleaded for mercy 'kne[lt] down, with their hands lifted up' (235) in a manner that seems to invoke the image of his first meeting with Friday, who 'came nearer and nearer, kneeling down every ten or twelve steps in token of acknowledgment for my saving his life' (*Robinson Crusoe*, 203). The Crusoe who acted in this episode, as he did on the island, as master, judge, civilizer and protective father, is replaced in the later sections of the novel by a merchant figure who has nothing but contempt for subjugated peoples apparently incapable of communication or commerce with other nations. Horrified by idol worship and determined to 'vindicate the honour of God' (*Farther Adventures*, 332), he proposes stealing an idol and leaving those who worship it an explanation of his reasons for doing so. Having reminded him that they cannot read or understand his language, the Scottish merchant then tells him the story of a Russian who tried to interrupt them in their worship and was sacrificed to their idol for his pains. To this, Crusoe responds by advocating extreme violence:

> I related the story of our men at Madagascar, and how they burnt and sack'd the village there, and kill'd man, woman and child, for their murdering one of our men, just as it is related before; and when I had done, I added, that I thought we ought to do so to this village. (333)

He conspicuously offers no reflection on this change of attitude. Neither the interpretive authority that he demonstrates on the island nor the self-doubt that he experiences on leaving it is available to mediate this contradiction. His violent plan is simply presented as the logical one in a land where the people are isolated, ignorant and pagan, in a 'wild uncultivated country' (347) where, we have already learned, there are no safe routes for traders to follow. In Siberia, where they next travel, things only seem worse as they encounter 'on the north side an unnavigable ocean, where ship never sailed and boat never swam' (357), and every other way 'byways clearly impassable, except by roads made by the governor'. While the company are trapped by the Siberian winter, Crusoe does speak proudly to the exiled Russian prince whom he meets there of what he calls his 'tyrannical' rule on the island, and of how as patriarchal sovereign he was 'universally beloved, ... yet horribly feared by his subjects' (351). This can only sit ironically next to his dread of travelling through this remote place which, being like his island 'far out of the road of commerce' (363), is naturally peopled by pagans and thieves.

Crusoe's final reflection in *The Farther Adventures* is on his at last having learnt 'the value of retirement and the blessing of ending our days in peace' (373). The peace of having finally abandoned the life of a wanderer, and returned home to a sober later life such as that of his father, is also the peace sought by a properly commercial nation. The law of nations into which Crusoe is educated in the course of the novel distinguishes between those societies that are capable of commercial intercourse and those that are not. To subjugate 'uncivilized' peoples and to set oneself up as their absolute ruler and master is to become de-nationalized and troublingly removed from the wider world of commerce. To make war on isolated 'savages and pagans' in the name of civilized trade, however, is as lawful as it is loyal to English interests.

Crime, vagrancy and trade in *Captain Singleton*

Crusoe's adventures can be usefully compared to those of Captain Singleton (*Singleton* was published one year later, in 1720) because their stories in many ways mirror one another even as they dramatize, in different ways, the same cluster of concerns about familial and national belonging. Singleton writes, as it were, from the other side of modernity. Unlike the middle-stationed Crusoe, for whom the abandonment of doting parents becomes as much a neglect of his social position as his absolute rule on the island becomes a betrayal of his responsibilities as an Englishman, Singleton has neither parents nor position. Rather than choosing to abandon family and nation, he is *forced* into a life of wandering. In remarking that he has no home and that 'all the world is alike' to him, he seems to embody both the deracinating consequences of travel and an ignorance of the world's cultural and biological diversity that Crusoe learns to respect, first as colonizer and then as merchant. Stolen from his parents when only an infant, Singleton has no familial identity, and is thrown early into a life of wandering as he grows up under the care of a gypsy who 'continually dragged [him] about with her, from one part of the country to another'.[31] With no experience of civilized culture in the form of either settled life or trade, Singleton 'naturally' turns to a life of crime, becoming, as he is later to repent, 'a thief, a pyrate and a murderer' (269). As a criminal and a vagabond, he has no obvious means of recovering his national identity and consequently no way in which to enjoy his wealth free of fear. In this respect, he is the counterexample to Crusoe: where the latter discovers that the geographical and cultural distance between English home and Caribbean colony can be bridged by trade, Singleton can only return to England by passing as a foreign merchant and can only enjoy his ill-gotten gains in the refuge offered to him at the end of the novel, which is a 'home' that only barely alleviates his rootlessness and that does not enable him to enjoy his wealth freely.

Like the first part of *Robinson Crusoe*, *Captain Singleton* dramatizes Locke's equation between children and savages since the improperly parented Singleton appears as savage as the isolated peoples with whom he comes into contact.[32] At the beginning of his adventures he is, the older and wiser narrator admits, 'perfectly unfit to be trusted with liberty' and 'ripe for villainy' (11). When, early on in the novel, he is punished for mutiny by being left, along with his fellow-mutineers on a Madagascan shore, he reflects that their desperation might make them 'more likely to eat [the Cannibal inhabitants of the island] than they us, if we could but get at them' (13). Finding himself in a savage state of nature, he does not hesitate to recommend an unprovoked attack on the natives with whom they are unable to trade for provisions, 'falling upon them with our fire arms; and taking their cattle from them, and sending them to the devil to stop their hunger, rather than be starved ourselves' (27). In the course of his journey across the African continent, however, he becomes the *de facto* leader of the mutineer band and begins to act with some semblance of respect for the laws that govern conduct between nations, and thin respect in turn initiates him into something almost like an affective community. When the mutineers are debating how they might force some of the Africans into slavery to help carry their belongings on the expedition, Singleton recognizes that according to the law of arms such violence must be justified by a prior attack, or at least 'knavery' (51) on the part of the natives. When the latter conveniently prove to be treacherous traders, the Europeans fire upon them, and take the survivors as prisoners. Although these slaves are on the whole so savage that they can only be managed by violence, Singleton does secure the loyal service of a prince who, in what seems like a repetition of Friday's subjection to Crusoe, encourages his followers to kneel before the European 'holding up their hands and making signs of entreaty' (57).

This brief experience as father/master is complemented by another role of surrogate son. During the same journey, Singleton makes a kind of substitute father out of the gunner, who is well educated in the sciences of mathematics and geography as well as in seamanship. This father-figure teaches him the rudiments of geography and astronomy and, in so doing, raises him out of the savage indifference to place that he demonstrated at the beginning of the journey when he remarked to his companions that 'whether we went or stayed, I had no home, and all the world was alike to me' (35). Moreover, the lessons stimulate him into the resolution to return to England and better himself in the world. At such moments, he begins to look very like Crusoe, looking hopefully (if not yet quite repentantly) towards the middle station of life and removing himself by his considered actions from the savage state that he formerly shared with the Africans, as well as with his fellow criminals.

Yet for the most part, Singleton's relationship to the civilized world, and to the home country to which he becomes more attached in the course of the novel, is a tenuous one. This is in part because the desperate acts that remove Singleton from any real possibility of national belonging, while they may originate in his lack of parenting, are set in motion by the experience of finding himself in remote and unproductive landscapes. The 'desperate resolution' that he and his fellow travellers make to travel overland through the 'unpassable deserts' and the heat and the dangers of the African wilderness, through 'the most desolate, desart, and unhospitable country in the world' (47), deliver them right back into a violent state of nature in which they have 'nations of savages to encounter with, barbarous and brutish to the last degree, hunger and thirst to struggle with; and in one word, terrors enough to have daunted the stoutest hearts that ever were placed in cases of flesh and blood' (48). The typically Defoean language of survey and calculation that the travellers use to try to assess and manage their circumstances is rhetorically overwhelmed by the narrator's constant references to the 'vast' and the 'infinite'. In the second half of the novel, when Singleton joins a pirate crew and cruises through first the West and then the East Indies, the 'vast unknown Indian ocean' (205) yields, if not the same terrors, at least the same savagery in the character of the natives who inhabit it: peoples who know little of commerce and who are violent and difficult to communicate with. These 'savage' landscapes are matched by the moral and physical unfixedness of the protagonist who robs and kills as the instinct of self-preservation dictates. Although his companion, William the Quaker, takes on the burden of recognizing what is and is not a just act of war, Singleton 'justifies' his acts of aggression against those who have done him no harm by arguing that he merely intends to prevent them from finding any opportunity to hurt him.

In the second half of his narrative, he undergoes a spiritual crisis during which he recognizes that his roving life may make him the object of God's just wrath. In the midst of a terrible storm he begins to 'feel the effects of that horrour ... upon the just reflection on my former life' (195). Yet the troubles of his conscience are not powerful enough in themselves to make him abandon this life because they are not, until the very last pages of the novel, linked (as Crusoe's were) to an idea of home. This becomes clear when, some time after the epiphany, William suggests to him that they are both rich enough to abandon piracy and suggests that 'it is natural for most men that are abroad to desire to come home again at last, especially when they are grown rich' (256). Singleton, however, replies that the world is his home and that he has neither relations nor friends in England nor any 'kindness for the country where [he] was born' (257). Despite his fear of God's judgement, his actions and decisions are determined less by the prospect of divine retribution than by his own deracinated condition. He still as rootless as he was at the beginning of his story when he revealed his indifference to the question of whether the party should try and return home, remarking that he would be happy to stay in Madagascar where plenty could be found to eat and drink and where, as a result, he might be 'rich as a king' (36). This arrogant, Crusoe-like dream of becoming sovereign in a savage land, like piracy, demonstrates either ignorance or defiance of his status as an English subject at the same time as it expresses resistance to God's law.

By the end of his story, however, he is convinced that he does indeed desire to return home, observing that 'a man that has a subsistence, and no residence, no place that has a magnetick influence upon his affections, is in one of the most odd uneasy conditions in the world; nor is it in the power of all his money to make it up to him' (276). The difference between wilful homelessness and melancholy homesickness has everything to do with money. While he applies the principles he learns about the rules and rights of war and responds to the fear of God's vengeance very erratically, he does take very seriously the lesson that wealth cannot be enjoyed without the assistance and guidance of friends and the security of 'a kind of centre'. The two halves of his story, which seem otherwise disconnected, find some symmetry in the paired events of return to England and in the prodigality into which circumstances force him each time. The first time he goes back, he is able neither to manage his money properly nor to establish any lasting affective ties. Having made the happy discovery of a huge supply of gold and ivory in Africa, he returns a rich man. Athough he very scrupulously documents the volume of each precious substance that he and his companions accumulate, the method of extracting and collecting, the value of the whole, and the quantity owing to each man, Singleton has very little sense of economy when it comes to managing his own share of the wealth. When he returns to England he squanders it and is back at sea within two years. Having no home to go to in the form of relation or friend (either of whom might have offered him financial guidance) he finds himself slipping into wastefulness, excess and indulgence. At the end of the novel, he again parts liberally and easily with his money, this time by giving it to William's sister, a poor widow with four children whom he eventually marries. Through this cultivation of home he is then able to enjoy what on the high seas he could only purposelessly accumulate. Yet this is only a half-won happiness since he must remain forever in hiding, disguised as a foreigner. The wealth he has accrued as a pirate cannot, therefore, be *directly* spent any more circumspectly than that which he found in Africa, and he is forced to excuse himself to the reader for having once again been so 'prodigal' (275) with his money.

Singleton thus finds himself in the same condition as the Kurtz-like English renegade whom he meets in central Africa (a former factor for the English Guinea Company in Sierra Leone who has become an independent trader in ivory).[33] This Englishman has given up collecting the precious goods of the desert because he had seemingly 'wandered beyond all possibility of return' (124) and believes he will never have occasion to enjoy the wealth they would bring him in England. In Africa, they will not 'buy clothes to cover [him], or a drop of drink to save [him] from perishing' (127). He identifies Singleton and his companions as his deliverers and encourages them to stay longer in the desert to collect a greater quantity of gold because value will be restored to it once they return to Europe. Their company and protection not only makes it possible for him to make the journey home but in so doing transforms a 'desolate, disconsolate wilderness' into 'one of the richest parts of the world' (126).[34] By showing them the way to the coast as well as the richest parts of the area, he, in return, delivers them out of a hand-to-mouth existence in which the gold they have found is valuable only as the material for fashioning trinkets that the travellers can trade with the natives in return for provisions or friendship.

The savage life that the Englishman has been forced into, that Singleton (has at least in part) embraced and the Africans have only ever known is therefore one of such isolation that it evacuates gold – the medium and the object of trade between states – of everything except use value. Obviously bullion has no value as a commodity when it is not in circulation, and only subjects of commercial nations are capable of circulating it. The mercantilist principles that gold should be circulated in order to promote a balance of trade and that exchange value should be protected against savagery and profligacy then become, more powerfully than the signs of God's wrath, instruments of adjudication with regard to the rules of warfare. William repeatedly reminds Singleton that his business is to acquire money and on one occasion (at the coast of Ceylon) points out to the ship's crew that to kill and conquer 'poor naked wretches' who have no money is not only to make no profit, but is also to commit cold-blooded murder. When it turns out, however, that the people of Ceylon treacherously offer a flag of peace when they mean to trap and imprison the Europeans, and moreover that they 'will not allow any trade or commerce with any European nation' (238), it becomes clear that firing upon them is quite justified. At such moments, the irony that, as a pirate, Singleton is guilty of the same disrespect for commerce as the Ceylonese is lost upon the narrator. (On one occasion Singleton's ship flies false colours in order to lure in a Portuguese sloop into the crew's clutches, and he congratulates their skill at passing 'for anything but really what we was' [169].) Yet his resolution to give up cruising and turn merchant seems implicitly to recognize Grotius's argument that pirates, like cannibals and others who offend the natural laws of sociability (in this novel, all non-commercial peoples), are legitimate targets of violent retribution.

* * *

The labour of transforming a wilderness into a garden, as in the first part of *Robinson Crusoe*, or of bringing home the profits of adventure, as in *The Farther Adventures* and *Captain Singleton*, can only be successfully accomplished by the subjects of commercial states. At the same time the strength of the state depends upon the accumulation of wealth through foreign and colonial trade and hence on the cooperative relationships between commercial nations producing, importing and re-exporting goods over and above what they can consume domestically. Defoe's mercantilist confidence in a favourable balance of trade overseen by a powerful and paternalist state is what gives coherence to the otherwise seemingly disconnected adventures of his seafaring characters. His correction of the errant behaviour of these characters, by providential law as well as by the hindsight of the 'older and wiser' narrators, orders these otherwise fragmented narratives into a coherent argument for the relationship between national wealth and state power. It is precisely this coherence and the violence it inflicts on those who are not the direct beneficiaries of mercantilist policy that

Swift will challenge in *Gulliver's Travels*. Here, as Swift's traveller becomes progressively more detached from the political and geographical principles that bind him to England, he also exposes the absurdity of mercantilist logic and the fundamental incoherence of a world that Defoe sees as ordered and organized for England's commercial taking.

4
Swift and the Geographers: Race, Space and Merchant Capital in *Gulliver's Travels*

> So geographers in Afric maps
> With savage pictures fill their gaps
> and o'er uninhabitable downs
> Place elephants for want of towns.[1]

I begin this chapter with these much-quoted lines from Swift's *On Poetry: A Rhapsody* because they argue so directly that 'savagery' is an invention of geography. Swift attacks geography as fraudulent learning, as a science that is always trying to cover the gaps and inconsistencies that it inevitably confronts by insisting on the barbarousness and barrenness of those regions about which it has little or no knowledge. Like the gaping lines of bad modern poetry, geographers' texts are filled with fantastic figures that expose their authors' want of knowledge more than they reveal the real character of the places and peoples they purport to represent. Formally linked by the couplet structure to such 'gaps', the 'unhabitable downs' are just as probably a convenient cartographic fiction as a reliable depiction of little-explored parts of the world. Rather than accounting for some existing geocultural reality or providing reliable documentation about the kind of human beings to be found in a continent as enormous and unexplored as Africa, Swift points out, 'savage pictures' are in fact the product of a dangerous modern ambition to map the entire globe fully and systematically.

Swift's distrust of geographical projects, I will be arguing here, is directly tied to his criticism of British mercantilist imperialism.[2] An advocate of Irish self-sufficiency, conservative opponent of the financial schemes tied to merchant capital, and vicious satirist of the scientific projects that put new discoveries at the service of commercial expansion, Swift was consistently a critic of English imperial excesses.

83

In this respect his work attacks precisely the kind of cultural chauvinism that puts England at the heart of a commercially expanding and integrating world. For Dampier and Defoe, as we have seen, both the epistemological coherence and the national identity of the travelling subject are secured by the growing congruity of the newly 'discovered' regions of the earth. As they describe the evolution of these travellers from renegade adventurers and uncertain observers of foreign cultures to merchants or men of science acting in the interests of the state, they organize representations of oceans crossed, lands traversed and peoples encountered into a comparative study of different parts of the world, a world that can then be comprehended as a hierarchically ordered whole. In so doing, they bring peripheral parts of the world into the commercial view of the British metropolitan core. Swift, on the other hand, puts an incoherent traveller-subject in an incoherent global space. In *Gulliver's Travels*, modern techniques of acquiring and systematizing knowledge repeatedly fail so that each encounter and each discovery progressively undoes both the sense of a stable self and of a world whose spatial and cultural logic can be fully and consistently mapped for English commerce.

My task here will be to look at how Swift's epistemological puzzles are responding to contemporary developments in the field of geography (the ways in which knowledge about places and peoples across the world is spatially arranged), and to suggest that, as such, they articulate not just an antimodern sensibility but also a thorough critique of the globalizing technologies of mercantile capitalism. Geography is more than an imaginative process of distinguishing between what is comfortably close and what is properly distant: it is also the instrument of an expanding commerce that needs to bring places closer together (opening up markets) even as it holds them apart (determining which parts of the world will deliver which products). *Gulliver's Travels*, I will not be the first to suggest, is as much a text written from the economic and political periphery as 'A Modest Proposal' or any of the Irish tracts.[3] This is especially so because it offers a critique of the penetration of the 'peripheral' world by the interests of merchant capital, and these interests are themselves bound to colonizing European states. As we shall see, Swift's anti-colonialism is articulated finally on the grotesque (and ultimately racialized body), as he turns Gulliver loose into a series of alien landscapes in which his body shape and size are hopelessly mismatched with those of his hosts; so much so that all his efforts to measure objects in impossibly small or impossibly large spaces and to use these measurements as the basis for cultural and economic exchange become patently absurd. The forced reorientation of the body to an unfamiliar environment highlights at once the peculiarity of that body and the empirical conundrum of trying to measure or describe accurately the landscape in which such a body finds itself.

To some extent, Swift's monstrous bodies resemble those of Mikhail Bakhtin's carnivalesque: both are irreverent, comic, and directly challenging of officialdom. For Bakhtin, as for Swift, these are the grotesque alter-egos of a properly proportioned body that provides the scale of measurement for humanist geography.[4] Swift's monsters, however, do not voice a radical vernacular or the culture of folk humour challenging official discourse in Bakhtin's reading of Rabelais. Instead they expose how the link between geographical science and commercial interests works to peripheralize and, in some cases, racialize those who are not the direct beneficiaries of modern global commerce. Swift, I will be arguing here, explores how geography and merchant capital together endeavour to create imperial and economic networks of connection between far-flung countries and cultures. His satires draw attention to the moments when geographers find they cannot assimilate those peoples that remain outside commercial modernity into measured global space and so construct such peoples as excessively remote, barbaric and physically grotesque. Turning the tables on the European explorer and transforming him into the deformed, racialized object of scientific investigation, he exposes travel writing and even geographical study itself as a flawed project.[5] The critique of mercantilism in *Gulliver's Travels* thus takes the forms of immeasurability, discontinuity and dislocation: the unsettlement of enlightened commercial and state-centred promises of geography.

Geography, merchant capital and the state

The field of knowledge known as geography represents a narrowing-down of the older subject of cosmography: the study of earth and its relation to the heavens. Unlike cosmography, geography is an earth-centred and primarily secular study of the environments in which human beings live. Geography encompasses both mathematical representations of the sphere – involving the sciences of cartography, chorography, topography, and the attendant skills of surveying and charting – and geological, ethnographic, botanical and zoological descriptions of the different regions of the earth. Early modern geographical treatises typically include a collection of maps and charts, as well as detailed reports of particular countries and documentation of the forms of government, methods of war, religion, commerce and manners of the peoples who live in them. Geography is at the heart of the new sciences of the sixteenth to eighteenth centuries, emphasizing the value both of empirical observation and of the systematic analysis of the data such observations recover.[6] It also belongs to an essentially mercantilist vision, serving the commercial ambitions both of the state and of a merchant class, each pursuing new markets and new sources of colonial revenue. Mapmaking in particular, as Jerry Brotton has shown, was coterminous with commercial expansion during the early modern period. From the sixteenth century onwards, maps of the east as well as of the new colonies in the west often included representations of the lucrative commodities to be found in the region, and were frequently drawn so as to emphasize points of commercial significance rather than conquered or desirable territories.[7]

At the same time, of course, the acquisition of colonies did combine commercial and imperial ambitions, and cartography provided data that served both the imperial archive and the centralized state. Elizabeth I's reign oversaw enormous cartographic enterprises, such as Christopher Saxon's 1575 atlas of maps of English counties (the Queen herself is standing on the frontispiece to Saxton's atlas in the famous Ditchley portrait) and the surveying of Ireland in the second half of the sixteenth century. A century later, in 1675, John Ogilby published his *Britannia*, a complete collection of road maps of England and Wales. Such large-scale projects were important as representations of the reach of state power, as well as instruments of both domestic and colonial administration.[8] The English map trade expanded significantly in the seventeenth and eighteenth centuries as England's imperial reach extended further into the New World: map publishers such as John Seller, William Berry, Moses Pitt and Herman Moll issued numerous atlases and geographical works that recorded discoveries and boundary changes in both the new and old worlds of which neither kings nor merchants could afford to be ignorant. Reconnaissance maps, maps to illustrate sites for settlement, and maps that would assist traders as well as settlers in established colonies were all obviously central to the acquisition and protection of new territories. Moreover, colonial boundary disputes were negotiated through competing national cartographic archives: in 1718, for example, the tussle between Britain and France concerning territories in the American west was articulated through the rival maps of North America by Guillaume Delisle and Herman Moll.[9] Maps at times performed a public function, illustrating and legitimizing empire; at other times they served as sources of military intelligence.[10]

Administratively, strategically and rhetorically, then, the imperial state was indebted to improvements in cartographical technology. Ptolemy's *Geographia*, rediscovered in the fifteenth century, provided the model for creating a mathematical depiction of the globe using lines of the equator, tropics and Arctic and Antarctic circles, as well as the coordinates of latitude and longitude. The Ptolemaic projection was challenged in 1569 by Gerhardus Mercator whose own projection increased the distance between the parallels until they formed perpendicular lines and so 'squared' the globe. By depicting rhumbs (the curving lines that mark the distance between points on the globe) as straight lines, Mercator's projection made navigation much more efficient. Several theories on how to improve the calculation of longitude at sea and the charting of lines of compass variation were also developed in England in the mid-sixteenth century.[11] By the late eighteenth century, mapmakers were relying more on original survey and on the growing sophistication of instruments used to calculate it. Altogether, maps became increasingly precise and useful for determining the accessibility and extent, as well as the natural and political boundaries, of a country, whether old or 'new'.[12]

The geographical genre of the atlas provided opportunity for more layered and complex representations of different parts of the globe. Instead of compiling a collection of sheet maps of differing sizes, atlases assembled a series of maps in a uniform size and with a uniform projection, providing information at once about a particular region and about its relationship to neighbouring countries and to other parts of the world. Atlases also often included descriptive information. Sixteenth-century editions of Ptolemy's *Geographia* accompanied each of the maps (drawn according to the coordinates he provided) with descriptive entries.[13] Subsequent atlas collections, such as those of Abraham Ortelius (1570) and Mercator (1585–95) in the Netherlands, and Johan Blaeu (1663) in Holland, included descriptive accounts of the location, boundaries, history, and ethnographic and botanical character of the regions represented cartographically.[14] At one level the atlas reflected the increasingly aggressive designs of sovereign states in the sixteenth and seventeenth centuries as they thought of their own territories in relation to the global distribution of power.[15] Yet atlases can also be seen to document other kinds of global relationships: natural-historical, ethnographic, and above all commercial.[16] In the combination of descriptive and mathematical representations, they demonstrate a relationship between cartographic uniformity and the diversity of objects of empirical investigation; this diversity is of course at the origin of international commerce. A range of cartographic modes – topography, charting and chorography – are combined with textual information so as to offer an expansive yet coherent account of a single, visible globe: all the different modes of geographical knowledge are fully reconciled so that the representation of the whole world (or in some cases a whole nation) appears as uniform, continuous and non-contradictory.[17] The very genre of the atlas proposes that the earth in all its variety can be comprehended by a single system of observation and measurement.

The seventeenth and eighteenth centuries also saw increasingly regular publication of what have come to be known as 'special geographies'.[18] Initially written mainly for adults, but by 1750 designed increasingly as instructional texts for young readers, these books boasted a highly ordered representation of the facts available on different parts of the world. They were typically organized by countries and divided up into sections according to the terrestrial, celestial and human-social features particular to that country. Subheadings for each of these sections would then cover topics such as longitude, situation and the natural features for terrestrial properties; climate, zone, seasons, and length of day and night for celestial properties; and arts, commodities, trade, government, manners, religion, and language for the peoples of that country or nation.[19] Often they also recorded these various features in analytical tables so that the characteristics of particular regions could be compared with one another and their differences immediately appreciated. The objective of such texts, according to Patrick Gordon, whose *Geography Anatomiz'd: Or the Geographical Grammar* went through 20 editions between 1693 and 1754,[20] was to reduce the whole body of modern geography to a grammatical method. For Gordon, such method could restrict the growth of vice among the idle young who were otherwise corrupted by the 'accomplishments and diversions so much in vogue among our gentry'.[21] Students of geography could be initiated into a more sober scientific lingua franca even as the diverse properties of different parts of the earth would be made visible by a single ordered system: universal knowledge would coincide with a coherent, singular geography.

The way in which the formal characteristics of atlases and of special geographies emphasize both the diversity and the connectedness of different parts of the world thus suggests that sciences of measurement coincide with mercantilist principles: they operate as much in the service of global commerce as of the competitive imperial state.[22] If commerce is to expand across the globe, if colonial and foreign markets are to grow and interpenetrate, then the cultural goods produced by one society must be measurable and quantifiable in terms of those of another society. This raises a more general question about how capital adapts, or perhaps more accurately 'naturalizes', spatial relationships. As Henri Lefebvre has shown, the idea of 'objective, neutral and empty space', a space that is 'luminous [and] intelligible', space that 'can be taken in by a single glance by that mental eye which illuminates whatever it contemplates', shapes our understanding of the relationship between perceiving subjects and grasped objects.[23] The notion that space pre-exists the productive activity that takes place in it obscures the ways in which space itself is *produced*. One of Lefebvre's examples is the division of contemporary Europe into the industrial north and the leisure-oriented perimeter of the Mediterranean. Here the 'unproductive expense' of tourism is stimulated by entrepreneurial initiative in the north; coastal landscapes identified for the purposes of tourism purely by the natural properties of sea, sand and sky are in fact inhabited not 'innocently' or naturally, but through what Lefebvre calls 'conceptualized space': that which is represented by 'scientists, planners, urbanists, technocratic subdividers and social engineers' (38). The way in which space is both managed and produced by such professionals is obscured for workers, bureaucrats and tourists alike by a geographical ideology whose first premise is that measured and calculated or conceptual space perfectly coincides with lived (and visited) space (58). This fetishization of abstract spatial relationships – presenting as natural what is in fact shaped by social relations of production – belongs to early eighteenth-century mercantilism just as powerfully as it does to the late capitalism of our own century.

Geographical texts produce space that can be readily accessed by merchant capital. Eighteenth-century geography endeavours to situate nations, landscapes and cultures in homogeneous, empty space, even as it takes pains to represent their extraordinary diversity and hence the great range of goods that can be bought, sold and exchanged through foreign and colonial commerce. This homogenization is what J. B. Harley has described as the substitution of space for place in which space is infinitely substitutable: 'if places look alike they can be treated alike'.[24] Geographical works of the late seventeenth and early eighteenth centuries demonstrate the dependence of capital on precisely this fusing of diversity and homogeneity, place and space. In the section that follows, I will look at the production of homogeneous space in a range of early eighteenth-century geographies. I will then consider where and when global space does remain troublingly discontinuous and contradictory, and how geography fills it with a barbaric and often racially marked outsider.

Early eighteenth-century geography: space, peoples and the global marketplace

Many of the advertisements and introductions to geographical texts explain the usefulness of measuring, comparing and classifying data collected from different parts of the world, emphasizing that such knowledge is central to the growth and sustenance of a commercial culture. Almost contemporary with *Gulliver's Travels,* a collection of maps by John Senex, *A New General Atlas of the World* (1721), opens with an account of the value of geographical knowledge in a commercial society. This preface points out how physical, environmental and demographic information about different parts of the world has a practical value that cuts across all class and professional differences in a society where there is a complex division of labour. The author remarks on the value of the atlas to 'noblemen, gentlemen, commanders by sea and land, divines, lawyers, physicians and merchants and indeed to persons of all ranks'.[25] He suggests that while geography is vital to the security of civil government, which needs to know the 'interests, extent, situation, wealth and strength of their own dominions and those of their neighbours' (1), as well as to the immediate survival of sailors and merchants, it is also central to the lives of those not directly engaged in foreign or even domestic commerce. Ordinary farmers, he points out, benefit from knowledge of the soil, air and water that gives them a livelihood. Geography is the apparently levelling science that benefits 'men of all ranks' [A3r.]; it is 'acceptable and useful to mankind in general' (1). Yet this claim that the accessibility of existing geographical facts erases established social differences actually points more to an *integrating* than a levelling influence. The author argues that no mode of knowledge – historical, medical, legal or providential – can avoid falling into 'gross errors' [A3r.] without a knowledge of geography, since only the latter can unlock the relationships between religions, histories, laws, customs, medical practices, histories and forms of trade that belong to different classes, peoples and nations. Geography does not democratize the community of observing subjects as much as it organizes the objects studied according to a single system of measurement, comparing and reconciling all historical and ethnographic data.[26]

It is thus not surprising that many geographical studies of this period take some trouble to establish the virtues of the atlas in bringing together the most up-to-date surveys, ethnographies and scientific discoveries. This concern with accuracy across a range of fields is clearly articulated in the work of one of the most prolific of the early eighteenth century cartographers in England, Herman Moll. His 1695 *Thesaurus Geographicus* remarks on the excellence of geography not only in describing all the parts of the earth, but also in 'intermixing accounts of what is valuable in each'.[27] This 'intermixing' is managed 'by means of commerce between nation and nation, [and by] the observations of learned and ingenious men, together with the relations of those many curious travellers that have survey'd almost all the earth' [A2r.]. In the advertisement for *A System of Geography* (1701), Moll suggests this accumulation of data is adequate to the geographical task of making the whole world visible to the enlightened (English) consumer:

> The art of making maps and sea charts is an invention of such vast use to mankind that perhaps there is nothing for which the world is more endebted to the studious labours of ingenious men. For by the help of them geography (a science so universally useful that no man pretending to knowledge, of whatever faculty he be, can with any excuse be ignorant of it) is made plain and easy, the mariners are directed in fetching us the commodities of the most distant parts, and by the help of them we may at home, with pleasure survey the several countries of the world, and be informed of the situation, distance, provinces, cities and remarkable places of every nation.[28]

Interesting here is the way in which knowledge of foreign parts and consumption of foreign goods are so intimately connected that the commodities produce the spatial knowledge rather than the other way around. The reader of a geography is able to grasp the world in its entirety, a world whose coherence is determined by the great variety of commodities that discovery and trade have brought to his doorstep. Unlike the country estate landscaped to suit the single perspective of the landowner, the globe is made visible to any consuming eye by the integrating power of merchant capital.

The concern of these geographers to represent homogeneous global space as the natural container of a global economy is visible in an earlier work by Robert Morden, entitled *Geography Rectified* (1688). Here even the labour of 'fetching', which for Moll, at least provisionally, distinguishes the merchant traveller from the consumer, loses its specificity. Morden, a mapmaker and mapseller of considerable reputation in the 1680s who drew the maps for and printed early editions of Patrick Gordon's influential *Geography Anatomiz'd,* anticipates the preoccupation of Gordon's geographical grammars both with the systematic organization of geographical data and with establishing a mode of equivalent value that can bring all the world's goods to a single market. He does this by identifying the special commodity status of money: 'Geometricians say that two lines equal to a third line are equal to one another; so is money a third line by which all things are made equal in value ... potentially to all'.[29] Anticipating by a century and a half Marx's analysis of money as the commodity that plays the role of general equivalent in exchange, Morden identifies this special commodity as a vehicle of measurement which erases the traces of labour and travel that still characterize Moll's commodities, and potentially eliminates the cultural barriers to the global circulation of goods.

Even as they endeavour to combine an enormously diverse body of data and a range of methodological approaches into a single, authoritative account, geographical texts are nonetheless quite selective of their sources and quite insistent on the credibility of the writers they depend upon. In order to bring together in a single text the world that 'no one man can possibly view ... in a lifetime', Moll's geographies claim to 'dispose in a regular local method' the accounts of 'the most credible travellers and historians and most judicious geographers'.[30] In *A View of the Coasts, Countries, and Islands within the Limits of the South Sea Company* (1711), he is careful to emphasize that the sources for any such project must not be found among 'historical and romantick accounts' of faraway places.[31] He explicitly locates the geographer's concern with accuracy in 'what we want to know most of' (A2v.): that is, the trade and product of those countries that fall within the limits of the South Sea Act. (The Act established the ill-fated South Sea Company that was supposed to pursue a commerce with the countries bordering on the South Sea.)

Since *A View* is devoted to making as thorough an account of the Southern coasts and territories of America as can be of use to the South Sea Company entrepreneurs, Moll suggests, such information is perhaps more usefully provided by a geographer than a traveller, since the latter is often prejudiced by envy and desire to outdo the reports of other writers (208). A geographical treatise 'collected from all authors' will be useful as well as diverting if it is 'made perfect by intelligence from judicious persons interested and conversant in these matters, [e]specially if it was done with care, impartiality, and by a person that is as well a lover of trade as letters'.[32] As one such bearer of expert knowledge, Moll here is also a *de facto* agent of the South Sea Company since he is assembling only such information as will help give a fair idea of the settlements, trade and profits that may be found on and around the southern continent of America. He describes how to navigate the Straits of Magellan, where to anchor between Queen Elizabeth's island and Saint Bartholemew, what the temperament of the Indian tribes in this part of the country is like, what these are prepared to trade, what winds blow in the South Seas, the desirability of the island of 'John Fernando' as a place to anchor and refresh, and the likely opportunities for trade in the Galapagos Islands. He also describes in detail the trade that the English might have with the Indians were they to establish a colony in this part of America: 'trifles and toys, powder and shot, will purchase [gold, silver, diamonds, pearl, etc.] for which men are ready to hazard ease, health and lives' (212). Here the criteria for what constitutes true and valuable knowledge about places and peoples are almost exclusively commercial.

A *View* is too explicitly an advertisement for the Company and too obviously designed as its instrument to be strictly an atlas. However, some editions of Moll's collection of sheet maps, *The World Described* (1715–54), include a version of the South Sea Company map depicting the parts of South America and the Pacific Ocean where the company had been given a charter to establish settlements and trade; the map was originally drawn for A *View* (see Fig. 4.1). Like most of Moll's maps, this one provides information about trade in and across the lands and seas that it represents.[33] In addition to marking trade winds, monsoons and the routes taken by European explorers, the map includes inset enlargements of the important regions covered in Moll's written account of the Company's jurisdiction. More detailed representations of Tierra del Fuego and the Magellan Straits, the Isthmus of Darien and the Bay of Panama, the Galapagos Islands, the island of Juan Fernando, the port of Acapulco, the port of Baldavia, and parts of Peru and Chile are the subjects of general and topographical studies that frame the general map of Central and South America.

This is not the only map in the collection containing information so specific to the commercial interests of Britain. The text inscribed on 'A New and Correct Map of the Whole World' (1719) boasts that it shows 'the situation of its principle parts viz. the oceans, kingdoms, rivers,

Figure 4.1   'A New and Exact Map of the Coast, Countries and Islands within ye Limits of ye South Sea Company ...' 1719 by Herman Moll. Reproduced by permission of the Newberry Library.

capes, ports, mountains, woods, trade winds, monsoons, variations of the compass, climats &c. with the most remarkable tracks to the bold attempts which have been made to find out the North East and North

West passages'.[34] The situation of each country and each ocean in relation to each other country and ocean is informed by the interests of
trade: both by the general and coasting trade winds, monsoons and climates that determine who can travel and when, and by the more and
less successful voyages of discovery that have sought to open up more
efficient trade routes. Other maps of North America, such as the
'Codfish Map' (1730, plate 7) and 'Beaver Map' (1730, plate 8: see
Figure 4.2) combine cartographic descriptions of British territories in
the New World with inset scenes of industrious commercial activity.
There is reason to believe that maps of America other than that which
Moll drew for *A View* were useful to advocates of South Sea speculation, including Defoe.[35]

Another major atlas from the period explicitly links credible geographical information to the commercial interests of Britain. In the
preface to the *Atlas Maritimus and Commercialis* (1728) the authors
(probably John Senex, John Harris and Henry Wilson[36]) remark that
knowledge of the globe is as yet incomplete. Yet far from suggesting
that the atlas itself might contain gaps or errors, they use this as an
occasion to point out that as an object of study, the 'world' is to be
understood primarily as the 'commercial world':

> our search has been confin'd to the practicable seas of the known
> world, and to those places to which our European ships go in
> common with one another, to fetch and carry merchant's goods.
> Such places as are not frequented, and cannot be come at, there was
> no occasion to concern ourselves much about: And this without any
> derogation from our title, or our pretension to a general view of the
> trading and navigating world.[37]

World history and trade, the preface emphasizes, are 'frequently
blended with one another' (iii), and for this reason the sections on
commerce are to be appended to the studies of each quarter of the
world (Africa, America, Asia and Europe) rather than combined in a
general section at the end of the text. Yet even this division is artificial,
for 'when we speak of the trade of Europe … we must speak of it com-
plexly … as it respects its correspondence with the other three parts [of
the world]' (99). Geography is caught in a paradox: it must isolate the
four major regions of the globe in order to identify the important cli-
matic, historical and cultural differences that are so important to
scientific investigation in the age of discovery, and at the same time
represent the increasing integration of these four 'quarters' of the globe

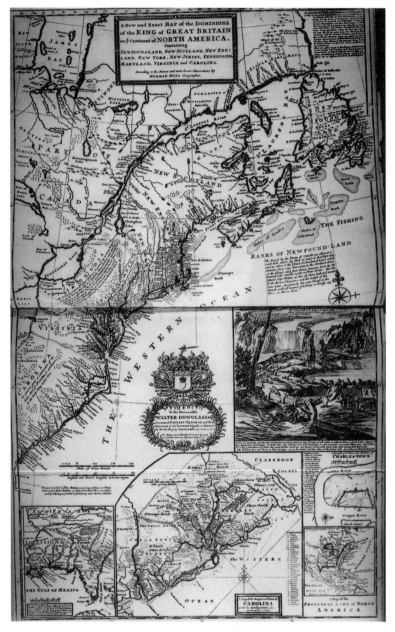

Figure 4.2 'A New and Exact Map of the Dominions of the King of Great Britain on Ye Continent of North America.' 1719 by Herman Moll. Reproduced by permission of the Newberry Library.

as the number of goods available for foreign and colonial trade is growing and the means of transporting them improving.

The *Atlas* is thus more than a description of distinct and different places; it is a means 'to trace our own manufactures into all the corners of the known world' (102). The authors describe how the trade in raw goods from the East and the American colonies and the manufacture and exportation of commodities to (in particular) colonial markets not only enriches England, but also provides other parts of the world with the necessaries and luxuries of life. Colonial countries are relieved of the burden of their surplus products even as new markets are created for the export of English produce and manufacture. The *Atlas* recommends expanding the trade in West Africa where an immense treasure in gold, ivory, slaves and drugs can be found for 'mere toys and trifles' (99), and reducing the trade to India whose powerful markets threaten to reduce those of Europe. Such mercantilist principles put England at the commercial centre of the world and demonstrate how she can maintain her economic position, selling more than she buys and 'exporting the greatest quantity of its own produce and of the labor or manufacture of its own people than any other nation in the world' (100). As it analyses the commercial interests of Britain county by county, the atlas as a whole perfectly expresses the movement of merchant capital out from this centre and into the new spaces of geographical knowledge.

This focus on the movement of consumable goods through global space is also a feature of collections of voyages which assemble (rather than edit into a single description) travellers' accounts of journeys to different parts of the globe. Awnsham and John Churchill's *Voyages* (1704) opens with an introduction that puts the sciences of discovery at the service of trade:

> geography and hydrography have received some perfection by the pains of so many mariners and travellers ... Natural and moral history is embellished with the most beneficial increase of so many thousands of plants it had never before received, so many drugs and spices, such variety of beasts, birds, and fishes, such rarities in minerals, mountains and waters, such unaccountable diversity of climates and men, and in them of complexions, tempers, habits, manners, politicks, and religions; Trade is raised to the highest pitch, each part of the world supplying the other with what it wants, and bringing home what is accounted most precious and valuable ... To conclude, the empire of Europe is now extended to

the utmost bounds of the earth, where several of its nations have conquests and colonies … drawn from the labours of those, who expose themselves to the dangers of the vast ocean, and of unknown nations … whilst the rest of mankind, in their accounts, without stirring a foot, compass the earth and seas, visit all countries and converse with all nations.[38]

As geography promotes commerce, trade becomes inseparable from learning. The commercial penetration of Europe into all parts of the globe has enabled Englishmen to converse with other peoples; their cosmopolitan skills are developed as fully in the consumption of foreign goods as in direct experience of foreign lands and cultures. Here not only the natural commodities of a country but also the 'complexions, tempers, habits, manners, politicks and religions' of the 'unaccountably diverse' range of human societies can be measured and compared once the earth's space is organized and made coherent by the flow of goods back and forth across the globe. This even plotting of cultural differences is the gift of merchant capital to the English consumer/cosmopolitan who can then see everything that his explorer compatriots have recorded in their journals. The mercantilist investment in geography is what makes the latter, in the terms that Patrick Gordon put it some years earlier, 'the eyes and feet of history'.[39]

Thomas Salmon's *Modern History: Or the Present State of All Nations* (1744–6) emphasizes the more reliable form of the *collection* of voyages rather than the single account. Salmon also remarks on the importance of drawing on a range of travel books so that the reader is not left at the mercy of the 'invention, credulity or superstition of the relators',[40] particularly with regard to the description of foreign peoples. Salmon combines the information from the journals of travellers with that which he has gathered from governors, consuls and merchants who have resided in foreign places. Even where he has first-hand experience of a foreign land, he compares notes with other travellers 'in order to obtain a more perfect account of [these nations'] present state' (1:vi). In the introduction to the octavo edition, he links the taste for 'relations monstrous and unnatural' to a contempt for truth and knowledge that is characteristic of the 'weak and indolent' (1:ix). A careless reading of voyages and travels 'without reflection or examination' encourages the notion that other nations are 'as different from us in their temper and turn of their minds as they are distant from us in situation; when human nature will really be found much the same over the whole face of the globe' (1:ix). A more enlightened reading, in his view, will recognize how cultures are interchangeable: 'nothing is more barbarous than the looking upon every distant nation as such'. This collection, Salmon claims, useful to 'the trading part of mankind as well as to men of quality and learning' (1:ix), brings these 'fabulous' distant parts of the world together into a single whole.

Salmon's text is illustrated with maps and engravings by Moll, drawn with 'exact observations … agreeable to modern history' (1:805). These include a map of the North Pole beside which Moll has described the attempts to find a North East passage to China and a North West passage through the northern coast of America; a map of the West Indies and Mexico that identifies where goods can be transported from the North to the South Sea and the trade winds and voyages made by galleons from one part of this region to another; and a map of New England, New York, New Jersey and Pennsylvania to which is attached an account of the postal routes in the continent of North America.[41] Together these illustrate how trade endeavours to bring 'distant nations' nearer to European commercial cores, as well as to connect remote and isolated parts of those nations to their own centres by improvements in trade and communications.

Yet this narrative of triumphant, enlightened global integration, which collections of voyages and atlases seem to present so confidently, also expresses, as we have seen, a certain anxiety about the truth status of travellers' reports, particularly with regard to the inhabitants of the countries described. Moll's concerns about the improbable reports of both exceedingly large and unusually small peoples in South America, and Salmon's dismissal of those travel diaries that make sensational claims about giants, monsters, cannibals and necromancers, are at one level distancing themselves from the kinds of extraordinary statements about non-European peoples that can appear even in a 'canonical' geographical text such as Gordon's *Geography Anatomiz'd*. Having made several prefatory claims about the contribution his treatise makes to a body of geographical studies with works hitherto 'too voluminous', 'too compendious', or 'confused' [B2v.], Gordon goes on to describe how he will more systematically and more efficiently lay out the important mathematical and descriptive elements necessary to both a general view of the globe and a knowledge of its particular parts. Part one provides the reader with the geographical theorems necessary to a general understanding of the terrestrial globe, and part two describes all the countries and their inhabitants that are to be found on it.

Having worked through a series of definitions, problems and solutions of geographical measurement, part one then offers a series of

'geographical paradoxes' that are designed to startle readers into thinking more deeply and expansively about their subject of inquiry. These
include such 'facts' as the existence of a place where, if two men meet,
one stands upright upon the soles of the other's feet; the condition of a
whole tribe of people in South America who are furnished with only
one of the five senses; and the existence of a place in Southern China
where the people appear to walk on their heads. Although the descriptions of such phenomena are designed to 'whet the appetite of our geographical students for a compleat understanding of the globe' [B3r.],
they in fact disturb the grammatical logic of Gordon's geography by
introducing incomprehensible figures and manners. They demonstrate,
that is to say, an interest in those regions of the earth that must remain
remote in the European imagination, or that cannot be absorbed by the
consuming eye because their inhabitants are so physically or culturally
alien. These primitive and outlandish peoples are associated with
incomprehensible space or geographical paradox. Allowing that there
are peoples so radically 'different in temper and turn of mind' from
Europeans, as Salmon put it, means perhaps that the world is too vast a
place to be made available to a single view, and that the appearance
and behaviour of one people cannot be fully and comprehensively
grasped by those of another.

This concern about the limits of geographical comprehension, this
lingering preoccupation with the blank spaces on the map that present
extraordinary possibilities to the viewer's imagination, also raises the
question of geographical reliability where there is no immediate
scientific means of verifying a traveller's report. Explaining both the
blank spaces and the few lines that represent what is now the west of
the United States and Canada in his 1710 Map of North America,
Senex writes on the map that 'the long river or dead river was discovered lately by the baron Lahontan ... [and] that which is more to the
westward was drawn by the savages of the nation of Gnacsitares on
deer skin', adding, 'unless the Baron has invented these things which is
hard to resolve. He being the only person that has travel'd into these
vast countries'.[42] Lahontan was a French officer in North America
whose *Voyage to North America* gave what subsequently proved to be an
entirely fictional report of the discovery of the River Long (to the west
of the upper Mississippi) and a romantic description of the idyllic societies that he supposedly encountered there. The English translation,
published in 1703, was instantly identified as the most authoritative
existing account of the region. Yet while Lahontan's map of the river
continued to be incorporated in many early eighteenth-century maps

of North America, other travellers in the region, such as Le Sueur (in 1700–2) and Charlevoix (in 1721), found no evidence of either the Long River or the tribes that Lahontan claimed lived along it. Senex's consistent nervousness about the unreliability of some travel writers anticipates the scepticism that was to emerge more fully later in the century about Lahontan's voyage. While he feels bound to acknowledge Lahontan's discoveries in the map, these accounts are too unconfirmed to properly begin to fill the blank space that remains in the western half of North America. Such uncertainties, it might be said, compromise the geographical enterprise whose usefulness is otherwise so generally acknowledged that 'it is reckoned a sort of disgrace for persons of any tolerable figure not to be in some measure acquainted with it'.[43]

Lahontan's *New Voyages to North America* itself is illustrated with several maps that, although of his own design, were engraved by Moll. The first of these, 'A General Map of New France', represents the expedition which Lahontan led against the Iroquois along the St Lawrence River.[44] The second map, extending west of the area covered in the North American map, shows the course that he claimed he steered through the Long River and marks the places that he stopped along the way (see Figure 4.3). Moll included this river and marked it as the territory of the 'Gnacsitares' in several of his maps of North America, including the postal map from his 1729 *Atlas Minor* (the map which then appeared in Salmon's *History*[45]). In an inset title, his map is identified as a direct copy of one drawn for Lahontan by the 'Gnacsitares who gave me to know of the latitudes of all the places marked on it, by pointing to the respective places of the heavens that one or t'other corresponded to'. Below the map of the river are two other insets showing the front and reverse of a medal of the 'Tahuglahuk', and just above it a drawing of a canoe used by the 'Gnacsitares' and the 'Esanapes'. To the extent that this map of the river became part of established geographical knowledge of North America in the early eighteenth century, its exposure as fiction represents a radical disturbance of the organization of global knowledge that we have seen above. A map of a possibly fictitious place whose representation is supposedly itself indebted to an indigenous source is doubly disorienting, since it introduces an alternative (non-European) cartographic epistemology, as well as a plethora of questions about authenticity and reliability. The very possibility that such a fiction could make its way into the cartographic archive challenges the realist confidence in the inseparable bond between conceptual (or measured)

102

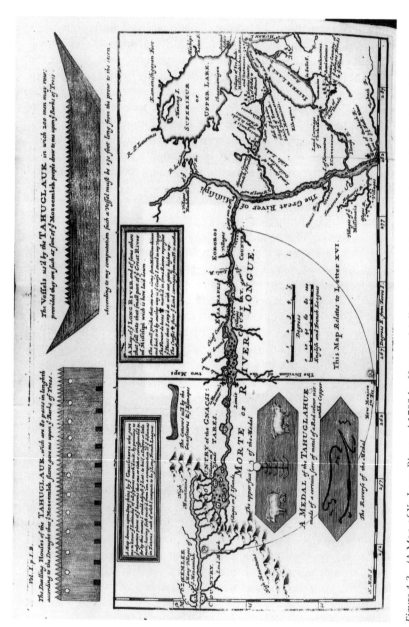

Figure 4.3 'A Map of Ye Long River ...' 1703 by Herman Moll. Reproduced by permission of the Newberry Library.

space and 'actual' (or lived) space. What I have tried to suggest here is that where such uncertainties are coded into the geographical production of homogeneous global space, they surface as the 'paradoxes' of savage customs.

The globalizing projects of geography in this period thus encounter several obstacles. In the first place they are to a great extent dependent on eye-witness reports of travellers that cannot be easily verified. Fantastic descriptions of foreign peoples and places that include accounts of human beings in sizes and shapes or with customs never seen before offer an epistemological difficulty for a geography committed to the production of homogeneous space, even as they also present the practical problem of unreliable data for merchant travellers negotiating new markets. Second, where these accounts are assumed to be true, they still frequently present human social possibilities that are incompatible with the global movement of capital. What travellers have described as remote, strange and commercially 'backward' countries cannot fall properly within the purview of geographical study since a worthy object of such study (as the *Atlas Maritimus* made clear) should be capable of commercial relations, and of negotiating equivalent forms of value with other societies. Unusual customs, unfamiliar needs, and human bodies attuned to their environments in ways that make no sense to European markets become (in the vocabulary of geographical study) 'brutish', 'idolatrous', 'bestial', 'ignorant', 'slothful', 'cruel' and 'savage'.[46] The result is that the social, and at times the perceived physical, characteristics of 'remote' peoples become connected to the degree of commercial civilization they have achieved. Swift is right; although the writers and publishers of geographical texts would like to dismiss accounts of the existence of some such peoples as the fictions of pseudo-science, it is not so much errant travel writers but geography's very anxiety about the uncharted 'gaps' where Europeans have no significant trade that constructs a racially marked outsider to the great society of commercial peoples.

Early eighteenth-century English geography thus finds itself accumulating potentially unstable knowledge about the arrangement of countries and peoples in global space. Together the cartographic and descriptive branches of geographical study identify the responsibilities of the observing eye and the organizing mind to bring the world into a single observable whole. They do this precisely in order to contain romanticizing and sensational discovery tales that challenge the mercantilist logic of a fundamental commensurability between peoples all across the world. Yet global space finds itself unable to cohere around the particularities of remote countries and unfamiliar customs. In what follows I will look at how *Gulliver's Travels* sets about articulating this incoherence. For Swift, I will argue, not only is the identity of the travelling subject radically unstable, but the world observed is equally so.[47] His satires challenge the spatial expression of mercantilist globalism by forcing his readers to confront impossible scenarios of measurement.[48]

This attack on the global mercantilist vision takes several forms. In his Irish writings, as we shall see, he articulates his disgust at the outrageous economic inequalities between imperial and colonized countries on the bodies of those whom he sees not as antagonists to global commerce, but as the most immediate victims of its uneven progress. The grotesque features and manners of the native Irish can, of course, be read as racialized signs of a degenerate or commercially backward national character that the, to some degree, Anglo-identified Swift wishes to distance himself from. Yet these 'monstrous' creatures are also the satiric vehicle for the attack on mercantile imperialism made by an Irish patriot.[49] As such, the bodies of the Catholic Irish expose the malevolent impact of mercantile capitalism on those at the commercial periphery. In *Gulliver's Travels*, the 'geographer' Gulliver tries to draw up equations between race, civilized 'achievement' and global space. He endeavours to give his readers an understanding of the relative condition of the peoples he encounters in every country he visits, and to show how commercially and politically backward isolated nations are and how physically repulsive those peoples remain who have not achieved civilized reason. Yet by the end of his tale he wilfully isolates himself from his own countrymen, and the body most grotesque and most vexed by the systematizing needs of global capital turns out to be his own. As a fantastic and monstrous spectacle, I will argue, Gulliver falls out of global space; the 'savage pictures' that he sends back to his English readers mark only the 'gaps' of his increasingly unreliable narrative and the improbable dimensions of the strange lands and peoples he describes.

Geography and monstrosity in *Gulliver's Travels*

Swift's hostility to the expansionist moneyed interests of the Whig administration belongs as much to his Anglo-Irish loyalties as to his Tory sympathies. Early eighteenth-century Ireland was impoverished by England's crippling restrictions on her wool trade, by the consequent lack of capital to develop her domestic trade, and by the loss of revenue to England through absentee landlords. In 'The truth of Maxims in State and Government Examined, with Reference to Ireland' (1724), Swift responds to these economic abuses by ridiculing the idea that one could ever engage in political and economic reasoning from a single (one's own) national example. The idea, for example, that a high price paid for basic necessities signifies a thriving commerce cannot be applied to Ireland where such prices are indicative of a state of near economic collapse. Similarly, where low interest in Holland or England suggests that there is plenty of money in circulation, in an economically frail nation such as Ireland it is a reminder that there is too little trade to support the borrowers. With the same taste for grotesque representations of radical physical incompatibility that more famously characterize *Gulliver's Travels*, he mocks those advocates for the economic improvement of Ireland who ignore its colonized circumstance, suggesting that 'if we could convince a nation where each of the inhabitants had but one eye, one leg, and one hand, it is plain, before you could institute them into a republic, that an allowance must be made for those material defects wherein they differed from other mortals'.[50] In drawing attention to the way mercantilism depends on radically unequal economic relations between the colonizing state and its colonized countries, he reveals an understanding of global commercial space very different from those of his geographer contemporaries, since according to the latter the penetration of commerce into the peripheral regions of the world brings different peoples closer together. In Swift's essay the Irish are deformed, 'defective' creatures, limping, blind, one-handed. Swift's critique of mercantilist imperialism and the cosy conclusions it manages to draw about trade, communication between different peoples, and the progress of knowledge is most forcefully located in this moment of spectacle: the representation of the colonized subject as the grotesque by-product of 'civilized' trade.

This is also the satiric strategy of 'A Modest Proposal'. Here the native Irish, driven by poverty to sell their own young for food, take on the figurative burden of savagery for the impoverished nation as a whole. Although it is the English landlords that are imagined as the cannibals (buying the children for meat to grace tables that have not seen enough venison of late), the native Irish families that sell them are the more horrifying figures in this gruesome picture, particularly as already their children are 'every day dying, and rotting by cold, and famine, and filth and vermin'.[51] They are the 'aged, diseased and maimed' (443), rather like the deformed creatures of 'The Truth of

Maxims': spectacularly other, physically inept, incapable of taking ordinary human care of their own kind. What the narrator presents partly as a consequence of Irish barbarism, having taken pains to show how 'our savages' (443) continue to breed children out of wedlock and beyond their means, Swift uses precisely as a means of attacking the notion that all Ireland has to do in order to improve the conditions of her people is to follow the enterprising lead of her wealthy neighbour (an assumption which of course ignores the economic facts of colonial oppression). The narrator demonstrates his skill at the kind of abstract economic reasoning that Swift despises when he suggests that in thus putting the bodies of Irish infants on the market 'the money will circulate among ourselves, the goods being entirely of our own growth and manufacture' (444). Yet at the same time he submits to English economic rule when he reminds his readers that such a scheme 'can incur no danger in disobliging England [f]or this commodity will not bear exportation' (445). Even as the viciousness of the colonizing, consuming English is satirized here, the grotesque shapes of the native Irish figure the anomalous condition of Ireland in the homogenizing projects of mercantilism.[52]

Although we do not really find representations of race difference until Book four, *Gulliver's Travels* makes similar points about the abuses committed by mercantile capitalism by satirizing measured space and measured differences. Gulliver's entire story revolves around the problem of the relationship of the travelling self to the foreign peoples 'studied' and about the improbable notion that members of different cultures can properly comprehend one another, a scepticism that is framed by Swift's suspicion of the mathematical grid that commerce lays over the different regions of the world. It is no coincidence, therefore, that Gulliver, Swift's modern traveller-hero, should try some one-up-manship on Herman Moll, claiming that the latter has made an error in his calculation of the longitude of New Holland; or that he should recommend to the geographers of Europe that they 'correct their maps by joining this vast tract of land [Brobdingnag] to the northwest parts of America' (89). Although it was probably the publisher's decision to include copies of parts of Moll's 1719 'New and Correct Map of the Whole World' (the sketched-in North-West coast of North America for Brobdingnag, and southern coasts of Sumatra and Van Diemen's land in the Lilliput map), Swift seemed to have no objection to this addition.[53] The fact that Moll had illustrated the 1703 edition of Dampier's *New Voyage Round the World* with a map showing the course of his travels from America to the East Indies and to New

Holland made him, in fact, the appropriate choice since Gulliver identifies Dampier as his cousin.

The maps, of course, represent a fantastic geography and hence the fraudulence of modern learning.[54] Lilliput is supposed to be north-west of Van Diemen's Land in the latitude of 30 degrees 2 minutes south. This puts it somewhere in the middle of yet uncharted territory.[55] If Brobdingnag is really 'a balance of earth to counterpoise the great continent of Tartary' (89), and size and distance are really as Gulliver claims, then a peninsula half the size of California is hardly going to represent it (see Figures 4.4 and 4.5). The meticulous care that Gulliver takes in recording latitude, wind direction and coastlines suggests that, despite the extraordinary character of the places he is describing, he believes he is capable of plotting them into the gaps in existing geographical knowledge. Once his travels are over, Gulliver claims (in the introductory letter to Sympson, the fictional publisher) that he has been persuaded to publish his journals against his better judgement, having little interest in impressing a Yahoo audience. Yet he adopts the geographer's trope of insisting on the veracity of his accounts, pointing out that his Hounyhnhnm education makes him incapable of saying 'the thing that is not' (3). In his address to the reader, 'Sympson' then remarks that Gulliver will be unhappy about an editorial decision to 'strike out innumerable passages relating to the winds and tides, as well as to the variations and bearings in the several voyages; together with the minute descriptions of the management of the ship in storms, in the style of sailors' (7). In other words, despite his mad, misanthropic withdrawal from the human world, Gulliver remains committed to a notion of spatial coherence, showing a modern man's faith in his own capacity to accurately record everything he encounters and in the value of that recording for the 'amendment' of a yet unenlightened race. In fact, as we shall see, the 'geography' of newly discovered parts of the world that he produces cannot logically chart the territories it is describing any more than it can plausibly document the cross-cultural encounters that take place within them.

Complementing his hours of leisure on board ship spent 'reading the best authors ancient and modern', Gulliver gains knowledge of the world through direct experience of it, 'observing the manners and dispositions of the people' in the countries to which he travels (16). Yet unlike Crusoe or Dampier he cannot properly fashion himself as a detached observer of those cultures; rather, he is changed as a consequence of his encounter with them. The most radical challenge to modern measurement occurs in Brobdingnag when, contemplating

108

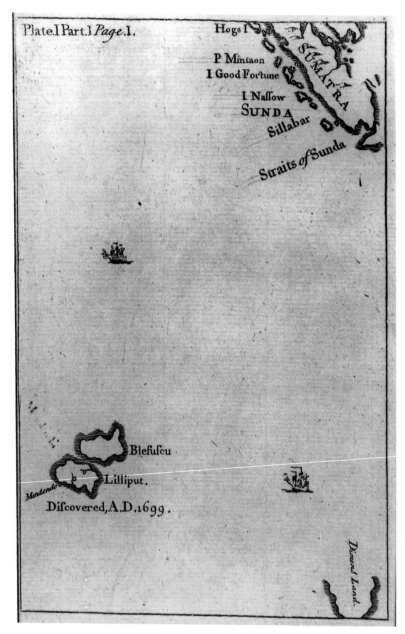

Figure 4.4   'A Map of Lilliput' by Herman Moll. From *Travels into Several Remote Nations of the World*, 2 vols (London, 1726), vol. 1, plate 1, p. 1. Courtesy of Kenneth Spencer Research Library, University of Kansas.

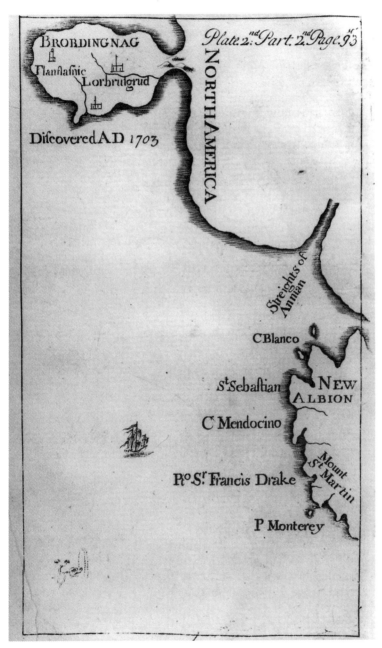

Figure 4.5 'A Map of Brobdingnag.' By Herman Moll. From *Works* (Dublin 1735), vol. 3, plate 2, p. 93. Courtesy of Kenneth Spencer Research Library, University of Kansas.

how large he must have seemed to the Lilliputians given his own diminutive size, he reflects that 'nothing is great or little otherwise than by comparison' (70). Here he seems to be, as it were, in the satirical 'know', reflecting upon the impossibility of maintaining a steady point of view, or of measuring differences of cultural perspective that are always inevitably shifting according to the circumstances of the encounter. This fluid cultural relativism of course hardens into the judgemental perspective of his hosts when on returning from Houyhnhnmland to England at the end of Book four, he cannot re-adjust to his human surroundings, or when he identifies as 'pygmies' the sailors who rescue him from Brobdingnag. The epistemological instability that occurs in these moments is also registered in the way that the travelling subject himself becomes an object of ethnographic investigation: in Books one and two particularly, a great deal of descriptive space is devoted to an account of the labours undergone to feed, house and clothe the giant or diminutive Gulliver. Travel turns scientist into bigot, subject into object of investigative encounter. What it cannot do is offer any epistemologically stable basis for acquiring geographical knowledge.

In Books one and two Gulliver's physical disorientation principally affects his status as an observer of political cultures. These two voyages are packed with instances of his failure to recognize precisely how size matters. At times he absurdly 'goes native', forgetting for some crucial moments that his physical size determines his relationship to his hosts. In Lilliput he defends himself against the charge that he has seduced a lady-in-waiting to the Queen, 'prostrat[es]' himself at the feet of the King in a formal expression of gratitude for his freedom (36), and swears loyalty to 'the monarch of all monarchs, taller than the sons of men' (35). In Brobdingnag, too, he speaks to the King as though he were the latter's physical equal. In part as a consequence of ignoring these physical differences while he converses with the heads of state, but also because he is so determined to abide by either contractual or cosmopolitan codes of responsibility, he becomes blind to the political realities of the societies in which he finds himself. He considers himself 'bound by the laws of hospitality' (19) to the Lilliputians to do them no harm despite the leviathan stature that he carries in their country, and acknowledges the contractual nature of his relationship with them so that, even though nature gives him such immense power over them, he will do nothing without 'their own consent and desire' (62). However, this abstract respect for political contract makes him blind to the local-political moments at which the king treats his subjects tyrannically, as when he is reprimanded for interceding on behalf of a thief who is condemned to death, and shamefully offers 'the common answer, that different nations had different customs' (47); or when he suggests that his failure to perceive the leniency offered in his own death sentence must be attributed to his having no experience of court life and therefore being 'an ill judge of things' (58).

Gulliver's Whiggish faith that rulers govern by legal principles rather than by tyrannical ambition or national prejudice is also linked to his confidence in the capacity of commercial relations between different countries to overcome national differences. When he reflects on the cultural and linguistic reciprocity between Lilliput and Blesfuscu that sometimes overshadows the rivalry between them, he remarks that:

> from the great intercourse of trade and commerce between both realms, from the continual reception of exiles, which is mutual among them, and from the custom in each empire to send their young nobility and richer gentry to the other, in order to polish themselves, by seeing the world, and understanding men and manners, there are few persons of distinction, or merchants, or seamen, who dwell in the maritime parts, but what can hold conversation in both tongues. (44)

Here cosmopolitan polish becomes the product not of rank but of mobility. Knowledge of 'men and manners' is as available to seamen as to the children of nobles. Travel can bring men into an understanding of their fellow beings that far exceeds their differences of rank, culture, or (by implication) size. Seeing himself as one such product of enlightened encounter, Gulliver conducts himself according to the laws between nations that respect the liberty of other peoples: while he allows the Lilliputians to harness his strength for the purposes of national defence when the Blefuscans threaten to invade, he nonetheless refuses to be 'an instrument of bringing a free and brave people into slavery' (42). Yet only a few pages later his radical physical difference from his hosts brings him, in his ignorance, to commit not only a cultural blunder, but also a capital offence when he puts out the fire in the Queen's apartments by urinating on them. The universal principles of justice that supposedly transcend local prejudices – principles that are supposedly the profit of travel – here discover their limit in physical size difference.

If in Lilliput Gulliver tries to conduct himself according to the rules of social contract and the laws of nations, in Brobdingnag he paints himself as a warrior hero and a servant of the public good, for whom every routine encounter with a garden animal – rats, wasps, birds, dogs – becomes an act of fantastic bravery. Here, of course, his heroic feats are of no value to the state and serve only to entertain his hosts. But of his uselessness he seems to have little sense, especially when, in his apology to the 'gentle reader' for adding to the account of his battle with the rats a mention of his need to 'discharge the necessities of nature', he suggests that knowledge of such scatological details 'will certainly help a philosopher to enlarge his thoughts and imagination and apply them to the benefit of public as well as private life' (76). Gulliver sees himself as a servant to the Brobdingnagian public too, when he offers their head of state knowledge of a more 'advanced' commercial and military nation. In his many interviews with the King, during which he gives extended accounts of the manners, government, warfare, commerce, religion and colonies of his own country (including a misleading portrayal of England as a *republic* where Members of Parliament are chosen for their 'valour, conduct and fidelity' and their readiness to defend the prince [103]), these details are designed not only to communicate the civic credentials of his own government but to bring the Brobdingagian king to a more informed understanding of countries his people have never had an opportunity to see. He flatters himself that this will make the King a better ruler since the latter remains, Gulliver suggests, narrow-minded in his contempt for Europe, just as Brobdingnag remains economically backward in its commercial isolation from the rest of the world. Confident that his account is quite unprejudiced, Gulliver imagines that he can overcome the 'narrow principles and short views' of his interlocutor so as to bring their two kingdoms into better correspondence.

Of course, to the king this ambassadorial exercise is little more than an amusing spectacle, although it does afford him the opportunity to reflect on the character of Gulliver's kind and to consider how in some parts of the world human beings have degenerated into the falsifying, destructive, ambitious and diminutive creatures that Gulliver represents. Where Gulliver attributes the King's distrust of European customs to the latter's ignorance of the world and to 'many prejudices, and a certain narrowness of thinking' (108), he also performs an absurd, Lilliputian-like demonstration of national-imperial pride, flushing with rage to hear 'our noble country, the mistress of arts and arms, the ... pride and envy of the world' (86) so much the object of the King's mirth. At this moment is it obviously not the King, but Gulliver himself, who betrays a lack of cosmopolitan breadth. In fact

Gulliver has no ambassadorial status in Brobdingnag at all, but merely a local value as a curiosity (a value which presumably is increased by his eloquent account of the customs and manner of his little nation). At the beginning of his Brobdingnagian adventures he is exhibited at market towns by his farmer-master, answering questions with speeches he has been taught, drinking from a thimble, and mock-fencing for the entertainment of audiences at local markets, before he is sold to the Queen for a thousand pieces of gold. Although he may fancy himself an ambassador, he is primarily a toy, a spectacle, an object to be consumed in one way or another by his giant hosts. Despite his pretensions to school the King in the customs of other nations, he himself unwittingly reveals that his place in the court is determined by his value as a curiosity: the Queen, he remarks, was 'surprised at so much wit and good sense in so diminutive an animal' (82); when the King inquires about the political culture of England, he is as much entertained by the rational performance of a 'diminutive insect' as he is engaged in learning about the administrative character of another nation. Gulliver's ability to give a full account of his own culture makes him an object of royal inquisitiveness, an elaborate piece of clockwork that, while it may be spectacularly capable of reason, certainly has no public standing. The roles that he thinks he has assumed – as ambassador, as warrior hero, and as informed discerner of the differences between political cultures – only serve to highlight his littleness.

Yet greater than the irony that the European discoverer has become a commodity in the foreign land he has discovered is the way in which he also becomes a piece of living evidence for the capacity of human beings to descend into barbarism. Linking Gulliver's physical size to the corrupt manners and government of his nation, the King reflects on how 'nature was degenerated in these latter declining ages of the world, and could now produce only small abortive births in comparison of those in ancient times' (113). Gulliver himself then reveals the synecdochic relationship between malformed body and corrupt body politic when, in a moment of embarrassed national pride, he admits that he 'would hide the frailties and deformities of [his] political mother' (107). Putting a mirror up to the racializing geographical grammars of the world that England uses to naturalize its own commercial interests, Swift here turns Gulliver into the grotesque savage subject of a grotesque state whose account of remote parts of the world can then only serve to destabilize global space.

As the scientific lens is turned back on the viewer (literally, when the scholars make a close study of his anatomy), Gulliver too begins to lose his sense of size difference (his physical and spatial *relationship* to the Brobdingnagians) and to 'imagine [himself] dwindled many degrees below [his] usual size' (87) or as an example of an aberrant and repulsive physical type. In Lilliput Gulliver had thought that his largeness marked both the extent and the limit of his responsibility to the state. In Brobdingnag he begins to reflect on the grotesque appearance that he must have made to the Lilliputians as he stares in horror at the Queen consuming a whole lark that is 'nine times as large as a full grown turkey' (85), at the monstrous breast of the nurse, and at the coarse, uneven skin of the maids of honour. The 'horror and disgust' (95) with which he responds to these assaults on his senses, and his reflection on what the skins of English ladies must look like through a magnifying glass, interfere with the spatial logic of scientific study that keeps subject and object firmly apart. Like his accounts of both English and Brobdingnagian civil society, his representations of the physical characteristics of this people do not reveal a stable or reliable subjectivity with which to view the world. Instead he becomes radically implicated in them: the grotesqueness of his own body is at the origin of every observation he makes.

It is in Houyhnhnmland that Gulliver's monstrosity is explicitly racialized. Here, more aggressively than in any other land he visits, Gulliver tries to represent himself as capable of rational exchange with the rulers of the country, and to conceal the aberrant features of his body. He does so not because he is repulsed by his hosts, but because he is afraid that exposure of his naked body will cause the Houynhnhnms to link him with the non-rational Yahoos, and then to exile him from their civilized circle. Once again, as in Brobdingnag, he continues to see himself in the role of ambassador even though, having (this time voluntarily) identified his equine host as 'master', he has already made this a discursive impossibility. The roles of ambassador that he plays for the Houyhnhnms, and of ethnographer that he still at least nominally offers to his English audience, are marked by the same incapacity to translate and mediate between different cultures that he experienced in Brobdingnag when he began to see himself as a 'little man'. This time he openly offers to explain to master the 'wonder' that his own kind are 'governing, rational animals' (193) in England, and begs the horse not to be offended by his extraordinary tale.

When he again lapses into the prideful assumption that, owing to their isolation, his hosts have an inferior understanding of the world, and proceeds boastfully to offer them the technological knowledge that the English have perfected in warfare, the horses respond with the same contempt and abhorrence towards his species as the King of Brobdingnag did. Again, the evidence of cultural degeneration that Gulliver's sort appear to offer this ostensibly kinder species is explicitly linked to the frame of a body 'ill contrived for employing ... reason' (195). Again, the potential for profitable exchange between representatives of different nations is thwarted by the character of this body as it is described by one Houyhnhnm to another as some part white, some yellow and some brown. This time, however, Gulliver is only minimally foreign. His body shape is the same as that of the Yahoos, and he is only physically distinguished from them by 'the whiteness and smoothness of [his] skin; [his] want of hair on several parts of his body; and [his] affectation of walking ... on [his] two hinder feet' (192). Once again Gulliver becomes the object of scientific observation as he is put together with one of the Yahoo 'beasts' tied up in the yard. To his horror he discovers 'in this abominable animal, a perfect human figure', whose difference from him is only visible in the features of nose and lips, which, using a favourite eighteenth-century racist trope, he attributes to the habits of 'savage' peoples 'suffering their infants to lie groveling on the earth, or by carrying them on their backs, nuzzling with the face against the mother's shoulders' (186).[56]

The geographical concern about mapping differences, which we have now come to see as a ritual of travel for Gulliver, is explicitly played out on the terrain of race difference. He then has to go to enormous lengths to demonstrate his curious difference from the Yahoos, strategically putting on and taking off his clothes and learning to mimic the manners of horses so that, instead of a pale Yahoo, he will be perceived as a two-footed horse. He must now *endeavour* to make a curiosity of himself. As the Hounyhnhnms persist in identifying him as an unusual Yahoo, he must insist on his physical difference from the latter, drawing attention to the whiteness and smoothness of his skin as the sign of his reason. Yet by the end of the book he too has begun to see himself as a racial inferior in a country where body type is thought to demonstrate a capacity for reason and self-government.

Perhaps for Gulliver the most disconcerting response that the Hounyhnhnms make to his account of his own species comes in chapter 6 when he describes the political economy of England. Responding to the horse's claim that 'all animals had a title to their share in the productions of the earth' (203), Gulliver gives a brief lecture on the necessary inequalities created by a commercial state: in order that the wealthy may enjoy extraordinary luxury they must be supported not only by the labour of the many poor, but also by 'sending vessels by sea to every part of the world' to collect the various goods that decorate a rich man's dining table. 'I assured him', he adds, 'that this whole globe of earth must be three times gone round, before one of our better female Yahoos could get her breakfast, or a cup to put it in' (203). The horse is astonished and appalled to hear of a country that cannot provide food for its inhabitants, but when Gulliver explains that in fact England produces three times the quantity of food that its inhabitants can consume in order to send the bulk of it to other countries, his listener is simply baffled. He tries to make sense of what Gulliver has told him first in class and then in race terms. Perhaps responding to the latter's observation that he himself carries on his body 'the workmanship of an hundred tradesmen', he comments that he is sure Gulliver must have been of some noble family since, along with his rudimentary capacity for reason, he seems 'to fail in strength and agility' when compared with the Yahoos. He points out that among the Houyhnhnms, however, the bay, the dapple-grey and the black are the natural rulers among the species since they are more exactly shaped and *therefore* have greater talents of the mind than the white, the sorrel and the iron-grey. In so doing, he offers a thoroughly racialized model of social order that, by reading Gulliver's capacity for reason through the shape and features of his body, marks him indelibly as a Yahoo. What the horse cannot not grasp conceptually about a complex division of labour because it involves drawing equivalencies between different kinds of value in a manner so radically foreign to the 'egalitarian' subsistence economy of Houyhnhnmland, it attributes to race difference. In the satirically-constructed inside-out geography of Gulliver's world, physical ineptitude is the product not just of class privilege (especially since Gulliver claims he has none) but of enlightened global commerce.

No wonder, then, that his story closes on a note of such extreme self-hatred. Gulliver the geographer has become his own object of racial contempt. The traveller returns bearing not the gift of knowledge about peripheral peoples that can be profitably communicated to enterprising students of geography, but a physical disgust at his own kind. For this reason he is obviously incapable of bringing home the riches of the world or of making men 'wiser and better, and improv[ing] their minds by the bad as well as good example of [what is to found in] foreign places' (235). Gulliver ends his journal with a remark on the revulsion he continues to feel in the prideful company of his own kind, from whose offensive smell he protects himself by stuffing his nose with rue, lavender or tobacco leaves, and by appealing to the insightful and sensitive reader never to appear in his sight. The 'lump of deformity and diseases both in body and mind' (239) that he perceives in his fellow Englishman makes the tribute to the English model of colonization (which he has delivered a few pages earlier) seem like empty rhetoric. Having compared the vigilance and virtue of English governors with the violence and greed of Spanish-style conquerors who make 'the earth [reek] with the blood of its inhabitants' (237), he then suggested as reasons for England's not attempting to colonize the countries he has visited not only that the people have no desire to be conquered, but also that none of these places abound in gold, silver, sugar or tobacco. This muddling of international legal and crude mercantilist arguments of course represents a radical compromise of both. Despite the geographer's tropes that he employs, Gulliver has no consistent vision of a globe integrated by civilized commerce and enlightened government. Everything he experiences is now filtered through his disappointed aspirations in Houyhnhnmland, and he can see only a progressive degeneration of the species that identifies the Yahoos as 'a race of brutes' descended from his own, already disgusting kind.

Book three differs from the others in the respect that it is more strictly an account of foreign places in which, although he may experience some desires and designs in relation to the peoples he 'discovers', the traveller's integrity and sense of self is never under the kind of serious threat that it is in the other three books. Here too, however, the arrogance of the geographer is aggressively satirized. On being told of the immortal Struldbruggs, Gulliver is invited to speculate on 'the scheme of living' he would adopt if he had been born one of them. His answer is framed with a fantasy of power, as he suggests that he is well prepared to speak about such a subject since he has so often indulged in fancies about what he would do if he were a king or a great lord. He then links this fantasy of rule (and wealth) and with his dream of assembling a single, coherent archive of knowledge:

> I would first resolve by all arts and methods whatsoever to procure myself riches. In the pursuit of which by thrift and management, I might reasonably expect in about two hundred years to be the wealthiest man in the kingdom. In the second place, I would from my earliest youth apply myself to the study of arts and sciences, by which I should arrive in time to excel all others in learning. Lastly, I would carefully record every action and event of consequence that happened in the public, impartially draw the characters of the several successions of princes, and great ministers of state, with my

own observations on every point. I would exactly set down the several changes in customs, languages, fashions of dress, diet and diversions. By all which acquirements, I should be a living treasury of knowledge and wisdom, and certainly become the oracle of the nation. (169)

Gulliver's promises to conduct an impartial and systematic programme of measurement in order to fully and accurately chart the development of a culture, combined with his dream of complete mastery of all the arts and sciences, are exposed as part of an egotistical fantasy at the moment that archive turns into oracle. The idea that he could be a 'living treasury of knowledge', an embodied archive, takes its most extreme form in his subsequent reflection that with immortality, astronomers could outlive their own predictions, thus being able to observe the movement of sun, moon and stars that they had anticipated. Speculations, too, about human culture, about longitude, perpetual motion, universal medicine 'and many other great inventions brought to the utmost perfection', could be seen at first hand. The degeneracy of human nature, he suggests, could by this method be corrected. Of course this embodied enlightenment meets its grotesque alter ego in the form of the actual Struldbruggs themselves who, it turns out, although they may be immortal, are nonetheless subject to decay. By the age of 90 they are hairless, toothless, disease-ridden and senile; and consequently they are deprived of all social pleasures and stripped of all legal and property rights.

This ingenious satirical move of locating all geographical knowledge in a decaying body turns modern learning into its own worst enemy. The grotesque body has become the very telos of modern knowledge and modern systems of global integration. In Balnibarbi the scene of physical decay belongs explicitly to the impoverishment of the colonized. Subject to the tyrannical colonial rule of the King of Laputa, the flying island Balnibarbi 'lies miserably waste, the houses in ruins, and the people without food or clothes' (144). Laputa is able to discipline any cities in the colony out of rebellion by flying over these and depriving them of light and rain. It does so by means of the giant loadstone (*sic*) in the astronomer's chasm at the centre of the island. As well as using technologies of navigation to bring a people into subjection, the Laputians have granted a royal patent to erect an academy of projectors in Lagado, the capital of Balnibarbi, in which absurd scientific speculations and projects absorb all the resources of the country. The projector who has the most striking effect on Gulliver is a man whose object is to turn human excrement back into its original food, and whose revolting appearance – 'his face and beard were of a pale yellow; his hands and clothes daubed over with filth' (145) – registers the futility of his labour. Specifically a dig at the Royal Society, the Academy of Lagado again situates modern learning in a decaying body, this time as an allegory for the way in which a colonized people are impoverished by the union of scientific speculation and imperial power.

* * *

Perhaps the best reason for putting Swift's satire in dialogue with the geographers of early eighteenth-century Britain is to show how he deploys the racist tropes of science against the teleologies of mercantile capitalism. 'Savage pictures', in *Gulliver's Travels*, expose rather than fill gaps in geographical knowledge, and in so doing they render the space through which merchant capital can flow discontinuous and contradictory. Swift's aggressive challenge to enlightenment cartography, voiced in the depiction of miniature kings who claim to be admired by 'all the world' (58) or travellers who imagine that they can assimilate impossibly small and impossibly large countries into their knowledge of the globe, leads geographical exploration to a series of epistemological dead-ends. Gulliver finds himself confronting either a relativist impasse – reflecting that 'different nations have different customs' – or else, more troublingly, a monstrous body that more often than not turns out to be his own. A geographer's terror associated with uncharted space where the traveller may 'become a morsel in the mouth of ... enormous barbarians' (70) is transformed in Books one, two and four not into the comfort (and ultimately profit) of knowledge secured by accurate measurement and documentation, but rather into self-hatred as every scientific endeavour turns the measurer himself into the object of amazed scrutiny. In his Irish writings, Swift draws attention to the bodies of those who are most impoverished and most disenfranchised by the movement of merchant capital into every crevice of the measurable earth in order to show how ill-distributed the profits of the commercial revolution have been. In *Gulliver's Travels*, he tries to imaginatively halt this movement by locating economic and scientific knowledge in a grotesque body of its own. His dystopic vision is one in which geography comes face to face with its own racializing systems of measurement and finds that the discovering self is always implicated in them.

5
Roderick Random, Rasselas and the Currents of Fancy

At the end of *Gulliver's Travels*, Swift's eccentric hero exiles himself not only from his countrymen but from all of humankind. Having been a self-styled ambassador between radically different cultures, and a sometimes open-minded student of moral relativism, he becomes instead a mad hermit who, in refusing the society of his fellow humans, also severs the potential for commercial and cultural exchanges between Britain and the countries he has discovered. Swift's satire reverses the enlightenment teleology in which patriotism, commerce and humanity converge. As mid-century social conservatives, Smollett and Johnson take up this inverted trajectory in the context of both official and popular attitudes to war and imperialism in the middle decades of the eighteenth century, the era that saw Britain drawn into several international conflicts over trade and territory, including the War of Jenkins's Ear and the Seven Years War. Neither, like Swift, sees mercantilist globalism as incurably tied to the corruption of humanitarian principles and ultimately of both psychic and social order. In fact, Smollett identifies a strong balance of trade as the source of security for Britain's social, as well as economic, interests, while Johnson sees in commerce the potential for the growth of cosmopolitan feeling. But, like Swift, both recognize a breed of so-called 'patriotic' moderns with little but their own interests at heart as the regrettable progeny of imperial and commercial expansion. Political culture, they lament, has become so imbued with commercial interests that what passes for patriotic sentiment or action taken in the interests of the public is in fact motivated by private ambition (the passions of faction or the greed of merchants) or by the blind jingoism of a barely governable mob that will sacrifice civil order and humanitarian feeling to its rage for imperial conquest. These war-mongering opponents of the government, they complain, care little about the enormous material cost that is accruing to the nation in lives as well as in money.

Aside from these shared grievances, Smollett and Johnson are also tied to one another by an objection that Johnson made to the kind of fiction which 'exhibits life in its true state, diversified only by accidents that daily happen in the world, and influenced by passions and qualities which are really to be found in conversing with mankind'.[1] Implicitly directed at Smollett and Fielding, his *Rambler* essay on 'the necessity of characters morally good' praises modern fiction for eschewing the machinery of romance, but criticizes it for taking too little care of the kind of moral examples it is inclined to offer to young, ignorant and idle readers for whom novels ought to offer lessons in conduct. While art should imitate nature, it should nonetheless distinguish the best models for imitation, 'cull[ing] from the mass of mankind, those individuals upon which the attention ought most to be employed' (*Works*, 3:22). Impressionable minds, he observes, are 'not fixed by principles' and therefore too easily follow 'the current of fancy' (3:21). This phrase, 'current of fancy', offers a convenient rhetorical bridge between aesthetic and economic issues since, while it describes the production of taste (in this case bad taste), it also evokes the movement of commodities across global space. In this respect, Johnson's criticism of novelistic realism ties the moral uncertainties of representing 'accidents that daily happen in the world' to the place of global commerce in the corruption of social and public life. Smollett himself is not blind to this connection. The morally itinerant protagonist of *Roderick Random* is a creature of the expanding commercial world in which wealth and power are increasingly divorced from any stable conception of virtue.

Patriotism and the picaresque

In the decades during which Britain came to establish its imperial ascendancy among European nations and in which navigation, the acquisition of colonial territories and the cultivation of profitable foreign markets took such powerful hold of the national imagination, a political journalist could scarcely fashion himself as a republican critic of the spirit of commercial enterprise. Smollett is unquestionably a critic of his times, and the civic personality that haunts the pages of Augustan satire – always just out of the irreversibly modern writer's reach – is barely to be seen in his work. His ideal character is more conspicuously a *national* subject: a new Briton whose frankness, honesty and industrious habits serve the nation's interests in the way that civic attributes served the political communities of the past.[2] Nonetheless, there is much in Smollett's writing of an 'ancient's' distress at social intrusions into the political realm, particularly in his attacks on the corrupting influence of luxury, faction and greed on the public interest and on the indifference of the appetites of the powerful to the suffering of the nation as a whole. Without retreating into a reactionary disgust at commercial life *per se*, *Roderick Random* concentrates on the corruption of metropolitan culture under the influence of global commerce and imperial aggression. Dramatizing the moral and public consequences of commercial modernity through the adventures of the picaro, Smollett can be seen to take satiric advantage, proleptically, of what Johnson sees as a capitulation to the 'current of fancy'. 'Fanciful' in its treatment of both moral and commercial matters, *Roderick Random* lets loose into the world a morally unstable character who mimics the public uncertainties brought about by commercial growth.

For Smollett, the moral itinerancy of the picaro emblematizes the limits to genuinely patriotic feeling in a commercial age. As the ancient bulwark against modern manners, patriotism signified party and principle over faction and interest in eighteenth-century political culture, and a Ciceronian loyalty to the public welfare that would not be compromised by individual financial and political ambitions. Patriots, as John Campbell described them in 1746, should be seen as those who can separate their schemes of government from their own interests so that their actions are driven by the 'dictates of public spirit'.[3] The patriot 'aims at inspiring counsels of general, not private utility' and 'deals fairly and freely with all characters and shows approbation or dislike as they tend to benefit or to dishonour, his country'.[4] In the middle decades of the century, the rhetoric of patriotism appeared in political conflict at all levels, both inside and outside Parliament. Accusations of insufficient or false patriotism were used as evidence of both ministerial corruption and of opposition factionalism. The terms 'true' and 'false' patriot were used by dissident Whigs as well as Tories to attack ministerial corruption. Walpole and his opponents accused one another of putting their own interests ahead of their duty to the nation. Pitt claimed to be driven by patriotic motives when he attacked the continental campaign early in the Seven Years War, and again when he reversed his position and argued that the war in Europe was necessary to secure territories in North America. Questions of patriotism also framed the popular radical demands for constitutional reform that consolidated around Wilkes in the 1760s, as well as the hostility to Wilkes expressed in pro-government political clubs.

Under the pressure of war, these distinctions between true and false patriotism became particularly loaded and the problem of faction particularly acute when 'in order to exert ourselves gloriously abroad, there [had to] be peace ... [and] tranquility at home'.[5] The debate over whether war with Spain in the early 1740s was restoring British pride and navigational strength or enervating her resources was framed against accusations of ministerial corruption during Walpole's last years. The case for pursuing war emphasized the interests of maintaining a free navigation and of censuring Spain for having infringed upon the right of British ships to sail unmolested through Atlantic waters, so that when Walpole signed the Spanish Convention in 1739 he was seen to have made Britain the dupe of a treaty that would weaken her naval power.[6] 'Patriot' objections to a delayed declaration of war came most powerfully from London merchants and through popular petitions and instructions to Members of Parliament[7] (the same constituency that attacked Walpole's system of patronage and the corrupting influence of placemen in Parliament, and that demanded constitutional reform).[8] Supporters of Walpole's efforts at diplomatic resolution urged that these complaints were the 'unjust clamours of a restless faction'[9] and that war involved unlimited expense of both money and lives, impoverishing rather than enriching the nation.[10] Yet once the war was under way, jingoistic exuberance over victories such as that of Admiral Vernon at Portobello tied the political future of the nation and public happiness to aggressively imperialist foreign policy and to the 'blue water' concentration of military effort in colonial arenas. As Kathleen Wilson has shown, popular agitation for building and maintaining the empire was tied to opposition to Walpole's ministry.[11] Although Walpoleans endeavoured to claim Vernon's victories as a triumph for the administration, colonial expansionism and mercantile ambition became the material of anti-government publicity.

During the early part of the Seven Years War, patriotic sentiments continued to forge links between opposition parliamentarians and non-parliamentary radicals with accusations of cowardice and rage at the incompetence and failing patriotism of politicians and generals crossing all social lines. The ritual 'executions' of Admiral John Byng's effigy by angry crowds all across the country for the failure of the expedition to protect Gibraltar and Minorca against the French were directed as much against the government's poor financing of the expedition as against Byng himself. Blame for the defeat prompted accusations in the periodical press against the ministry for neglecting the nation in its incompetent direction of the war. These called for a change of government, parliamentary reform, and the establishment of a militia of 'true Britons'.[12] Ministers, John Shebbeare's *A Fourth Letter to the People of England* complained in 1756, carried more responsibility than Byng for the failure because 'instead of ... securing the liberty and property of the nation ... [they sacrificed] everything to their ambition and avarice'.[13] Conversely, the victories over France in North America, India, the West Indies and Africa between 1758 and 1762, which put Britain unequivocally at the centre of the Atlantic economy, turned Pitt into a national hero. With British victory so nearly in sight, imperialism became demonstrably the source of not only economic security but also of public integrity and liberty as it delivered the nation from the decadent influence of French commodities and culture. The war for empire, as Wilson puts it, 'recovere[d] British patriotism and manliness'.[14] When Pitt resigned in 1761 in protest against the privy council's rejection of his proposal to declare war on Spain, he was replaced by the King's favourite and mentor, Lord Bute, whose programme for securing an end to the war met with contempt from opposition journalists. These voiced the popular sentiment that France could and should be forced into an even more ignominious defeat and the British empire expanded to its fullest potential. Much of this popular patriotism, mobilized by the press and by the multitude of urban political societies and clubs that formed during the middle of the century, was then converted into Wilkite demands for constitutional reform under the banner of 'liberty' in the 1760s and 1770s.

In his political journalism and editorship, Smollett opposed the politically radical and aggressively imperial 'coalition' of opposition members, moneyed city men and wage-earning activists. *The Critical Review*, which he edited from 1756 to 1762, criticized John Shebbeare's *Letters to the People of England* and articles in the anti-ministerial journal, the *Monitor*, which defended English rights and liberties and endorsed popular challenges against corrupt government policy. Through his editorship of the *Review*, he expressed sympathy for those who advocated an end to a war that was generating an over-corpulent imperial pride while significantly depleting national resources. He was recruited by the ministry to provide journalistic support in *The Briton* for Bute's peace and to condemn the conquest-hungry outcry of the *Monitor* against Pitt's resignation. In the *The Briton* he attacked the integrity of patriotic sentiment with his remarks on not only the inhumanity and misery of war, but also the discouragement it gives to commerce. How, he asked, could merchants and tradesmen support the protraction of a war that 'throws such a variety of restraints, clogs and trammels upon commerce; subjecting them to the imposition of severe duties, the grievance of pressing, the delay of convoy, the risk of capture and the exorbitancy of insurance?'[15] *The Briton* stimulated the publication of Wilkes's anti-ministerial *North Briton*, and as such linked Smollett by association with the controversial arrest of Wilkes for his attack on the King. Those who profess themselves 'free-born Englishmen' and patriots, Smollett commented in *The Briton*, have no real interest in their country, but are driven instead by political ambition and factious jealousies.

In its assessment of the major political and literary essays that appeared during its time of publication, *The Critical Review* regularly distinguishes between true patriotism, which is characterized by care for one's fellow creatures as well as for the glory and advantage of one's country, and false patriotism, which is visible in an appetite for luxury and a 'total immersion in pleasure'.[16] In this respect, the periodical joins philosophical hands with critics of commercial culture such as Rousseau and Ferguson, who argue that the profits and products of empire have replaced civic with commercial relationships and in so doing destroyed the basis upon which a healthy state ultimately depends. The *Review* and its allies challenge the principle, advanced perhaps most aggressively by Mandeville and furiously debated among mid-century writers, that unrestrained self-interest would ultimately produce economic and social good. In his attacks on the Whig moneyed interest, Smollett wholeheartedly opposed Mandevillian economics. He identified luxury as the enemy of a healthy balance of trade, as the social environment in which private commercial gain is privileged over the greater public interest – and in which, consequently, political corruption is allowed to flourish – and as that which collapses necessary distinctions between people of different social rank. This last symptom of luxury is one of the most dangerous for Smollett as it generates both insubordination and sloth among the lower classes, thereby creating further disruption in the economic and political life of the nation.[17]

Provoking interest-driven faction and disloyalty to the state, false patriotism and luxury therefore also produce moral decay and political corruption in the culture at large. True patriotism, on the other hand, provides a cohesive influence in its struggle against the atomizing effects of interest. A review of Thomas Leland's *Orations of Demosthenes* in August 1756 approvingly quotes the author who hopes to reanimate 'a people renowned for justice, humanity and valor, yet in many instances degenerate and corrupted; to warn them of the dangers of luxury, treachery and bribery' and to 'revive and enforce the generous sentiments of patriotism and public spirit'.[18] The same issue contains a severe review of Shebbeare's *Fourth Letter to the People of England*, attacking the conduct of the ministry over the war. This 'obscure scribbler', the reviewer accuses, 'assumes the character of a patriot and reformer' while 'sowing the seeds of civil dissension'.[19] 'Pseudo patriots', such as Shebbeare, are those who profess to have the interests of their country at heart, but who are in fact the instigators and beneficiaries of ministerial corruption and the perpetrators of party faction.[20]

Identifying the need to protect public life against luxury and faction, the *Review* supports solidly conservative arguments about the negative effects of economic growth. The reviewer of John Brown's *Estimate of the Manners and Principles of our Times* laments that public spirit no longer exists in a nation whose people are inflicted with a 'vain effeminacy', the source of which is exorbitant trade and wealth, producing avarice and luxury.[21] Another review endorses Malachy Postlethwayt's mercantilist arguments for a balanced trade and for reducing the public debt. The reviewer concurs with Postlethwayt that the increasing debt, raised to support the war, creates clamour and discontent among the people of England. Moreover, importing too many foreign goods will lead an otherwise industrious and manufacturing people into 'debauchery and faulty exuberance', thus diminishing production even while the consumption of foreign goods is on the rise.[22] In support of the author of *The Contest in America between Great Britain and France*, the *Review* agrees that, while the state should take measures to secure trade and dominion, foreign policy has been influenced too much by the opinions of merchants who are only interested in their own profits.[23]

With growing hostility towards Pitt and the expansion of the war, *The Briton*, even more aggressively than the *Review*, attacked the city interests that backed this expansion and lamented the popular support that it commanded. The 'base unthinking rabble'[24] who back the trading interest are 'without principle, sentiment or understanding'. They are 'undistinguishing babblers that open on every scent with equal clamour; the [servants] ... of faction, supplying fuel to every incendiary'.[25] The charge of the truly patriotic writer is to 'pluck the mask of patriotism from the front of faction'[26] and to expose the cry

against peace and Bute's administration as the unscrupulous politick-
ing of the least public-minded members of the nation. Those who
profess as 'free-born Englishmen' the right to challenge their government are not the fundamentally 'just, generous and discerning'[27]
people of England or the 'thriving sons of industry' but the 'forlorn
grubs and garreteers, desperate gamblers, tradesmen thrice bankrupt,
prentices to journeymen, understrappers to porters, hungry pettifog-
gers, bailiffs' followers, discard draymen, hostlers out of place and
felons returned from transportation', and the public spaces in which
they assemble are not only coffee houses but also 'ale houses, cellars,
stalls, prisons, and public streets'.[28] A corrupt urban underclass, in
other words, is the symptom of faction and luxury-induced indolence,
the creature of an overly commercial culture that has transformed a
public of respectable and industrious Englishmen into a self-serving
rabble. Anticipating some of the anti-populist and anti-radical vitriol of
The Briton, a frustrated writer of tragedies in *Roderick Random* accuses
the opposition press of being staffed by hack writers who seek to please
'*the most polite* of the chairmen, draymen, hackney coachmen, footmen
and servantmaids',[29] and whose work is 'calculated to foment divisions
in the commonwealth' (377).

    The distinction between true patriotism and seditious factionalism
and the arguments for peace and an economy built on honest industry
and a favourable balance of trade therefore linked the commercial and
financial interests of the nation to the moral character of its subjects.
In *The Briton*, in particular, Smollett seems horrified at the spectacle of
itinerant exiles and subcitizens worming their way into the heart of
public life. The perverted form of patriotism that they represent is
magnified, however, by those who make use of the war to pursue their
own interests: 'an iniquitous band of money-brokers, usurers, contractors and stock jobbers who prey upon the necessity of their country
and [act as] hackneyed retainers to a desperate faction'.[30] The culture of
appetite to which this greedy financial sector and criminal subprole-
tariat both belong demonstrate how the aggressive expansion of the
commercial empire has damaged, rather than improved the nation.
The industrious part of the people (hardworking landholders, [honest]
merchants and manufacturers) on the other hand, not only contribute
to the economy by bolstering the balance of trade, but at the same
time value the 'blessings of peace' over the 'calamities of war' (324).
These same 'honest, sober and thriving souls of industry'[31] are humane
enough to wish to see an end to the death of their countryfellows and
the distress of those who are made into widows and orphans. It is only

the 'idle and the profligate' who remain indifferent to both the private suffering and the public calamity that the protraction of the war has caused.[32]

Yet while Smollett assumes that strength of national character is enervated by wasteful wars and the indolence and selfishness of those who try to profit by them, he nonetheless sees the protection of British colonies as essential to both the economic and (less directly) the moral infrastructure of their mother country. In his account of the North American colonies in the *Present State of all Nations*, he observes that the colonization of parts of this continent and the wealthy islands around it was one of the 'most important consequences of the happy discovery of the compass and the improvement in navigation'. Without these colonies, he suggests, the trade to the East would only have drained Britain of all her gold and silver, whereas the natural wealth of the colonies has enabled her to supply eastern markets with commodities.[33] Protecting a profitable balance of trade also means emphasizing exports over imports and therefore, at least in theory, cutting back on the quantity of luxuries brought into the country from the East. Moreover, owing to its sheer effort of productivity, imperial Britain has been able to keep most of its subjects (particularly the English, in whom Smollett is most interested here) usefully employed and in so doing to protect them against the 'effeminacy and indolence' that attend a life replete with luxuries. The manly vigour characteristic of an industrious people also encourages a spirit of liberty, illustrated by the difference between the English, with their 'contempt of danger and ... admirable spirit of independence', and those Asian countries where the ease and splendour of the lifestyle stupefy the subjects into obedience to a tyrannical state (*Present State*, 7:5). Britain's virile mercantilism keeps the nation free as well as powerful.

A national character shaped by commerce, however, is as vulnerable to change as the fortunes of those who look for profit on the high seas. The English (the most commercial of Britons) are indeed, *The Present State* argues, naturally honest, frugal and fired by a spirit of trade and adventure or a 'mercantile disposition', but these very virtues make them susceptible to the tricks of 'those who can amuse them with plausible schemes of turning their money to good account' (2:214). What is more, the maritime climate of Britain has helped to make the tempers of its freedom-loving, trading inhabitants as variable as their weather and they are inclined to be 'whimsical, capricious and inconstant' (2:216). Curiously, the quintessential Englishman appears to be, for Smollett, a sort of alienated picaro, vulnerable to the ways of the more worldly and yet himself something less than a shining example of virtue. The variegated landscape of the picaresque is for Smollett sometimes England, sometimes Britain, and sometimes the wider commercial world in which the picaro is alternately a victim, a swindler, and an honest merchant. In one sense, *Roderick Random* is a straightforward social satire, describing the gradual exposure of its innocent hero to the corrupt urban culture in which any demonstration of 'virtue' is only ever a means of securing place or favour or of cheating one's way into money. More complicatedly, however, the novel explores the inevitable conflict between public spiritedness and private ambition that arises once the hero is immersed in commercial culture. Random, whose very name evokes the (sometimes sexualized) haphazard and disconnected quality of his adventures, is recognizably a picaro, not merely because he is forced into a life of wandering, but because his travels are characterized by moral inconsistencies and motivated by scruples as contradictory as his fate is capricious.

Random is not English but Scottish, yet he manifests all the qualities of the ambitious, spirited and yet naive Englishman of *The Present State*. He is repeatedly swindled out of all his money and thrown into destitution, and as a consequence finds himself in company unsuitable both to his birth and to his naturally good hearted and industrious disposition. In the preface to the novel, Smollett explains that he has made his traveller-protagonist a Scot rather than an Englishman because his simplicity of manners would only be plausible at a considerable distance from London. A North Briton, in all his unpolished eccentricity, exhibits the characteristics of the Englishman of *The Present State*.[34] Random's 'whimsical peculiarities' are to 'appear as nature implanted them' (5). Yet with his exposure to the vicious subcultures of the metropolis, his ingenuous state of mind mutates into a more self-conscious and calculated disposition. Smollett promises that his novel will reform the taste of mankind by 'point[ing] out the follies of ordinary life' (4) and he invests his hero with 'dignity of sentiment and practice' rather than with the hyperbolic qualities of a romance hero. He represents 'modest merit struggling with every difficulty to which a friendless orphan is exposed'; virtue pitted against the 'selfishness, envy, malice and base indifference of mankind' (5). Yet Random only manages to surface from the criminal underworld when the hodgepodge of unfortunate events and bizarre adventures begins to take shape under the tropes of romance that conclude the novel. Having been thrown about by life – orphaned in infancy, mistreated by his family, abused and cheated by the people of the town, pressed into service and confronted with the horrors of naval conditions, employed and mistreated by the French army, seducing of and seduced by fortune hunters, jailed, robbed and captured by smugglers – Random is miraculously reunited with his living father who provides him with the money he needs to marry Narcissa, the woman of his dreams, and to retire from the tormented life he has lived thus far. It is not, then, the impenetrable innocence and steady virtue of the hero but rather the artifices of romance that bring about a happy and morally comfortable resolution to his story.

Since the conventions of the romantic plot substitute for the moral reformation of the hero and the world through which he has travelled, Random learns no lessons. Although he is happily restored to the class that he was born into, his character is unable to anchor class status to any code of moral or affective behaviour and, as a result, both seem highly unstable. His companion Strap, he observes earlier in the novel, 'retains notions of economy and expense suitable to the narrowness of his education' despite (or perhaps because of) his 'invincible attachment to me' (312). Random, on the other hand, continually crosses class boundaries, in circumstance as well as in appearance. In so doing, he becomes as emotionally unreliable and unscrupulous as the confidence tricksters, fortune hunters and thieves that surround him in London. He may not be as corrupt as a Strutwell, who poses as a man of power and influence in order to rob and seduce his victims, but by the time he has plotted counterdeceptions against those who have cheated him and involved himself in a series of matrimonial schemes, he inspires scarcely more admiration. By the last quarter of the novel, he is clearly at home in the culture of fluid social identities where fortune and patronage reward not industry but deception.

However, there are moments (in the first half of the novel particularly) when Random does appear utterly innocent of the ways of the world. At such times, he seems as honest as Strap (who regularly bails him out of financial and legal trouble) is loyal. Just after Strap has declared that he will beg, steal and starve with him, Random learns that he has been conned out of all his money by 'a rascally money dropper' who has cheated him at cards. He is 'confounded at the artifice and wickedness of mankind' (79), particularly as part of the cunning of this 'gentleman' was to warn him of the snares in which innocent young people are likely to be caught in the metropolis. Even later in the novel, when he has spent considerable time trying to win the hearts of wealthy women in order to secure himself money and position, he is accused of being 'too honest and too ignorant of the town to practise the necessary cheats of [his] profession' (283). He is enough of a stranger to metropolitan life that he is capable neither of recognizing confidence tricks when they are performed on him nor of practising them very effectively himself. Yet he is no Strap who, driven only by a 'disinterested, voluntary inclination', remains steadfastly attached to him. Neither is he quite like his uncle Bowling, who is so 'unacquainted with the ways of men in general' that he fails to see that his good hearted schemes for his young nephew's welfare at the beginning of the novel will be thwarted by the selfishness of those he entrusts to carry them out. Bowling, like Random, is an incorrigible adventurer and, like his literary successor in *Humphry Clinker*, Matthew Bramble, a gruff and unpolished Scotsman who makes no secret of his contempt for the conceited and selfish behaviour that attend the luxuries of modern living. Yet unlike Bowling, Random is changed by his exposure to both the desperation and the decadence of London life. He is more than once brought to such a state of destitution that he gambles away money that is rightfully Strap's and forgets what he feels for Narcissa while on his hunt for a wealthy bride. The progress of one of his courtships lifts him to such a degree of pride that all thoughts of Narcissa give way to 'planning triumphs over the malice and contempt of the world' (300).

These vicissitudes in his character as much as in his fortune are indeed provoked by the brutality of an unfeeling world. I want to suggest that the 'world' in this novel should be understood both literally and morally: it is at once the commercial reality of an expanding globe – the greatest part of which is divided among the most powerful trading nations – and at the same time the cultural phenomenon of an unfeeling competition for wealth and privilege. So-called 'patriotic' clamour for the destruction of the French empire, we have seen in Smollett's political journalism, was so often driven by faction or greed that it was difficult not to see the temptations of the colonizable world stifling public life with private ambition rather than nourishing it with trade. In *Roderick Random*, the war against Spain to protect navigational privileges, despite its initial successes, is shown to be mismanaged by vain and ambitious generals whose peevish decisions result in the pointless slaughter and suffering of thousands of men. It is therefore quite possible to connect the scenes of sickness, death and naval abuse that take place on board the *Thunder* man-of-war to those that depict the decadence and selfishness of metropolitan life where the destitute are at the mercy of those who seek to gratify their ambitions. In the preface, Smollett attributes such inhumanity both to the 'base indifference of mankind' and to the 'sordid and vicious disposition of the world' (5). If the 'world' is understood both in geographical terms – that is, as the totality of appropriated resources including colonies and navigable oceans – and in moral terms ('worldliness' denoting a lack of concern about the suffering of one's fellow creatures), then 'indifference' is less a fundamental quality of human nature than a product of commercial modernity.

'Worldliness', of course, describes everything that is barely visible to the innocent and good-natured traveller, and in this respect it is encapsulated in London life where social interactions amount to little more than duplicitous, malicious or calculated exchanges. The 'world' in which, literally speaking, Britain has invested so many lives and so much money is at times metaphorically reducible to a corrupt system of patronage, to a social landscape in which merit counts for nothing and connections for everything, and to the preoccupation with wealth and place that leaves no room for genuine affection. Random smiles at his uncle's ambition to gain the attention of the Board of Admiralty because he '[knows] the world too well to confide in such dependence [him]self' (235); a good match with an only daughter of a wealthy gentleman will make anyone 'independent of the world' (206); a marriage that takes place without parental consent or approval will result in being 'deserted by the whole world' (216); Strutwell, the fraudulent 'earl' who robs Random by convincing him that he will place him as an ambassador in a foreign court, ironically warns him that there is 'little merit in the world' (305); and Narcissa rails against 'the prying curiosity of a malicious world'. At such moments the globe seems to shrink to the dimensions of London society or to become merely a prop for the schemes of confidence tricksters. The profound sense of duty owed to 'king and country' (184), which Random witnessed among the most honest and stoical of the injured on board the *Thunder* is mocked by a staged coffee-house debate about patriotic loyalty designed to cheat the credulous of their money. Indeed, coffee houses in this novel are, like taverns, home to tricksters and prostitutes rather than to public-spirited gentlemen ready to debate the advantages and hazards of the war or the conduct of ministers.

Yet the world is also, specifically, the Atlantic world, and as such the medium of mercantile capital. Towards the end of the novel, Random is reunited with his uncle Bowling and the two set sail on a merchant ship which the latter has been given command of. Their 'advantageous voyage' (392) takes them to the coast of Guinea, where they acquire slaves, to Buenos Aires in New Spain, where they sell them for silver, and to Kingston, where they take in a cargo of sugar. It is on this voyage that Random is reunited with his father, and it is (in keeping with the conventions of romance) his father's gold rather than the profits of the voyage that enable him to claim Narcissa on his return to England. Nonetheless, the notion of a world in which profit and status are acquired without any consideration for the suffering of one's fellow creatures applies as strongly to the global arena of exchange as the metropolitan one. We need only compare Random's indifference to the lives of the African captors on board his ship (he complains of having been *their* 'miserable slave' [403] between Guinea and New Spain!) with Smollett's observations on the slave trade elsewhere to see that this is another instance of the hero's slide into 'worldly' insensitivity. In volume 8 of *The Present State*, Smollett recommends introducing industry and the arts among the African natives as a means of stimulating a demand for English produce and manufactures that will always be lacking in Asia. He suggests therefore that it might be of more advantage to make Christians rather than slaves out of the Africans and 'give a relish for the blessings of life, by extending traffic into the country' (8:61), and he remarks too that the plantations in America might easily be worked by hired servants so as to prevent 'this scandalous commerce in human flesh' (2:236). Mercantilist and humanitarian interests could in this way be combined. Random experiences no such moral outrage, precisely, one might say, because he is by now so thoroughly a creature of the 'world'.

Yet because his adventures bring him misfortune as often as they do reward, Random is sometimes an unwilling servant of mercantile imperialism and the moral economy that underpins it. Pressed into service on board the *Thunder*, which is sailing to the West Indies as part of the expedition commanded by General Wentworth and overseen by Admiral Vernon, Random experiences the mass slaughter and brutal conditions of a war for commercial ascendancy first hand. He describes bitterly how the how the ship's company was kept unnecessarily on a diet of putrid salt beef, salt pork 'which, though neither fish nor flesh, savoured of both' (187), maggot-infested biscuit, and an insufficient quantity of water for the hot climate, with 'a view to mortify them into a contempt of life, that they might thereby become more resolute and regardless of danger'. In his account of how the sick and wounded were crammed into 'hospital ships' where they received no care and where their wounds putrefied, he blames General Wentworth, whose feud with Vernon raised his pride to such a pitch that he would not ask for extra surgeons. The mishandling of the expedition against Cartagena in which Vernon refused to use ships to create a diversion and support the land forces can be attributed, he satirizes, 'to the generosity of our chiefs, who scorned to take any advantage that fortune might give them, even over an enemy' (181).

The *Compendium of Authentic and Entertaining Voyages* (1766) puts the history of this expedition (in which Smollett as a ship's surgeon took part) in the context of support for the larger aims of the war, which 'if properly conducted might have reduced the whole of the West Indies under the dominion of Great Britain'[35] and which accordingly celebrates Anson's destruction of Spanish ships as the profit of a 'spirit of prudence and intrepidity [and] love of glory and his country' (*Compendium*, 7:366). It ascribes the failure of Cartagena, however, to the weakness, vanity, mutual dislike, and 'overboiling passions' (6:334) of its leaders, who were unable to summon up the necessary patriotic zeal and unanimity to protect the lives of those under them and to defend the interests of their country. The fruits of this war, as he describes them in *The Complete History of England*, were 'a dreadful expense of blood and treasure, disgrace upon disgrace, and additional load of grievous impositions, and the national debt accumulated to the enormous sum of eighty million pounds'.[36] In the portion of the novel that represents this expedition, Random is genuinely patriotic enough to recognize the difference between a necessary and glorious war and one that is run according to the whims and ambitions of powerful men and at the cost of so many lives. The nation, he observes, is ill-served by squabbling military chiefs, whose discord he compares to the cooperation of a joint stool and a close stool through which the public interest can only 'hang an a–se at its disappointment' (189).

Although he is demonstrably possessed of more patriotism, humanity and sense than his betters on this expedition, Random's return from the West Indies finds him in the position of ignominious outcast rather than veteran-hero. During the last stages of the voyage, the ship runs into a sandbank on the south coast of England and the crew riot. In the struggle to get to shore, Random is forced out of the boat by his captain and challenges the latter with a pistol. The fight ends when Random is struck from behind by one of the crew members, and when he wakes he finds himself alone and stripped of all his clothes and belongings. At first his search for help proves fruitless, 'nobody having humanity enough to administer the least relief to me' (215). He is finally rescued by an elderly woman, herself shunned because she is suspected of practising witchcraft, who warns him against returning to London where he will be treated as both a deserter and a mutineer, and who places him as a servant in the house where he first meets Narcissa. His declaration of passion for Narcissa forces him to flee to the coast where he is captured by smugglers who transport him to France and threaten to kill him if ever he should return to England. This unfortunate sequence of events, the bitter reward of for his service in the Caribbean, ironically highlights how the 'outlaw' who is forced out of his class and his country is in fact the victim of those who care much less for their nation and their fellow men than he does: self-serving officers, a riotous crew, cold-hearted country people and genuine maritime criminals.

It is perhaps during the period of his exile in France, 'transported into a strange country by force' (231), that Random seems to be at his most patriotic. Even while he is serving in the French army, fighting against the English, he is perfectly capable of recognizing the 'vicious ambition' of the French King, whom he reviles for inflicting the miseries of poverty, oppression, disease, mutilation and death on his soldiers merely to satisfy his own vanities. In the course of debating precisely this issue with a fellow soldier, Random discovers that the subjects of this oppressive monarch abhor the 'rebellious principles' of the English who are so insolent to their kings. He responds by rehearsing the basic principles of Lockean contractualism – a king is only a king by the will of his people – and by observing that the so-called insurrections of the English are in fact 'the glorious efforts to rescue that independence which was their birthright, from the ravenous claws of usurping ambition' (245). Describing the battle with the Allies at Dettingen and the French flight, he praises the humanity of the King of Great Britain for personally putting a stop to the carnage, and mocks the French for their ability to praise their own generosity and courage in the face of defeat. It is only once he is back in London that he again finds the title of 'Englishman' to be less than synonymous with liberty and humanity. Struggling once again to find a living, he complains that to set himself up and 'rise in the state' would require that he 'flatter [or] pimp for courtiers' or else 'prostitute [his] pen in defence of a wicked and contemptible administration' (253). However removed he feels from such corruption, he rapidly adapts to the culture of appetite and deceit. Resolved to marry into a more comfortable lifestyle, he hires lodgings beyond his means and goes to the theatre dressed in a Parisian-cut suit mimicking, he believes, the 'cosmopolitan' fashion of the London set and its taste for foreign, particularly French, styles and commodities. In his less-than-successful attempts to find a wealthy wife, he becomes affected and effeminate, 'guilty of a thousand ridiculous coquetries' (256) and yet more blind than ever to the deceptions of his rival tricksters and fortune hunters.

Thrown back and forth from the position of the world's victim to the worldly entrepreneur, Random aspires to the condition he believes he is rightfully born into in which, as another of the fraudulent gentlemen he meets in London describes it, 'the world is made for me and not me for the world' (264). This is the situation of comfortable retirement which he does indeed achieve at the end of the novel where, with the help of the devices of romance, he is finally removed from the vicissitudes of metropolitan life and the desperate hunt for wealth and position. In the closing scene, he learns both that his wife is pregnant and that he is entitled to her fortune, and delighted by this first piece of happy news, declines to go to London even to recover the money that is now rightfully his. The 'impetuous transports of [his] passion are now settled and mellowed into endearing fondness and tranquillity of love, rooted by that intimate connection and interchange of hearts which nought but virtuous wedlock can produce' (427). Finding himself settled on his Scottish estate and at last beyond the world of exploited and exchanged desires and needs that are excited by poverty and luxury, and having already seen plenty of the world, Random can take the same advice he gives another character earlier in the novel, and retire to his estate to 'improve' himself (87). Yet it is hard to argue, as Smollett does in the preface to *Roderick Random*, that this 'interesting story' has inflamed the humane passions or improved the reader's heart by example. If Random has luckily ceased being the world's creature, the world itself is no better for what he has done in it. He leaves it with all the dishonesty and discord that he found in it. The happy marriage, the recovered property, and the pleasant society of neighbourhood gentlemen that Random comes to enjoy, thanks to his father's generous interventions, do nothing to correct the worldly commercialization of intimate relationships and the corruptions of public office that continue to take place in the city he has left.

Rasselas and cosmopolitanism

The moral and social chaos that *Roderick Random* finds at the heart of worldly metropolitan life and to which the novel gives narrative life in the fall of the well-meaning, true-hearted Briton into the unreliable picaro is also at the centre of Johnson's political thinking. Johnson, like Smollett, identifies the social consequences of commercial imperialism at two levels: the first lies in the corruption of public spirit (which he associates with Walpole in his early career and with popular patriotism and Wilkite sentiment in his later writing), the second is to be found in the immediate suffering of those who are most directly affected by colonial greed and war. Smollett tries, and fails, to imagine a polity commercially powerful, yet at the same time morally reinvigorated by a virtuous national subject. Almost always anti-imperialist and often anticolonialist, Johnson tries to correct the ills of rapaciously commercial culture with a universalizing Christian moralism. He rejects histories of national character that concentrate on differences of climate, contingencies of contact with other peoples and, in their most racist form, innate characteristics,[37] arguing that all human beings are equally capable of reason and therefore entitled to equal rights and equal happiness. The governments of imperial states ought to respect such equalities, and powerful nations ought not to be allowed to ride roughshod over the rights of less powerful ones simply because by fortunate accident they have the technological advantage. But he also highlights the fallibility of most efforts to remedy such ills. Proposals for political reform and theories of social order are easily waylaid by what he describes in *Rambler* 89 as 'the luxury of fancy' from which one can only return peevishly to society, frustrated by the impossibility of modelling it according to one's own will.[38] In what follows, I will look first at Johnson's political writing to show how he shares with Smollett a concern about the evacuation of moral and humanitarian feeling from a society shaped by the 'world' of mercantilist imperialism. His political writing is therefore, like Smollett's, focused on the corruption of manners, a corruption that he then extends to the behaviour of states. I will look at how the cosmopolitan vision of the royal travellers in *Rasselas* promises to restore moral order to the world, but proves to be as vulnerable as the narrow view of the picaro to the distractions of fancy.

Johnson identified as a Tory, but the trajectory of his political allegiances – from patriot opponent of Walpole's peace to a later supporter of it, and from editor of the pro-Pitt *Literary Magazine* to advocate for the policies of the North administration – makes it clear that any account of his political views based on party affiliation would be misleading.[39] His political writing from the 1760s and 1770s is consistent, however, in identifying the adverse effects of imperialist passions on national institutions and British manners. In articles written during the

Seven Years War he chastises the English people for a blind jingoism that has caused the innocent to be charged with wrongdoing (Admiral Byng), the honour of the nation to be compromised by the public celebration of minor conquests, and improper complaints to be made against the King.[40] In *The False Alarm* (1770), he defends the House of Commons for having declared Wilkes ineligible for the seat of Middlesex against widespread demand that, as the winner of the most votes, he be given the seat. Such opposition to the Government, Johnson insists, is 'raised only by interest and supported only by clamour'.[41] The rabble who support Wilkes are over-enthusiastic patriots who continually invoke the bill of rights and the imagined shackles of violated liberties. 'Patriotism' of this kind only inspires labourers to quit their work in order to assemble at an alehouse where they raise themselves to a pitch of fury at the actions of the Government, which are in fact perfectly legitimate. 'The sense of the people is the sense only of the profligate and dissolute' (341). Since in other of his writings Johnson is not so virulently antidemocratic (and sometimes defends the rights of the people to question the decisions of government[42]) this position might be taken less against the phenomenon of collective protest than against 'liberty' as the creature of Wilkite jingoism. In his capacity as editor of the *North Briton*, Wilkes accused Bute of betraying British pride with the peace of 1763. The association of Wilkes with liberty in the wake of the election therefore also revived the excessive patriotism of the war years.

This perverted case for liberty is therefore partly responsible for the volume of suffering caused by unnecessary wars. *The Patriot* (1774), like *The False Alarm*, condemns the opportunistic rhetoric of patriotism for its populist war-mongering over the Falkland Islands incident in 1771 where, 'let it not be forgotten, that by the howling violence of patriotic rage, the nation was for a time exasperated to such madness, that for a barren rock under a stormy sky, we might now have been fighting and dying, had not our competitors been wiser than ourselves' (10:396). While maintaining peace promises to keep down the national debt, he argues in *Thoughts on the late Transactions Respecting the Falkland Islands*, war threatens 'the death of multitudes and expense of millions [in exchange for] sudden glories of paymasters and agents, contractors and commissaries' (371). Those who are the most direct sufferers experience neither profit nor glory: they [languish] in tents and ships, amidst damps and putrefaction; pale, torpid, spiritless and helpless; gasping and groaning, unpitied among men, made obdurate by long continuance of hopeless misery'. Meanwhile those who are 'without virtue, labour, or hazard are growing rich as their country is impoverished' (371).

If imperial wars represent the corruption of public spirit in direct proportion to the degree of suffering that they inflict, they also destroy political community at the level of interstate relations. Apart from the direct assault on the lives and lived conditions of millions, war also indirectly impoverishes the nation by transforming the 'confidence and friendship' between nations into 'a cold and sluggish rivalry' (354). Neither mercantile men nor mercantile nations, he argues in *The Political State*, are capable of maintaining friendships any longer than their immediate interests are served by such friendships (143). With their concern for their own interests over and above respect for the rights of other nations, the commercial powers have violated laws of nature and nations with respect to their treatment of first peoples in the Americas. They have assumed themselves entitled by prior right of seizure to huge tracts of land, and they have laid claim to inland territories where they are only rightfully in possession of coastal regions. They have extorted titles through violence, fraud, threats and empty promises, forcing cessions and submissions 'against the precepts of reason and the instincts of nature' (187). For this reason, there are no just grounds upon which to initiate war with France. Although the French are guilty of intrusions onto British territory, neither the French nor the British 'can show any other right than that of power, and ... neither can occupy but by usurpation, and the dispossession of the natural lords and original inhabitants' (186). Indeed, one of the causes of Britain's weakness against French encroachments is that it has treated the Indians unkindly and 'no people can be great who have ceased to be virtuous' (150).

Virtue, however, proves difficult to isolate from the moral ills of the commercial world, particularly when such virtue is identified as the product of cosmopolitan learning. In the introduction to *The World Displayed* (published in the same year as *Rasselas*) he complains that the Europeans 'have scarcely visited any coast but to gratify avarice and extend corruption; to arrogate dominion without right and practice cruelty without incentive'.[43] Yet the brutality of European colonialism (the slave trade, the illegal dispossession of first peoples, and the emphasis on profit over human rights) cannot quite be separated from the enlightened cosmopolitanism it has made possible. Through European colonization:

distant nations have been made acquainted with one another, unknown countries have been brought into general view, and the power of Europe has been extended into the most remote parts of the world ... What mankind has lost and gained ... it would be long to compare and very difficult to estimate. (1:11)

'Columbus', he goes on to say, 'gave a new world to [both] European curiosity and European cruelty' (1:23). The atrocities committed by colonizing states belong to the same set of events that enabled the opening-up of different parts of the world to one another. In the ambiguous syntax of the first sentence, European power could be either expanding into or *offered* to 'less enlightened' countries. The 'displayed' world – a standard trope of eighteenth-century geography – is thus more than the archive of knowledge about the world's places and peoples. For one thing, the very act of displaying reveals as much about the history of European colonial greed as it does about the progress of geographical science; for another, the question of what the world has gained or lost by discovery and conquest cannot be calculated accurately. The text that should stand as an exhaustive survey in fact cannot successfully weigh and balance suffering against scientific progress.

This identification of an epistemological frustration at the heart of enlightened knowledge – a frustration characteristic of Johnson's voice – is especially strong when he writes about travel, since his travellers, like Smollett's, move in and out of metropolitan spaces and from remote or isolated countries and towns into more 'civilized' and aggressively commercial ones. In his early writing, the moral status of this traveller is relatively fixed. In *London*, published in 1738 during the period of his affiliation with the patriot opposition to Walpole, he depicts a Briton rather like that of Smollett's *Compendium* who maintains the qualities of modesty, honesty and industry, and who can only retire in disgust from a metropolitan scene in which English rights are mortgaged by corrupt, pensioned politicians and where 'all are slaves to gold'.[44] The threat of mob violence and the culture of bribery, flattery and deceit sets this Briton literally, but not morally, adrift:

> Then through the world a wretched vagrant roam
> For where can starving merit find a home?[45]

The 'world' into which this innocent is launched is simultaneously the foreign landscape into which the virtuous are exiled, the disputed colonial territory of imperial powers, and the corrupt metropole in which honesty is inevitably homeless. This patriotic exit from London is in a sense reversed in a much later essay from *The Adventurer*, which describes a traveller leaving a remote part of Britain for the capital. This traveller, endeavouring to divide his attention 'among a thousand objects',[46] is struck by the enormous diversity of manufactures, by the merchandise that 'attract[s] his eye and solicit[s] his purse' (384), and is astounded that so much can be consumed all at once. The shops he passes are full of luxuries whose use he does not recognize. His confusion and disorientation, however, are corrected by the eye of another observer in the essay, one whose perception is so broad that he can 'take in the whole subordination of mankind' (386) and who therefore appreciates 'the secret concatenation of society' (386) that prevents both superfluity and want and unites all the members of a society by a 'general concurrence of endeavours' (386). While society depends on the industry and application of all its members, no single one standing as an idle spectator to the labour of others, such order can only be appreciated by one who can step outside the 'universal hurry' (386) of manufacture and commerce. This spectator, capable of discerning order where his unworldly counterpart saw only the confusion and extravagance of the crowded city, also travels further afield than his fellow citizens.[47] In order to appreciate the pleasures of London, the happiness it offers, and the efficient relay between production and consumption that its numbers make possible, he must spend time 'in a distant colony, or those parts of our island which are thinly inhabited' (387). There he will see how much harder life is without a sophisticated division of labour or easy communication between sellers and buyers. Along with the material pleasures that the city offers, its booming economy also releases this spectator from labour so that he can enjoy the very activity of reflection that he is engaged in. His role as enlightened traveller and observer to the display of the secret whole seems to provide the epistemological remedy to the excesses of commercial culture.

Yet the spectator-speaker retains some ambivalence about the satisfactions that this busy world offers. Londoners, he observes, are exposed to a vast number of commodities that they quickly begin to find essential, and the more of these they acquire, the more they find they need. They then 'forget the paucity of our real necessities' (387) and the skills needed to satisfy these, becoming dependent for every article they imagine they require on the labour of a great many others. Their happiness, therefore remains imperfect, and the 'rude Indian' (388) who supplies all his own needs with fortitude and skill has no envy of it. Contemplating how the comforts of modern life lead us more into unsatisfied desire than satisfied enjoyment, and yet, at the same time, how 'savage life ... shews likewise how much society is to be desired' (388) given the danger, discomfort and uncertainty of life without it, the spectator finds himself unable to draw any final conclusions about the best route to happiness. It is a task worthy of a philosopher, he suggests, 'to examine how much is taken away from our native abilities, as well as added to them by artificial expedients' (387), but he seems to be unable to make the calculation himself. Hence as much as he may claim to be able to 'rate [the] proper value' (387) of the city from his traveller's perspective, he makes no final theoretical claims about the relationship of changes in material culture to the improvement of society.

This ambivalence is thematized in *Rasselas* where the protagonists set out to find the best routes to private and public happiness and end up no more able to say how these can be achieved than they were at the beginning of their journey. Yet the tale ostensibly sets out to correct precisely the moral ambivalence of Smollett's picaresque. Johnson's criticism of popular novels such as *Roderick Random* and Fielding's *Tom Jones* (novels that 'exhibit life in its true state')[48] is that in order to faithfully represent human manners they make their adventurers as vulnerable to vice and folly as the rest of the world and 'mingle good and bad qualities' (23). A narrative freed from the constraints of verisimilitude, on the other hand, can incite pleasure through the representation of virtue, and disgust through vice. Art should 'distinguish those parts of nature which are most proper for imitation' (22). Its capacity for moral discernment comes from the ability to survey the progress in manners of different societies across time. A more instructive kind of literature than the picaresque novel, this suggests, is able to transcend the everyday realities of commercial life in which interest so powerfully influences perception. Hence while the tale's setting provides Johnson with an opportunity to reflect on both the civilized achievements and the political tyrannies of the East, its Abyssinian protagonists are primarily disinterested observers of foreign countries and cultures with the enlightened (rather than national) ambition of identifying the political conditions that best serve human happiness. In this respect, *Rasselas*'s 'artistic' achievement seems to be the discovery of a morally stable, cosmopolitan point of view that in other of his writings, such as *Journey to the Western Islands of Scotland*, remains precarious and self-contradictory.[49]

However, the kind of cosmopolitan breadth that is capable of such discoveries, and that lifts a rational observer beyond the muddle of good and bad belonging to the 'true state' of things, is made possible, in *Rasselas*, by the very knowledge technologies that have accompanied the expansion of the globe by colonialism and commerce. The characters who are capable of seeing more and further than their narrow-minded, satisfaction-seeking fellow beings are technicians of the new sciences: as geographers, they can look at a variety of countries at a variety of stages of progress all at the same time; as ethnographers, they can compare the manners of one country or social class with those of another. Even when they study the heroic past it is in order to investigate behaviour, or 'the most powerful motivations of action',[50] in human beings rather than to find models of virtue or civic responsibility. It is true, of course, that Rasselas and his philosopher-teachers travel extensively and look at the world they see expansively so as to try to plot the moral and political coordinates for universal good. In this respect they do introduce civic motives to the study of social behaviour. And to a large extent they transcend the condition inflicted on most of their contemporaries by a commercial age in which 'every man is placed in his present condition by causes which acted without his foresight and with which he did not always willingly co-operate' (*Works*, 16:67). Yet there is no avoiding the contradiction at the heart of their study: in an effort to know the world in all its diversity and at the same time find a political cure for the moral torpidity into which it has descended, they must pursue the same kinds of investigation that have brought far-flung places and peoples into commercial contact. Their task is like that of the artist, to rise above the earth so as to look down on 'all its inhabitants, rolling beneath ... and presenting ... successively, by its diurnal motion, all the countries within the same parallel' (26). This geographer's vision offers a degree of moral discernment, yet in the end no moral certainties, no reformed rulers or subjects and, consequently (given that this highly allegorical story is driven by moral imperatives), no satisfying conclusion to the plot.

The two spectators from the essay in *The Adventurer* are combined in the characters of the royal travellers. Rasselas and his sister are at first dazzled by the 'tumults of a port and the ruggedness of the commercial race' (62), and perplexed by money, which they cannot understand as having a value equivalent to the necessities of life. Yet by attempting the enormous geographical study of all the ranks and circumstances of mankind, they come to exercise a more confident judgement about the moral condition of those they observe. Like the spectator in the essay, however, they have difficulty arriving at strong conclusions about what they see. The more they inquire after the sources of happiness, whether in public or intimate life, the laws of nature, solitude, social station, fame or learning, the fewer answers they find and the more they encounter moral contradictions such as 'disagreeing virtues' (104), a disproportion between virtue and happiness, or reason contaminated by powerful passions. Moreover, in their search for an Olympian wisdom that transcends passions and interests – one that will enable them to align forms of government with 'schemes of happiness' (175) derived from fixed principles of virtue – they find themselves unable to calculate the relationship of bad and good to political and natural evils. Vice and virtue are 'confounded in the misery of a famine, and not much distinguished in the fury of a faction; they sink together in a tempest and are driven together from their country by invaders' (102). Like natural disasters, political strife and colonial violence expose the discerning eye to scenes of confusion.

The royal travellers leave the happy valley to explore the world in which 'the miseries of public life' (11) and the rage of discord are fuelled by luxury and the constant stimulation of the appetites by the prospect of different pleasures. They leave the 'garden' in which all the natural goods of the world are brought together, but which is also, paradoxically, protected from the world by impassable mountains. The happy valley is at once, fantastically, both of the commercial world and beyond it. It is an emblem of global mercantile capital, the product of elaborate systems of exchange negotiated across enormous distances where 'all the diversities of the world were brought together [and] the blessings of nature were collected' (9). And yet it is also a remote, isolated country, protected against the miseries of appetite and want inflicted on those who live in the stream of commerce. It represents everything that is gained in a commercial hub such as London without the pangs of desire that metropolitan life inevitably stimulates. Equally fantastically, the valley offers consumption without production: 'here is neither labour to be endured nor danger to be dreaded, yet here is all that labour or danger can procure or purchase' (15). Being at once remote and metropolitan, it removes the imperative for travel; being a place where desires are satisfied instantaneously, it has no history of commercial progress or of the social change that progress brings about, and so the spectator is relieved of the task of assessing what is gained or lost by its commercial sophistication. Without geographical or historical shape, the valley is a place in which judgement is neither clouded by desire nor refined by reason and reflection. Rasselas is motivated to leave in part because of the fundamental human quality of desiring something beyond what one already has; in part because what he desires is knowledge (he has a 'longing' to see the miseries of the world). He is drawn into the world in all its spatial and historical dimensions, in other words, by his wanting to be two different kinds of spectator: the dazzled consumer and the detached observer.

Accordingly, the instruction of the prince and princess in the ways of the world beyond the valley takes two forms. The first is that of experience-by-immersion, as they are introduced to the commercial centre of Cairo by their companion; the second that of geographical instruction as Imlac describes to them the 'various ranks and conditions of mankind' (65), setting the world before them for them to review at their leisure. They are at once actual adventurers, terrified by the immense vacuity of the landscape beyond the happy valley and by the danger of contact with strangers, and students of history and geography who can compare one region, class, or mode of subsistence against another. As innocents 'unpractised in the world' they face 'the tumults of a port and the ruggedness of the commercial race' (62). As detached observers, they examine the conditions of life most conducive to virtue and happiness, but discover that both privilege and poverty breed corruption: the wealthy and powerful are continually caught up in 'faction and treachery' (91), and the poor are inflicted with narrow thoughts, 'petty competitions and worthless emulation' (92). These findings bring each of the characters at the end of the tale to plot a scheme of happiness, whether a life secluded from the vicissitudes, 'expectation and disgust' (175) of the world, or an institution in which 'models of prudence and patterns of piety' (175) might be encouraged, or a dominion over which a good prince will exercise reasonable government. In agreeing to return to Abyssinia they concede that none of these plans will be realized, and that the 'stream of life' along which their wiser and more modest companions are content to be swept will continue to harbour ambition, faction, viciousness and ignorance.

Over the course of the tale, however, they interview a number of philosophers who seem to offer a model of detached observation from which moral judgements can be made and the source of happiness discerned, but all of whom fail to do so. In his dissertation upon poetry, Imlac describes the business of a poet which demands an extraordinary perception: one that can observe nature in all its variation and the passions in all their combinations, 'trac[ing] the changes of the human mind as they are modified by various institutions and accidental influences of climate or custom' (44). In order to make such a study, the poet must 'divest himself of the prejudices of his age and country … disregard present laws and opinions, and rise to general and transcendental truths, which will always be the same' (44). He must become 'superior to time and place' (45). Imlac describes how, having travelled through the Middle East, Asia, and through northern and western Europe, comparing the men in these different kingdoms and their comforts and hardships, he found himself frustrated by the indifference of his countrymen to the wisdom he had accrued and retired in frustration to the happy valley, resolved to 'hide [himself] forever from the world' (54). The artist who contructs wings with which he hopes to rise above the earth and observe all its inhabitants and countries at once, 'tower[ing] in the air beyond the malice or pursuit of man' (27), finds that flight is impossible. The philosopher who teaches Rasselas that rational fortitude should prevail over the vicissitudes of passion turns his back on truth and reason in the midst of grief. The astronomer who seeks solitude in order to devote himself entirely to science succumbs to the mad hubris of believing that he controls the seasons. The effort to rise above time and place therefore risks creating disorders of the intellect, allowing fancy to take power over reason in the mind: 'fancy, the parent of passion, usurps the dominion of [reason, and] nothing ensues but the natural effect of unlawful government, perturbation and confusion: [fancy] betrays the fortresses of the intellect to rebels, and excites her children to sedition against reason, their lawful sovereign' (71). The psychic and political disturbance caused by fancy blurs the distinction between high and low spectators: the superior vision of poet, artist or philosopher assisted by the technologies of the geographical sciences is as vulnerable to disorder and confusion as the raw traveller who steps unpractised into the world.

'Fancy' therefore denotes both the riotous pressure of the imagination fixed on a single object or a particular train of ideas, and the determining influence of desire on the activity of the mind (which provides the psychic ground for the expansion of commerce). Under the reign of fancy it proves impossible to calculate the conditions most conducive to happiness or entirely to distinguish bad effects from good in the impact of commercial imperialism. This is for two reasons. The first is that the mind itself rejects the disciplining force of reason, most obviously in the cases of the philosopher and the astronomer, but also in Rasselas himself who is driven into the world by his *appetite* for knowledge and who learns that the 'love of knowledge' sits side by side with 'the hope of gain' (53). The second reason is that, as Imlac counsels, no one intellect, however philosophical, is so singular as to be able to transcend the 'mass of humanity' (163).

The philosophical spectators of *Rasselas*, in other words, are no better equipped than those of the *Adventurer* essay or of *The World Displayed* to assess the effects of commerce on the total happiness of all the human beings it affects. If their observations are not distorted by enthusiasm or appetite, then they are frustrated by the quantity of contradictory data they receive. Inequalities of fortune, political faction, national jealousies, the subjection of indigenous peoples in colonized countries, the terror caused by wars, private greed, laziness and frivolity (to name only some of the consequences of commercial progress that Johnson identifies) represent as vast a network of suffering as the conveniences afforded by modern technologies of production and exchange represent an overwhelming number of pleasures. Hence, while Rasselas admires European powers for their superior power and knowledge, for having sent armies and fleets into the remotest parts of the globe and for having developed systems of communication across vast distances and 'a thousand arts of which we never heard' (46), he is reminded by Imlac that colonial power and the sophisticated pleasures it makes possible do not guarantee happiness. Yet no less unhappy are the Arab women who attend the Lady Pekuah during her imprisonment and who have 'no ideas but of the few things that [are] within their view' (139), and who therefore cannot properly enjoy friendship and society. These women are the slaves of Arab men, but also the victims of foreign invaders who have taken their lands and forced the former occupants into a primitive way of life supported by war and plunder. Neither Rasselas nor any of his companions attempt to compare the virtues and vices of primitive with modern life, or to put these ways of life into historical dialogue. They do not, for example, compare European with Arab violence, and neither do they try to assess whether the suffering in one region of the world is historically tied to the pleasures available in another region. There is conspicuously no conclusive geographical or historical analysis of the data about different ways of life offered at the end of the tale.

Instead the tale ends with the travellers' effort to circumscribe the arena of their study and influence. Rasselas, Pekuah and the princess all try to imagine a polity in which virtue would provide a principle of order or a 'fixed invariable state' (175) against the vicissitudes of the world. This task, they recognize, cannot be achieved in the greater world and they return to Abyssinia where the seclusion of the history-less happy valley once again offers to contain both their desires and the geographical region of their moral and political concern. At one level, analysis of commerce's muddle of social consequences, the impossibly intertwined advantages and evils, is resigned to the inscrutable will of the Supreme Being, whom no spectator, however high he flies, can hope to emulate. But at another level Johnson's travellers show how the new sciences fail to calculate and hence to offer anything like an autocritique of the commercial expansion in which they are so heavily implicated. Worldliness and fancy – which, I have argued here, are powerfully connected – for Johnson, as for Smollett, spell social disorder and moral confusion. In *Roderick Random* true patriotism and national identity fail to provide the moral glue for a crumbling polity; in *Rasselas* moral calculations arrive only at unreliable conclusions about the past or the future of an inevitably more commercial world. Neither political morality in the form of true patriotism nor cosmopolitan humanity provide the solution to the material contradictions created by global commercialism: affluence and suffering.

6
South Seas Trade and the Character of Captains

In a scene from Lewis Milestone's 1962 film, *Mutiny on the Bounty*, William Bligh is reprimanded by members of the Admiralty for having dispensed unusually cruel punishments on board his ship. Justice, they remind him, is carried not in the articles of war, but in 'the heart of a captain'.[1] Although this wholly fictitious scene takes considerable liberties with the facts of eighteenth-century naval discipline, it nonetheless offers quite an accurate depiction of the moral economy operating in later eighteenth-century voyages to the islands of the South Seas. The imperial ambitions of these lengthy journeys were, in many ways, inseparable from the principles of moral sympathy since, for the later eighteenth century, sympathy offered a theory of social order (the sublimation of aggressive and dangerous passions) that privileged commercial growth. In the journal records from Cook's three voyages into the Pacific and from Bligh's breadfruit expedition to Tahiti a decade later, passions are everywhere: in tensions among the crew and between sailors and their indigenous hosts, both on board the ship and on shore. Both Cook and Bligh encounter South Seas 'savagery' in the tempers and appetites of sailors as much as in the barbaric or licentious customs of Pacific peoples.

Between the time of Cook's first expedition in 1768 and the mutiny on HMS *Bounty* in 1789, the British empire had weathered the crises of the American Revolution and exposure of the East India Company's misrule in South Asia. Hence, in the larger imperial context, the questions of what constituted good government in the arena of colonial and commercial enterprise was particularly pressing. As commanders in chief of the 'wooden world' of the ship, captains modelled forms of government appropriate to British and non-European 'subjects' far from the imperial metropole. In the later eighteenth-century Pacific voyages, this meant that the captain had several administrative identities. He had to be the ambassador of an apparently humanitarian state that promised to deliver Pacific peoples into a more prosperous, comfortable and law-abiding way of life and, at the same time, he had to exercise firm but benevolent 'rule' over his sailor subjects and manage the often unpredictable and volatile exchanges between members of his crew and the peoples of the islands visited. The first of these tasks was to be accomplished through plant exchange, 'gifting' the botanical wisdom of enlightened states to nations that were apparently in need of it and opening up new regions of the world for global trade, which promised prosperity to all. The South Seas expeditions made by Cook and others after him were charged not only with the navigational tasks of exploring coastlines, harbours and food and water supplies in new territories, but also with collecting data about their soil conditions, climate, potential for plant cultivation, and animal and human populations. The second task was to correct the raw affections and impulses of natives and seamen, both of whom were inclined to act on their immediate desires rather than in the service of finer and greater social ends. Disciplining labour as well as socializing savage subjects required the 'compassion' of a global commercial vision alongside the authority of command.

The humanitarian promise that horticultural science would deliver prosperity and civility to countries that knew neither was of course also wedded to state and colonial interests.[2] The cultivation of plants in foreign soils would potentially reduce the costs of running colonies and supply the English market with goods that would otherwise have to be imported. In 1754, the Royal Society of Arts, Manufactures and Commerce tried to diversify crop production in the West Indies and mainland colonies by offering bounties for the cultivation of crops such as indigo, coffee and breadfruit in these non-native soils. As president of the (original) Royal Society, Joseph Banks sponsored Bligh's two expeditions to Tahiti to collect breadfruit plants and transport them to Jamaica, where it was expected (wrongly, it turned out) that the fruit would provide a cheap source of food for slaves. Banks began this work in his *Endeavour* journal, where he included a detailed assessment of the quality of soil and the crops it supports in each country. Occasionally he commented on plants (such as New Zealand flax) that might be hardy enough to thrive in English soil, or on the amount of labour needed to cultivate the soil in a given climate.[3] Cook also participated in plant interchange. He left English garden plants and root vegetables, corn, beans and peas as well as pigs and goats in New Zealand, and an assortment of garden seeds and domestic animals in Tahiti. With the help of the journals of the natural scientists who accompanied him, he also observed how and where indigenous plants grew and where else they might thrive. He was, Georg Forster observed on the second expedition, 'determined to omit nothing which might tend to the preservation of European garden plants in this country, prepar[ing] the soil, sow[ing] seeds, and transplant[ing] the young plants'.[4]

However much plant interchange served national interests, those who were most immediately involved in it often emphasized the disinterested, humanitarian implications of introducing new technologies, commercial as well as agricultural, to peoples who knew nothing of them. Although often concerned about the corrupting influence of European vices on the peoples of the South Seas, the journal records of each of these voyages for the most part reflect on the potential of contact between metropolitan Europe and the primitive South to emancipate native peoples of the Pacific from their isolated and sometimes brutal lives. Improvements in their agriculture, they suggest, will assist the progress of their manners, and education in the principles of commerce will liberate them from the poverty and savagery created by isolation.

Nonetheless, if the visits of European ships are to set these transformations in motion, and if the inhabitants of the South Seas are to benefit from the contact without, in return, influencing European sailors for the worse, then the exchanges must be overseen by a steady and authoritative, impartial and detached, yet morally sensitive captain. In the journal records of these expeditions, the instances of commercial or sexual contact, of friendship and conflict with native peoples that take place both on board and off, sometimes illustrate a larger theory about either the progress or the 'degeneration' of human passions. In such accounts, the larger historical outcome of such exchanges – the moral improvement or decline of societies that enter into commercial relations with one another – becomes contingent on the success or failure of a captain in managing the affections and impulses of his crew. He must restrain those who are more nearsighted than he from their inclinations to act on an immediate desire rather than in the interests of a distant advantage. At an enormous distance from 'civilized' metropolitan England, however, the sometimes attenuated authority of the captain was not always sufficient to preserve peace between crew and natives or to prevent desertion or mutiny. At such moments, the responsibilities of beneficent instruction and sympathetic command – responsibilities that entailed the infusion of moral sentiment into commercial imperialism – were also compromised.

Sympathy, commerce and character

By the time Cook sailed for the last time into the Pacific, plenty had been said about the relationship between social order and the passions. In *The Fable of the Bees*, Mandeville argued that human beings are driven entirely by their selfish desires, and that the passions that we affect to be ashamed of are in fact the very means by which a society flourishes. Shaftesbury, on the other hand argued that a society can only cohere through a 'right application of the affections'.[5] His argument, that through an 'exercise of the heart' that he calls 'reason'[6] we can identify passions as either virtuous or vicious, was adapted by Hutcheson into the theory of a moral sense that recognizes virtue as the touchstone of social being. Where Mandeville argued that society coheres only because the ambitious, prodigal, greedy, vain and lascivious create such a demand for luxuries that they support the working poor, Shaftesbury and Hutcheson countered that the acquisitive and jealous passions are in themselves entirely dissociative. These selfish passions, they claimed, must be moderated either by the reasoning of the heart or by the natural leaning of social beings towards virtue.

With Hume's *Treatise of Human Nature* the passions are not so much tamed as directly channelled into social order through the vehicle of sympathy. Human beings, Hume agrees with Hobbes, Pufendorf and Locke, are motivated to form and maintain societies out of their own self-interest, since without institutionalized justice they cannot hope to enjoy peaceably what they have acquired by their industry and fortune. But this contractual society then coheres neither through the power of the sovereign nor through the exercise of reason, but rather through the operation of sympathy. 'Rules of morality are not conclusions of our reason', he suggested, since reason is 'perfectly inert' and cannot adapt itself to the 'heedless and impetuous movement' of the passions.[7] Rather, the difference between virtue and vice must be *felt* rather than reasoned, and the mechanism for feeling justice is sympathy: competitive differences are effaced at the moment that we are able to enter into the feelings of others, converting their sentiments into our own. The passions pass from one person to another, producing 'correspondent movements in all human breasts' (*Treatise*, 605). Only here, in this conversion of someone else's ideas and sentiments into our own, are we are able to exercise approval or disapproval. We do so not according to the merit or criminal nature of a given action, but according to what we perceive as the motivating sentiments behind the action. Our sympathy is drawn to the character and disposition, rather than the actions of another person. Commerce, which depends on peaceful relations within and between societies, relies on this conversion, and sociability it makes possible.

Since, however, our feelings are naturally strongest for those closest to us, sympathy in itself is an undependable conduit of justice in a society of any considerable size. What Hume identifies as our partiality and unequal affection naturally affects our understanding of vice and virtue; acts of moral judgement must look to the artificial remedies of 'education and human conventions' (483) if they are to be properly just. One of these conventions, of course, is government, 'entered into by all the members of the society to bestow stability on the possession of ... external goods' (485). The artificially enforced sympathy for those who are not close to us, a sympathy into which we must be educated and one that takes the form of regard for the public interest, becomes the basis both for protecting our own interests and for exercising moral judgement. Because human beings cannot extend their concern beyond themselves to any great distance, their interest is best served by 'an universal and inflexible observance of the rules of justice, by which alone they can preserve society and keep themselves from falling into that wretched and savage condition which is commonly represented in the state of nature' (534).

Yet because we are perpetually drawn to what is close, present and immediately advantageous, there is no innate principle which determines that we will look to our more distant advantage through the aegis of justice and government, rather than pursue the immediate gratification of our desires at the expense of others about whom we care little. Thus, Hume argues, 'the commerce of men [is] rendered dangerous and uncertain', and the desire for 'great present advantage' (534) might make us overlook our more remote interests in preserving the peace of society and lead us instead to rebellion. The solution offered by Adam Smith in *The Theory of Moral Sentiments* is for us to sympathize with the happiness or grief of strangers through our respect for a man of more extensive humanity than our own. For Smith, the person who is capable of 'exquisite sensibility' and of 'the manhood of self command'[8] – a man, for Smith, who can suppress his own immediate passions in order to respond sympathetically to the feelings of others – is not only a cut above his fellows, but also likely to be able to guide and manage the impulsive behaviour of others. Sensibility of this finer kind is, according to Smith, determined by the degree to which a feeling agent is able to identify with an 'impartial spectator' who can judge with the moral strength of detached sympathy. This 'great judge' or 'man within' adds 'reason, principle and conscience' to the felt response he has to another's joy or suffering, and in so doing demonstrates 'the propriety of generosity and the deformity of injustice'.[9] He represents, in fact, the general moral rules and principles of justice endorsed not by custom, but by the central mechanism of moral community itself: in order to be part of any properly cohesive society one must judge oneself with the eyes of others independently of one's own visceral response to an apparent injustice. Smith's spectator – the well-informed judging figure within the breast who moderates and softens the raw desires of self-loving individuals – is not so impartial that he does not recognize where we owe *most* loyalty. Moral judgement is 'interested' for the society as a whole. It is simply that this judgement can only be effective if it is exercised through the normative authority of a moral arbiter: one who is represented abstractly in the impartial spectator, but who comes to life as the man of exquisite feeling and self-command. This spectator is a natural leader and someone who is capable of acting in the greater interests of his nation, while his inferiors are perpetually blinded by their own passions.

Thomas Haskell has argued that humanitarian feeling is an offshoot of capitalism because the kind of calculating and forward-thinking 'cognitive style' that the market rewards is necessarily one that respects the moral consequences of an act. At the same time, he argues, 'capitalist thinking' recognizes how people far removed from one another in space and time might be differently affected by a particular transaction.[10] 'The very possibility of feeling obliged to go to the aid of a suffering stranger', he suggests, 'was enormously heightened by the emergence of a form of life that made attention to the remote consequences of one's acts an emblem of civilization itself'.[11] His account of the genesis of the modern promise-keeping 'man of principle', who combines the self-control that belongs to market discipline with the expanded affection that arises out of remote interests, also describes Smith's impartial spectator. Even alongside his seemingly ruthless defence of the alienation of labour, Smith reserves a place for the moral spectator in an economy driven by radical specialization. *The Wealth of Nations* famously opens with the chapter on the origin of the division of labour in which the progress of society is traced not to the human capacity for reason, but to the coincidence of passions that drives human beings to trade with one another:

> This division of labour, from which so many advantages are derived, is not originally the effect of any human wisdome, which foresees and intends that general opulence to which it gives occasion. It is the necessary, though very slow and gradual, consequence of a certain propensity in human nature which has in view no such extensive utility; the propensity to truck, barter, and exchange one thing for another.[12]

From the disposition to trade arises the diversification of tasks, and ultimately the kind of specialized division of tasks – such as that of the pin manufacture – that has magnified labour's productive power. Yet even alongside this seemingly ruthless defence of the division and alienation of labour, Smith reserves a place in modern industrial society for the philosopher, although he is as specialized as any other labourer, and is 'often capable of combining together the powers of the most distant and dissimilar objects' (*Wealth of Nations*, 1:14).

Of course philosophers are, in this context, inventors; men who deduce how the arts of manufacture can be improved and time saved. But their ability to discern relationships between diverse and remote objects where other labourers are focused entirely on the minute task in front of them also gives them a role something akin to that of the impartial spectator. Smith wanted to ensure that the effects of industrialization, the expansion of commerce and a market-driven economy did not strip self-interested subjects of moral understanding and compassionate imagination. He recommended government-subsidized education for workers who might thereby be freed from the 'torpor', stupidity and ignorance that come with performing the same simple task over and over again. Workers needed to be invigorated with generous, noble and tender sentiments, not least in order to be able to appreciate 'the great and extensive interests of [their] country' (2:782). The apparently *laissez-faire* doctrine of the 'invisible hand' is therefore complicated by Smith's vision of the role of the state in the moral education of labouring subjects.[13] Such intervention is analogous to the moral arbitration of the spectator-philosopher: most people are incapable of the kind of moral refinement that enables them to recognize interests greater than their own, and they require the guidance of superiors – or what, in the *Theory of Moral Sentiments*, Smith calls 'men of exquisite sensibility' – to direct them into a recognition of the greater needs of the community as a whole.

For both Hume and Smith, the concept of a society regulated by sympathetic feeling recognizes that relationships between social beings are inherently commercial and as such, paradoxically, inevitably moral. Yet for both, social order demands that the passions be subjected to the moderating influences of education or government. Smith's impartial spectator represents an internalization of the moral authority exercised through what Hume called 'human institutions'. In *The Wealth of Nations*, this spectator comes to life again in the figure of the philosopher who, by virtue of his ability to combine the distant and dissimilar, becomes capable of an exquisite feeling and greater humanity than his fellows. The less perceptive cannot be depended upon to respond to what seems remote and disconnected from their own interests. Thriving industrial and commercial societies, according to Smith, are able to achieve a global vision of the accumulation of wealth, and as such depend as much upon a well-regulated moral economy as upon the 'invisible hand' of a self-regulating system.

The South Seas voyage narratives that I will be looking at here recognize the captain as a moral spectator of the kind that Smith proposed.[14] In the confined space of a ship, sailing enormous distances from home, captains had to be more than mere disciplinarians. In some respects its own floating society-in-miniature, the ship housed passions that were potentially quite volatile, given the conditions in which seamen worked and their distance from the 'civilized' world. The humanity and self-command of captains, just as much as their direct authority, should have ensured that they were able to manage such passions, whether these arose among crew members or in the sometimes violent interactions between sailors and their indigenous hosts. Captains were therefore required to be exemplary moral subjects, whose own conduct and capacity to recognize the distant consequences of an action was directed by a restraining inner judge. Yet, at the same time, they also had to act as flesh-and-blood moral spectator-arbitrators, correcting the self-serving passions of their ignorant, violent and greedy inferiors (whether seamen or natives) with their own humanitarian foresight. In this respect, they also represented the cosmopolitan vision of commerce over the nearsightedness, jealousy, and self-isolation of unenlightened nations.

Cook's three expeditions into the Pacific were successful in a largely negative way. He settled once and for all the non-existence of a Southern Continent and of a North West Passage. Bligh unsuccessfully commanded an expedition whose project – to ship breadfruit plants from Tahiti to the West Indies where they would provide a cheap source of food for slaves – was thwarted by mutiny. His failure as a commander to manage the heightened passions of his sea-weary crew directly embarrassed the commercial objectives of the voyage, whilst Cook's expeditions merely disappointed theirs. In the mythology surrounding the achievements of both captains, relative degrees of success and failure seem to come down entirely to a matter of character: Cook was magnanimous and self-controlled; Bligh was ungenerous and hot-tempered. These portraits clearly borrow from the vocabulary of sympathy, contrasting the restrained humanitarian with the passionate bully. Yet neither Cook nor Bligh, we shall see, entirely succeeded in exercising the kind of moral authority that could contain the passions of frustrated or amorous crew members and affronted natives. The cosmopolitan promises of British voyages into the Pacific – in which moral philosophy would join hands with commercial interests – terminated in Cook's death and in Bligh's expulsion from his own ship.

Aside from native violence and mutiny, captains also had to worry about the fascination with local customs seducing European seamen away from their duty, perhaps even provoking them to desert and 'go native'. Smith argued that the general rules of morality are so firmly rooted in the passions of human nature that they can never be entirely perverted by custom, however much the latter might cause moral mischief by provoking discordant opinions. Yet since the bulk of mankind is incapable of the proper sentiment that gives rise to these general rules and thus enables us to recognize the monstrosity of certain customs, social order can only survive exposure to such customs through the authority of an 'impartial' man of feeling. Once this authority is challenged, then general moral rules might splinter into morally relative customs. Apart from the real possibility that sailors might turn their backs on home forever, another likely consequence of this failure of moral authority was that commercial enterprises of this kind would become separated from the humanitarian vision that was supposed to underpin them. It might suddenly seem possible, in other words, that contact with other cultures in the Pacific did not, in fact, represent events on the progressive timeline of commercial enlightenment (whereby commerce and civility were delivered to the impoverished, isolated, and either indolent or excessively martial nations of the South Seas) but rather scenes of social degeneration provoked by the greed of more 'advanced' and prosperous nations.

Captaincy and humanity

Although it is a long time since history has been told through the stories of great men, Cook's heroicization survived well into the twentieth century. A nineteenth-century fictional account of his early life, entitled *The Adventures and Vicissitudes of Captain Cook, Mariner, Showing how by Honesty, Truth, and Perseverance, a Poor Friendless Orphan Boy became a Great Man* (which narrates the boyhood adventures of James Cook and his friend Ike), was written 100 years earlier than Daniel Carrison's *Captain Cook: Genius Afloat* (1967), yet both titles preserve Cook as the national hero that he became following his death in Hawaii.[15] Carrison does not stray far from late eighteenth-century sentimental discourse when he says of the reactions of Cook's crew at his death that 'these tears would have been memorial enough for the austere, capable and unpretentious Captain Cook'.[16] Even the formidable Cook scholar, John Beaglehole, emphasizes the exceptional character of the man. In his biography of Cook, Beaglehole scans the journals for evidence of the character of which we lack any 'intimate' account:[17]

> His was not the poetic mind, or the profoundly scientific mind. He was the genius of the matter of fact. He was profoundly competent in his calling as seaman. He was completely professional in his trade as explorer. He had, in large part, the sceptical mind: he did not like taking on trust. He was therefore the great dispeller of illusion. He did have an imagination, but it was a controlled imagination that could think out a great voyage in terms of what was possible for his own competence. He could think, he could plan, he could reason.[18]

In Beaglehole's elegy, Cook becomes at once the thorough empiricist, the forward-thinking and practical sailor, and the man of exemplary restraint. His scrupulous attention to detail is complemented by the same 'controlled imagination' that Smith identified as a feature of sympathetic spectatorhood. Beaglehole locates Cook's professionalism in his capacity to plan and reason ahead, recognizing that such professionalism included the ability to discipline the passions that draw lesser men to excessive ambition or to fascination with the 'illusions' of either irretrievably monstrous or blissfully idyllic societies in the South Seas.

Immediately following his death, Cook was eulogized as a man of extraordinary compassion and as the benefactor of 'backward' nations whose economies he helped to diversify, and to whom he introduced modern technologies of crop and animal cultivation. Anna Seward remembers him both as the steward of an allegorical 'Humanity' who 'unite[s] the savage hearts and hostile hands' and 'strew[s] her soft comforts over the barren plain' and as a national hero furthering the power and glory of Britannia, who in turn commemorates his 'virtues just'.[19] The dedicatory preface to a collection of cloth specimens gathered during Cook's voyages describes a heart expansive enough to spread happiness into every corner of the globe, declaring, presumably of Cook:

> there is none more ready to feed the hungry and clothe the naked: would to God it was as much in your power as it is in your heart to wipe the tear from every eye, but that is impossible; for while you was teaching Indian nations how to be happy, you was as much wanted at home where it is our constant wish that heaven may long preserve you the support of science, and the idol of family and friends.[20]

In the journals written by members of his crew (mainly officers), Cook is praised for his bravery, his skill at managing interactions with the natives, his restraint, his superior judgement, his ability to focus on the great objectives of the voyage, his skill as a navigator, and his care for the health of (and compassion towards) his seamen. Such tributes are, unsurprisingly, most frequent in the journals of the final voyage from which Cook did not return. James King, who commanded the expedition following the deaths both of Cook and of Charles Clerke (the captain of the companion vessel *Discovery*), spoke of the 'very unfortunate and tragic death of one of the greatest navigators our nation or any nation ever had', and of the powerful loss that his crew felt when he was killed.[21] Midshipman George Gilbert recalls that the 'gloomy dejection' of the crew was 'more easy to be conceived than described, for as all our hopes centred in him, our loss became irreparable'.[22] Able Seaman Heinrich Zimmermann also depicts Cook's death as something too terrible to relate, recalling that everyone on the ships was 'stricken dumb'; and he adds that every man felt 'as though he has lost his father'.[23] These testimonies, equally weighted between memories of his paternal tenderness and testimonies to his superior seamanship are, however, oddly contradicted by passing remarks about his temper, such as Gilbert's observation that 'he had but little command over himself in his anger',[24] or William Ellis's report that Cook punished a Tahitian who had stolen the ship's quadrant by flogging him until his 'skin came away in shreds',[25] or Zimmermann's account of the same episode in which, he says, Cook cut off both the thief's ears.[26] Such incidents do not seem to compromise his reputation as a humanitarian, however, in part because punishments of this kind were not perceived as extraordinary in England, but also, perhaps, because in the wake of Cook's death, the crew saw their captain as having protected them precisely against what Zimmermann called 'the momentary impulse[s] of passion' that afflicted native peoples.[27] All the accounts of his death are careful to observe that he tried to keep his own people from firing on the Hawaiians (an act that would certainly have resulted in more English deaths).[28]

More probably, however, the representation of particular incidents in which Cook revealed a shortness of temper and a willingness to inflict punishment on those who inspired his rage would have compromised the perceived 'humanitarian' successes of the voyages. Although the scientific objectives of each of his expeditions – to study the transit of Venus, to explore the Southern Pacific for a continent, and to search for a North West passage from the Pacific to the Atlantic oceans – were very precisely laid out in the directions Cook was given by the Admiralty, the definition of 'discovery' was expanded in accounts of his achievements to include the introduction of new plant and animal species to remote regions of the world. A surgeon on the *Discovery*, David Samwell, commemorated him through the figure of the 'grateful Indian' who:

> in time to come, pointing to the herds grazing his fertile plains, will relate to his children how the first stock of them was introduced into the country; and the name of Cook will be remembered among those benign spirits, whom they worship as the source of every good, and the fountain of every blessing.[29]

Similarly, George Anderson saw Cook executing the benevolent plans of George III to gift the achievements of a superior civilization to the native peoples of the South Pacific: 'The very introduction of our useful animals and vegetables, by adding fresh means of subsistence, will have added to their comfort and enjoyments of life.' Such plans, he pointed out, excuse British commerce from the brutality associated with the Spanish conquest of America, for the former aims to promote general knowledge rather than to enlarge Britain's dominion, and in so doing to deliver the peoples of the South Seas into a more civilized condition in which they might abolish 'their horrid repasts, and their equally horrid rites', and thus come to hold 'an honourable station amongst the nations of the earth'. 'We wish to learn they exist', he

adds, 'in order to bring them within the pale of the offices of humanity, and to relieve the wants of their imperfect state of society'.[30] Based
on a principle going back at least as far as Bacon's hope for science as a
'relief of man's estate',[31] these commentators saw horticulture and
improved husbandry diversifying the economies of less advanced
countries, which will then necessarily support more peaceful societies.

It was precisely the presumed link between a great man's 'acts of
humanity' and the progressive effects of empirical science that Georg
Forster satirized in his vitriolic letter to the Earl of Sandwich, com-
plaining of the treatment his father had received from the sponsors of
the second voyage. Johann Forster, he reminded the Earl, had been
promised the rights to his own published account of the second
voyage. As it turned out, however, he was given neither the right to
publish a connected narrative (instead, his observations were to be
included in the official publication of Cook's journal) nor any compen-
sation for the financial loss. His son complains of those in influential
circles who professed friendship and then refused to support the
Forsters' appeal that 'a great man always requires, that his friend
should even on philosophical subjects ... implicitly adopt his fancies',
and that:

> if the patron maintains that salt-water cannot freeze, and his friend
> ventures to trust his own eyes and believe the contrary; or if the
> great man dreams of a Southern continent, and his client has the
> audacity to divulge, that he has sailed over the spot where it should
> have been found ... not the sea, but his patron's heart will be
> instantly frozen into ice, and from thence forward to find one single
> sentiment of philanthropy or even common justice in the frozen
> mass, will be as utterly impossible as to meet with lands where it has
> pleased heaven to place an ocean.[32]

Where 'great men' have more authority than eye witnesses, then character cannot be trusted and humane sentiment barely masks vanity
and self-interest.

In his defence of Cook against Johann Forster's claims that he
pushed his crew beyond a reasonable limit, the astronomer on board
the *Resolution*, William Wales, accuses the naturalist of trying to dis-
credit his captain as a man who has very little feeling for the lives of
his own people.[33] Forster, he suggested, has had the audacity to challenge public confidence in Cook's strength of character: namely, his
expansive capacity for fellow feeling combined with considered and

informed judgement. He could only manage to do so, Wales suggests, by flatly contradicting himself: one moment he praises the great and generous intentions of the British Crown to bestow the gifts of agricultural science on less fortunate peoples, and the next he argues that 'the dictates of philanthropy do not harmonize with the political systems of Europe'.[34] The contradictions in Forster's journal are important, however, precisely because they do point to the moments where, under the pressures of long-distance travel, the moral economy both on board and off fails to operate properly. He raises the possibility that at an enormous distance from home, exposed to foreign customs, subject to violent passions provoked by the conditions of life at sea, sailors might sink into the indolent and degenerate behaviour that they were exposed to in the manners and customs of Pacific peoples. Early on in the journal he praises the 'mild government' exercised on an English ship where 'the meanest of subjects is always treated with tenderness and care, vice is punished and virtue is rewarded'. At sea, he declares, 'no subject can be happier than an English one'.[35] By the end of the voyage, however, he is warning that maritime life stifles the tender affections. Every 'spark of humanity', he complained, is extinguished:

> among the stern aspect of the boisterous sea, the dashing of the enraged waves, and the fury of the winds, among the sight of so various and strange nations, the harsh manners of rough cursing and often cruel sailors, and the unnatural life we lead after so long an absence from any European port.

At once emotionally heartless and 'insensible to the enjoyments and comforts of life', seamen remain unblessed by the material benefits of commercial culture and the powerful social ties that it makes possible.[36]

Cook himself takes considerable care in describing how he managed the passions and appetites of his crew in their interactions with their indigenous hosts.[37] Drawing on instructions from the Admiralty that he should show 'every kind of civility and regard' to the native peoples, he gave explicit orders that no violence was to be offered against any native unless absolutely necessary. In an effort to try to control the spread of syphilis, he prohibited infected sailors from going on shore and forbade any of the crew members from bringing native women on board the ship. He also gave his crew detailed directions about how trade was to be conducted with the natives in order to stabilize the value of the goods exchanged: only the officer appointed to trade with the natives for provisions could do so; any arms or working tools lost by any of the crew were to be charged against their pay; and iron and cloth were to be traded for provisions, not curiosities. He comments in the journal:

> I thought it very necessary that some order should be observed in trafficking with the natives: that such merchandize as we had on board for that purpose might continue to bear a proper value, and not leave it to every one's own particular fancy which could not fail to bring on confusion and quarrels between us and the natives, and would infallibly lessen the value of such articles as we had to traffic with.[38]

The danger of conducting trade according to 'particular fancies' is of course especially acute in a new market where supply and demand can fluctuate with the very unstable conditions of contact. Georg Forster commented on the danger of allowing sailors to trade for curiosities, particularly given that there was no anticipating what a given commodity (such as nails, or the red feathers which members of the ship's company acquired in Tonga) would fetch on another island or in a different region. The price of provisions could be raised to such an unreasonable height that the market in curiosities and sex stifled trade for provisions altogether. The protection of 'proper value' is thus an important labour of command designed to control the diversity of needs and desires that arise in a virtually unregulated marketplace.

There was more than the micro-economy of the ship at stake in such interventions since, according to what Europeans thought they had observed in the study of Pacific peoples, the free expression of passions stifled productivity and commercial enterprise. A sailor who, as Forster puts it, 'rushes headlong after the pleasures of the present moment'[39] is not so different from a Tahitian who 'spend[s] his life in the most sluggish inactivity and without one benefit to society' (*A Voyage*, 1:296). Emphasizing their difference from the Tahitains, Cook praised the islanders in the Tongan group for cultivating their soil so well and observed that it must have been divided as private property, since 'interest is the great spring that animates the hand of industry'. He also observed that not only was theft severely punished on Tonga-tabu but that the people were of a mild and benevolent character (*Voyages*, 2:270). In Tierra del Fuego, on the other hand, he complains of natives who have such a passion for beads that 'in this consists their whole pride', and he implies that with such primitive passions it is little surprise that they appear to have no form of government and 'are perhaps as miserable a set of people as are this day upon earth' (*Voyages*, 1:45). On the east coast of New Holland, he observes, a poor, nomadic people 'move from place to place like wild beasts in search of food and ... depend wholly upon the success of the present day for their subsistence' (*Voyages* 1:396). Fully engaged in satisfying their most immediate and daily needs, they have been able to make no improvements in agriculture, and neither have they organized themselves into large stable communities (1:312).

The Dusky Bay Maori in New Zealand, 'far remote from the trading part of the world' (1:131), live 'a wandering life in small parties' (2:134), and are frequently at war with their neighbours. Those in Queen Charlotte Sound are similarly grouped in small, isolated communities and are therefore 'subject[ed] to many inconveniences a well-regulated society under one head or any other form of government are not subject to' (2:171). He also observes that the North Island Maori seem generally to have formed stable enough laws that they are not vulnerable to the attack of every stranger, whereas those of the South Island, 'by living a wandering life ... are destitute of most of the advantages which subjects them to perpetual alarms' (2:171). They are more martial cultures as a result, with 'even the women ... not exempt from carrying arms' (1:172). Given the emphasis that Hume and others put on peace for the success of commerce, this in turn explains why the South Island Maori remain developmentally, as well as geographically, 'remote from the trading world'.

Despite his personal disagreements with Cook, the elder Forster endorsed the former's ranking of South Seas cultures according to the civilized achievements each had made in mode of subsistence and manners. Societies, he argued, are more or less degenerate depending on the influence of climate and the degree to which they have retained knowledge of the technologies and civilities of former ages. Using the expansive historical method of Kames, Millar and Ferguson, his *Observations Made During a Voyage Round the World* examines the relationship between customs, climate, property, commerce and government.[40] He argues, for instance, of the New Zealanders that, blessed with a mild climate (which softens the manners) and a sizeable population (which makes agriculture necessary), they have remained relatively civilized (*Observations*, 208). Nations that inhabit the frozen extremes, on the other hand, have become degenerate and debased. These extremely primitive peoples, he argues, are originally descendants of more enlightened tribes which, living closer to one another, shared 'useful knowledge, established principles, regulations ...

mechanical trades ... [and] the arts, manufactures ... and principles of Egypt' (196). Forced to travel beyond the reach of their enemies, and compelled with every generation to 'wander across a great space of unoccupied land' (196), such peoples gradually lost the memory of these ancient systems.

It is hard not to see Forster's account of the degeneracy caused by wandering too far from the civilized world as a warning about the possible consequences of European sea travel and the danger that, in remote parts of the world, sailors might mutiny or desert. Despite his frequent condemnation of metropolitan decadence and the taste for luxuries which obscures 'that spirit of benevolence and real goodness' (223) that can be observed in some South Seas societies, he warns that, at the furthest distance from well-regulated and well-governed parts of the world, the people are the most miserable. This relationship between a geographical region and the happiness of the people who inhabit it can only be gleaned through a detached and reflective assessment of the various cultures of these remote parts, an assessment that, like Cook's, will then prevent the collapse of value into fancy:

> a mind accustomed to mediation, and able to afix to everything its true value, must certainly perceive, that this situation of the savage or barbarian, is nothing more than a state of intoxication; his happiness and contentment founded on mere sensuality is transitory and delusive; the sum of his enjoyments is so small, so defective in its particulars, and of so little value, that a man in his senses cannot but think himself happy that he was born in a civilized nation, educated in a country where society is as much improved as possible; that he belongs to a people who are governed by the mildest laws, and have the happiest constitution of government, being under the influence of civil and religious liberty. (199)

With respect for the kind of detached observation and attention to the 'bigger picture' of human improvement or degeneration that his father recommends, Georg Forster promises in *A Voyage Round the World* that his remarks praising or censuring the South Seas nations are influenced neither by attachment nor aversion to that people, but by 'a retrospect to our general improvement and welfare' (*A Voyage*, 1:xii). Customs and traditions, this suggests, should be responded to with scientific detachment as well as with the sympathy that can embrace even distant objects, and not with the immediacy of either shock, revulsion or delight. Cook, too, learns how to become a detached rather than an enthralled or horrified spectator of savage customs by putting what he sees into an evolutionary context. In Tahiti, he observed that the regular practice of infanticide is 'a custom ... inhuman and contrary to the first principals of human nature' (*Voyages*, 1:128). His remark is uncannily anticipated by Adam Smith, who in *The Theory of Moral Sentiments* said of infanticide that 'our disgust at a particular custom should never pervert our sentiments with regard to the general style and character of conduct and behaviour'. 'No society', he added, 'could subsist a moment in which the usual strain of men's conduct and behaviour was of a piece with [that] horrible practice' (211).

This is a lesson that Cook seems to put into practice in his record of events in the South Island of New Zealand when, during the second voyage, he first became convinced of the existence of cannibalism among the Maori. In Queen Charlotte Sound he asked that a piece of human flesh from a body that had been brought on board the ship be cooked and offered to his Maori visitors. Suppressing his own visceral horror at the spectacle of cannibalism, he offers a calm diagnosis of the cultural shortcomings that provoke such appallingly violent acts in a people who are to some degree civilized:

> the New Zealanders are certainly in a state of civilization, their behaviour to us has been manly and mild, shewing always a readiness to oblige us ... This custom of eating their enemies slain in battle ... has undoubtedly been handed down to them from the earliest times ... [A]s they become more united they will of consequence have fewer enemies and become more civilized and then and not till then this custom may be forgot. (*Voyages*, 2:294)

Finding that commercial isolation and a lack of settled life and government is responsible for the persistence of savage customs such as cannibalism, he goes on to observe that this primitive condition itself prevents these societies from allowing the proper mechanism of sociability – the exercise of normative moral judgement – to evolve. 'At present', he goes on to say, 'they seem to have but little idea of treating other men as they themselves would wish to be treated, but treat them as they think they should be treated under the same circumstances' (2:294). Without an impartial moral spectator they are guided only by their own powerful passions of fear and vengeance. In the absence of any such judging figure within their own communities, Cook stands in as moderator and compassionate observer of their actions. His own suppression, in this instance, of what Smith calls 'the insolence and

brutality of anger' (*Theory*, 24), in favour of a kind of reasonable dis-
taste as he responds thoughtfully and 'historically' to the spectacle of
cannibalism, distinguishes him as much from the ship's crew as from
the Maori themselves. The former were, as the younger Forster
describes them, extremely affected 'beholders', some of whom were so
heartlessly amused as to consider joining the feast, while others were
inspired with such disgust they were ready to murder the cannibals for
a crime 'they had no right to condemn' (*A Voyage*, 1:512).

In the same historicizing vein as Cook, Forster also commented of
cannibalism that:

> the action of eating human flesh, whatever our education may teach
> us to the contrary, is certainly neither unnatural nor criminal in
> itself. It can only become dangerous in as far as it steels the mind
> against that compassionate fellow feeling which is the great basis of
> civil society; and for this reason we find it naturally banished from
> every people as soon as civilization has made any progress among
> them. (*A Voyage*, 1:517)

Yet Forster is frequently less than confident about the firm distinctions
between savage and civilized upon which such observations depend.
He cites Las Casas on the brutality of Spanish colonialism in America,
and reflects that, however brutal cannibalism might seem, Europeans
continue to 'cut one another's throats by the thousands' (1:516).
Moreover, with the same inconsistency that Wales accused his father
of, he complains of the 'mercenary principles that commerce inspires'
(2:190) and suggests that it would be better for both discoverers and
discovered 'that the South Seas had still remained unknown to Europe
and its restless inhabitants' (1:386). At the end of the second volume,
he tells the story of Mrs Milton, whose son was one of the party from
the *Adventure* who was killed and eaten in New Zealand, reflecting that
'no heart [could] refuse a sympathetic tribute' to her grief, and lament
the enterprising spirit that had caused it (2:586).

This spirit of regret, a kind of expansive sympathy gone awry, is also
visible in Cook's journals. Despite the self-conscious acts of moral arbitration that Cook engages in, he also from time to time offers a less
confident reflection on the impact of European arrival on the native
peoples of the South Seas. In Queen Charlotte's Sound, he regrets that
the prostitution of Maori women is clearly the consequence:

> of a commerce with Europeans and what is still more to our shame,
> civilized Christians [for] we debauch their morals already to prone to

vice and we interduce [*sic*] among them wants and perhaps diseases which they never before knew and which serves only to disturb that happy tranquility they and their fore Fathers had injoy'd.

He then invites anyone sceptical of his argument to consider 'what the natives of the whole extent of America have gained from commerce with Europeans' (*Voyages*, 2:175). The natives of New Holland, too, he suggests, are happier without the desire for riches that plagues Europeans, and 'live in a tranquility that is not disturb'd by the inequality of condition', and the European observer who truly believes them to be 'the most wretched people on earth' is simply blind to the corruptions of his own world and time (1:399). At such moments, he is not an impartial, reflective spectator at all but rather an affected eyewitness frozen, like Forster, in feeling tribute to those who are likely to suffer from the influence of result of European appetites and ambitions.[41]

The other challenge to the theory of commerce's benevolent influence comes from on board the ship itself. In his account of the voyage on the *Resolution*, Midshipman Elliott praises Cook for his bravery, his coolheadedness and his humanity, and insists that 'no man was better calculated to gain the confidence of savages'.[42] Yet commenting later on Cook's decision in the New Hebrides to flog a sentry who shot a native dead, Elliott remarks that 'I must think that here ... he lost sight of both justice and humanity'.[43] This incident brings Cook's role as humanitarian statesman into conflict with his task as captain: he is appalled by the 'inhumanity of the act' of killing a man who was merely showing the visitors that he was armed, while members of the crew in turn accuse Cook of excessive discipline (*Voyages*, 2:498). A like conflict arises in the accounts of the decision to sail the *Resolution* back by passing south of New Zealand in 1774. Cook reports the readiness of the crew to make the expedition, praising their obedience and alertness and insisting that they were 'so far from wishing the voyage at an end that they rejoiced at the prospect of its being prolonged another year' (2:328). This directly contradicts the account of their reactions given by Georg Forster, who reports with a very different emphasis that 'the only thoughts which could make them amends [for this voyage south] was the certainty of passing another season among the happy islands in the torrid zone' (*A Voyage*, 1:526). 'The hope of meeting with new lands', he recalls, 'was vanished, the topics of common conversation were exhausted, the cruise to the south could not present anything new but appeared in all its chilling horrors before us, and the absence of our consort doubled every danger' (1:524).

It is tempting to link this horror of the icy south and the evacuation of social spirit from the ship that it provokes to the incidents of 'depravity' among the sailors who, in their associations with native women, Forster reports, 'disclaimed all acquaintance with modesty' (1:577). His father, having praised the entire expedition into the Pacific as motivated by 'principles of humanity',[44] then went on to complain of the 'boasted civilization [and] parade of humanity and social virtues'[45] that characterize European sensibilities, contrasting them with the natural tenderness of a Tahitian man who wept when he saw the Maori men eating human flesh in Queen Charlotte Sound. What he identifies as hypocrisy, however, seems more like a process of social breakdown and growing disaffection among members of Cook's crew as the Captain's acts of moral judgement cease to appear uniformly humane. The consequences seem trivial: members of the crew thought increasingly of their own discomforts and longed for the pleasures of the torrid zone. Yet such 'unsociable' inclinations, attached as they were to a fondness for Tahiti rather than a longing for home, could be enormously troubling for British commerce, as a later expedition into the South Seas was to show.

Mutiny on the *Bounty*

Tensions on board Cook's ships, of course, never achieved crisis proportions in the way that they did aboard the *Bounty* in 1789. Bligh's expedition, however, faced much the same set of problems as Cook's: in particular, the enormous distance that had to be travelled and the need to manage trade between European sailors and their island hosts carefully. Bligh's task was to collect a large number of breadfruit plants in Tahiti, half of which were to be delivered to the King's botanical gardens at St Vincent, and the other half to Jamaica, where the fruit might provide cheap food for plantation slaves. The *Bounty* reached Tahiti on 26 October 1788, where it remained for 23 weeks while the breadfruit was collected. A short way into the return voyage, on 28 April 1789, the crew mutinied, and Bligh and 17 others were set adrift in an open boat in which they managed to cover 3500 miles to Timor. Bligh then travelled on through the East Indies to Batavia in a schooner, during which voyage he nearly faced another mutiny, and finally returned to England as a passenger in a Dutch vessel. Two years later he returned to the South Pacific on a second breadfruit expedition. Fletcher Christian's mutineers returned to Tahiti briefly and then sailed on to Pitcairn Island where they settled, and where most, including Christian, died in a conflict with the Tahitians who had accompanied them. Several of the mutineers who remained in Tahiti were captured and brought back to England for court martial.

Beaglehole has pointed out that while Cook was revered as a great humanitarian and mourned as a loss to the entire world, and while Bligh was and is remembered as a bully and a failure, there was not much to distinguish professionally between the two of them. Both were strict disciplinarians, and both, in Beaglehole's words, 'were exceedingly humane men, careful of the lives of those who served under them'.[46] Like Cook, Bligh was scrupulous about his seamen's general health, but also like Cook, he was known to lose himself from time to time in violent fits of temper. Bligh, who had sailed in the final voyage of the *Resolution*, to a large extent modelled his management skills on those of Cook, strictly regulating trade by determining who among the crew could conduct it and which goods were to be exchanged, and relying on the power of chiefs to capture and return deserters. However, in his log entries prior to the mutiny, Bligh actually expresses more interest in the diet, exercise and cleanliness of his crew than in their behaviour in Tahiti, and he is less concerned about how they are affected by the unfamiliar customs they witness than either Cook or the Forsters were about the impact of such observations on the crew of the *Resolution*. It is only when he comes later on to reflect on how the experience of a lengthy stay in Tahiti might have precipitated the mutiny that he observes how tempting the ease of a life on this island must have appeared to men who were so far away from the comforts of home.

A large portion of the log is devoted to a detailed account of Tahitian customs and with the means that he used to maintain 'a very friendly and affectionate footing with the principal people'.[47] He observes, for instance, how gifts are given by the chief both as signs of patronage or friendship and as a means of securing political alliance or loyalty. Because it is so crucial to keep the chiefs' good will, Bligh uses gifts in the same way: he keeps some 'favour[s] in reserve' (*Log*, 1:410) to ensure that he has a means of restoring good relations when necessary; and even while he 'rewards all classes of people, both men, women and children' (2:68) with European goods, he often distributes these according to the status and situation of the person whose affection he most needs to secure. He often does this according to the direction of his principal host, Chief Tynah. Wary of the more radical measures that Cook took to recover stolen objects or deserters given their consequences in Hawaii, Bligh avoided holding chiefs to ransom whenever possible. On the one occasion that he did so, he soon released his weeping prisoners, calculating that the return of the stolen object was not worth the distress their detainment was causing them. But in imitation of Cook, he noted when and where he had planted trees and how he had tried to encourage the breeding of sheep and cattle.

There are ways of accounting for why a mutiny took place on the *Bounty* and not on the *Endeavour* or the *Resolution*. Greg Denning has argued that 'spaces of ambivalence' profoundly affected the culture of the ship: the sense of placelessness created by being in port for so long as routine is disrupted, the lack of ceremonial distance between captain and crew in the small and crowded vessel where the main cabin was turned into a nursery for the breadfruit, and the blur between public and private that Bligh created in his punishments as he flogged men whom he felt were personally 'against' him. Bligh in fact, Denning shows, flogged his sailors less than any other British captain who travelled into the Pacific in the eighteenth century, including Cook.[48] However, the punishments that were dealt out were often individually excessive: he was known to give 120 lashes when the navy limit was 36.[49] Moreover, he was not able to convince his crew that his decisions about reducing food allowances or about replacing one food with another more cheaply were motivated by anything other than private greed, since he stood to profit personally from such parsimony.[50] Bligh was, according to this account, hot-tempered and too apparently self-serving. The idea that the mutiny was the direct consequence of flaws in Bligh's character which disturbed the hierarchical order of the ship is borne out by John Fryer, master on the *Bounty*, who accompanied Bligh on the open boat journey to Timor following the mutiny. Fryer complains that the captain continued to behave abusively in the launch. In his account of a conflict between Bligh and the carpenter, he argues that the former put himself on a footing with a member of his crew whenever he made a personal challenge, and in so doing justified the crew member's violence against him.[51] James Morrison, the boatswain's mate, reported that Bligh routinely cut provisions, replaced one foodstuff with another which was cheaper (such as pumpkin for bread), and deprived the crew of fresh meat even when it was readily available.[52] Bligh himself answered Morrison's complaints point for point, defending his decisions as based on dietary needs, general shipboard rule, and 'acts of kindness, not oppression'.[53]

Fryer recorded in his journal that only a couple of the men were attached to any particular women in Tahiti (Christian not being one of them), and that Bligh's treatment of the officers was so disrespectful – and his own self-interest so apparent – that he was himself to blame for what took place.[54] Such observations are ignored in Hollywood's long-lived romance with the story of the *Bounty*, where the theory that mutiny was provoked by Bligh's brutality is combined with the assumption that sailors were seduced by the charms of Tahitian hospitality. In its celluloid version, the mutiny is seen as the effect of sudden exposure to the pleasures of the South Seas after many months of subjection to Bligh's brutal discipline. Charles Laughton's Bligh, in particular, is the sadistic creature of an outdated system of naval discipline who, among other crimes, publicly flogs an already dead seaman, inflicts cruel and unnecessary punishment on a well-meaning midshipman, and over-works and starves a crew already stretched to the limit to serve his own greedy and sometimes vengeful ambitions. The members of his crew are so delighted by what they find in Tahiti, particularly in its women, that the prospect of a lengthy return journey seems suddenly unbearable. At the end of the film his 'methods' are repudiated in favour of 'a new understanding between officers and men' that will raise patriotic spirit and enable future expeditions to 'sweep the seas for England'.[55] In Milestone's adaptation of the story Bligh's brutality stands in contrast to an aristocratic Christian's decency and humanity. Brando's Christian not only moderates Bligh's fits of passion, but he also tries to convince the all-too-comfortable mutineers on Pitcairn (most of whom have Tahitian brides) that it is their duty to return to England and make their case to the Admirality so that their captain's inhumanity can properly be put on trial. In both versions, the tension between an extended period of subjection to naval discipline and the 'temptations' of the South Seas is the consequence of a spectacular form of discipline that will eventually be superseded by a 'humane' and more hegemonic model of military order. (In Frank Lloyd's film, Cook, unreservedly admired by anyone – European or Tahitian – who mentions him, becomes the precursor figure for this regime.)

The difference between these fictionalized versions of events and Bligh's own account of what happened before and after the mutiny is that Bligh represents *himself* as the detached humanitarian against whom, however, the passions of his crew finally prove too strong. In his log entry following the mutiny, and in the two written narratives that he published after his return to England, Bligh attributed the mutiny to the sailors' attraction to a happier life among the Tahitians than they could possibly have in England, including the formation of strong attachments to Tahitian women.[56] (A fraudulent 'first hand' account of the fortunes of the mutineers, which claimed to be written by Christian himself, makes the same case, excusing Bligh of all wrong-doing and confessing that he and his followers were seduced away from their duty by 'certain tender connexions which banished the remembrance of Old England from our breasts'.[57]) In Bligh's reconstruction of events, then, the sailors lose their ability to maintain a reflective distance on Tahitian customs and give in to their passions. This surrender to the pleasures of the moment explains why they reject his more far-sighted authority. In his 'Dispatch to the Admiralty', Bligh describes in detail the tattoos that several members of the mutinous party – Christian, Morrison, Peter Heywood and Thomas Ellison – had made in Tahiti, implicitly identifying these gestures of 'going native' as proof of the guilt of the men who had made them. He suggests that these men are more likely to be 'led away' because they are 'void of connections'.[58] They become like the protagonists of Defoe's travel fictions: unattached to family, home or country and therefore easily seduced into a life of crime.

In his 1792 *Voyage to the South Seas*, Bligh revises his account of an incident in Tahiti when the ship was cut adrift. In the logbook he assumes this was an act of native mischief; in the *Voyage* he reflects that 'this was probably the act of some of our own people, whose purpose of remaining at Taheite might have been effectually answered, without danger, if the ship had been driven on shore' (74). Yet at the time, he observes, he had no suspicion that the crew had 'so strong an attachment to these islands … as to induce them to abandon every prospect of returning to their native country' (72). Also in the later narrative (but missing from the logbook) is the concerned observation that within a short time such an intimacy grew between the crew members and the natives that 'there was scarce a man in the ship who did not have his *tyo* or friend' (38). Once again assuming in retrospect that the crew were immediately drawn to the pleasures offered by their Tahitian hosts, he comments in the *Voyage* that on their arrival in the islands, every sailor was inspected by the surgeon for symptoms of venereal disease, since 'it could not be expected that the intercourse of my people with the natives should be of a very reserved nature' (34). In the logbook, on the other hand, he merely observes that, as the Tahitians have not been visited by any European ships since Cook's, they might well now be free of the complaint, and he orders that the ship's company be inspected by the surgeon 'to prove this and to free us from any ill-founded suppositions' (1:369).

If Bligh is concerned to show, looking back, how vulnerable the members of his crew were to the charms of the South Seas, he is also anxious to demonstrate that he could not have anticipated the violent measures to which their fancies would lead them. In the *Voyage* he elaborates on the remark in his log that 'the secrecy of this mutiny [was] beyond all conception' (*Log*, 2:223), maintaining that while a commander might, at the utmost, have been prepared for a few desertions, he could not be expected to guard against anything as radical as mutiny unless he were to 'sleep locked up and when awake be girded with pistols' (*Voyage*, 94). The mutiny was not, he insists here, the result of any lack of foresight or reasonable preparation on his part. In fact, he points out in his 1792 account of the voyage of the launch how careful he was to prepare against unforeseeable events. During this voyage, he recalls, he was 'constantly assailed with the melancholy demands of my people for an increase of allowance which it grieved me to refuse' (*Voyage*, 134). He did so, however, knowing that a rigid economy was their best hope of survival, and congratulates himself that on their arrival at Timor they still had provisions for 11 days, which would have enabled them to sail on to Java had they missed the Dutch settlement at Timor. He also reflects on the 'caprice of ignorant people' (134) who, without his guidance, would have gone on shore as soon as they reached the island of Timor and before they reached a European settlement. Here he is taking pains to counter any inference that he might lack the foresight and vision of a commander such as Cook. It is not surprising then, to find him explaining the failure of the expedition to Joseph Banks and the Admiralty by insisting that in his careful preparations for the voyage home he demonstrated 'that foresight which is necessary to the well doing of the voyage', but that 'in the present instance I must have been more than a human being to have foreseen what has happened'.[59]

Indeed, as he looks back on events in Tahiti in an effort to clear himself of any charge of incompetence or lack of foresight, Bligh comments more broadly on the nature of a society in which present passions determine the way people act towards one another more powerfully than they do in a more 'advanced' culture. Even in the logbook he notes how unrestrained the passions of the islanders tend to be. He wonders, for instance at how 'in so prolific a country as this' the men are led into 'deviant' practices such as homosexuality and oral sex, or at how an expression of great sorrow and distress can change to laughter in an instant (*Log*, 2:17). In the *Voyage* he revises some of his descriptions of his exchanges with Chief Tynah to show that the latter is governed by passions and ambitions very remote from the humanitarian calculations that motivate British interest in South Seas societies. In both the log and the narrative, Bligh records Tynah's account of how neighbouring tribes killed and ate the cattle and sheep that Cook left on Tahiti to breed. Bligh responds to this news by telling the chief that King George will be very angry to learn of it, and in the log Tynah is reported to be 'much pleased and satisfied' to hear so (*Log*, 1:379). In *A Voyage to the South Seas*, however, Bligh reports that Tynah's satisfaction had nothing to do with the loss of the cattle, 'about which he appeared unconcerned and indifferent' (41), but that he is pleased to think that the English will take vengeance on the people who have robbed him. His desire for vengeance, Bligh also suggests in the *Voyage*, is only matched by his hunger for European commodities, which are highly valued by high-ranking Tahitians for their status rather than their usefulness.

In this later version of events, then, Bligh supplements his account of how skilfully he has managed to establish and maintain important friendships with remarks intended to illustrate the difference between Tahitian passions and English prudence. In so doing he highlights the perspicacity of his many efforts to plant foreign seeds on the islands and to secure the remaining livestock. In their contributions as editors of the *Voyage*, Joseph Banks and James Burney enlarged the scope of Bligh's compassionate calculations by adding (as though in his words) a lengthy proposal to transport natives from Tahiti (where infanticide appeared to function as a means of controlling population growth) to under-populated New Holland, thus 'forwarding the purposes of humanity by bringing a people without land to a land without people' (46).

Bligh's efforts to present himself as a forward-thinking humanitarian in the style of Cook also become a means of defending himself directly against the charges of excessive discipline. In the log he comments of one incident of flogging that 'I punished Isaac Martin with nineteen lashes for striking an Indian', and 'I had ordered him two dozen by the desire of Tynah he came off with less' (2:27). In the *Voyage* this episode is reported rather differently, and the reaction of the chief carries no political weight next to the more extensive view of the captain: '[I gave] nineteen lashes to a seaman, Isaac Martin, for striking an Indian. This was a transgression of so serious a nature and such a direct violation of my orders, that I would on no account be prevailed to forgive it, [although] intercession was made by some of the chiefs' (*Voyage*, 68). Like his item-by-item defence of the nutritional reasons why certain foods were given to the sailors in place of others, this justification for the flogging is calculated to represent him as a human-itarian in his strict discipline. It shows him able to recognize where the violation of an order might precipitate serious conflict and so compro-mise the objectives of the voyage, while the chiefs are capable only of a softer and more immediate sympathy for the suffering seaman. In this way, Bligh credits himself with the greater vision of a captain as he pre-pares the reader of the *Voyage* for the account of the mutiny. He pre-sents himself as a thwarted humanitarian whose service to a commercial enterprise that promised to bring prosperity to all the nations involved in it was to be reversed by a conspiracy 'render[ing] all our past labour productive only of extreme misery and distress' (87).

Bligh's insistence on the near-sighted, passion-driven characters of his crew members is challenged, however, in the journal of James Morrison, boatswain's mate on the *Bounty*. Morrison stayed on board with Fletcher Christian following the mutiny in 1789. He was then arrested in Tahiti and brought back to England for court martial, found guilty, but given a royal pardon. In his journal record of the voyage, he argues that the mutiny was provoked by Bligh's brutal treatment of his crew rather than, as Bligh later represented it, by a rebellious longing for the pleasures of Tahiti. The Tahiti that Christian and his crew return to, Morrison shows, is not a world that romantically defies the moral calculations of British imperial culture (a world where the pursuit of pleasure is the first principle of social life), but rather an unhappy island of exiles on to which the mutinous sailors have been forced by desperate circumstances.

Morrison's journal undermines many of the assumptions made about the sailors' Tahitian experience in representations of the *Bounty* mutiny, ranging from Bligh's published narratives to the twentieth-century celluloid versions of the story. Where Bligh reconstructs events in *A Voyage* to show that the sailors intended to remain in Tahiti, Morrison remarks that on the voyage out 'everyone seemed in high spirits and began to talk of home ... and one would readily have imag-ined that we had just left Jamaica instead of Tahiti, so far onward did their flattering fancies waft them' (*Journal*, 35–6). Once the mutineers had irreversibly changed their fortunes by casting both Bligh and the breadfruit plants out of the ship, Tahiti offered neither a refuge from the abuses of maritime life nor a satisfying alternative to the oppressive economy of the ship. Christian, Morrison reports, promised to become just as much of a tyrant as Bligh, threatening with his pistol and clap-ping in irons two men who refused to recognize his authority and who declared that they were now their own masters. Describing the life the mutineers tried to make for themselves in Tahiti, he also complains that the Tahitians are so 'backward' in their agricultural methods that the fertile soil of the island is wasted. In particular, he reflects on how the experiments in planting begun in Cook's time have been thwarted by the islanders' passions for new and curious commodities. These passions, he observes, have brought all Cook's humanitarian intentions to nothing, for although:

> when he first thought of stocking these islands with cattle, poultry and the fruits and roots of Europe, [he] intended it for the good of mankind, ... these people knew not the value of them and for want of Europeans to take care of them they were soon destroyed. [T]he curiosity of the natives to see such strange animals made each wish to have one, by which means they were separated and their increase prevented; the poultry soon became extinct; the sheep, who did not as in other warm climes lose their wool, died for want of sheering; the black cattle alone thriving tho mostly kept separate; the seeds and plants were destroyed by being removed as soon as they made their appearance, everyone wishing to possess some part of the curiosities which they esteemed the whole and would part with the best cow for a good axe, setting no value on them for food tho' they kill'd several and eat part of them in the wars, but having no method of taking the hides they clean'd them as hogs but could not fancy they were good, therefore took no pains to save a breed. (238)

This appetite for European curiosities has thrown them into what is virtually a state of war, and made them incapable of cooperating in the achievement of long-term agricultural goals. They sacrifice economic forethought to envy and greed. Morrison then goes on to describe how certain plants, some (such as shaddock) introduced by Cook's ships, some (such as Indian corn) by the *Bounty*, should be properly cultivated, and he speculates on how well they might grow in such a climate if the native inhabitants were educated in the first principles of capital and persuaded to take the trouble to produce more food than they actually consume, or to labour for more than than 'what nature has abundantly supplied them' (150). The irony here is that such observations, particularly his inclination to see the trade in curiosities as the obstacle to commercial progress, correspond very closely to Bligh's comments about Tahitian neglectfulness: 'Thus all our fond hopes, that the trouble Captain Cook had taken to introduce so many valuable things among them, [and that] would ... have been found to be productive of every good, are entirely blasted' (*Log*, 1:318).

Morrison's journal and his account of Tahiti were probably transcribed from notes after his return from England, and perhaps while he was in prison in England awaiting court martial. His discussion of the backwardness of the Tahitian economy, along with his accusations against Bligh, might therefore constitute a defence of his own character as a loyal British seaman. But, if so, it is a truly radical defence, for what Morrison demonstrates is the extent to which the 'humane' undertakings of eighteenth century global capital are tied to the brutal exploitation of labour, not only on the slave plantations of the West Indies but also on the high seas. Sailors, in his account, are not at all the easily seduced, near nationless creatures of passion that they are in Bligh's writings. In an acute observation of the role of primitive accumulation in the development of civilized societies, Morrison uses the evidence of 'backward' Tahitian culture to illustrate how unappealing forced exile from the commercial world is for men who so recently had rejoiced at the prospect of home.

Morrison's journal offers a defiant response to Bligh's equation between South Seas indolence and the recalcitrance of seamen. In many ways this presents a stronger case against the captain's 'humanitarianism' than do the accusations about his excessive discipline. Yet Bligh's version of events, unsurprisingly, was the one to prevail, and he was given command of a second breadfruit voyage to Tahiti. It was, of course, easier for Bligh to demonstrate that he had exercised moral strength of character in the face of the uncontainable passions of his crew than for Morrison to argue that men who had wilfully severed all ties to home were attuned to the kind of economic prudence characteristic of a civilized and settled people. This perhaps explains why Christian, when Bligh last spoke to him, declared that he was in hell. Bligh, on the other hand, as he looked back on the experience of the open boat voyage, observed that even with scarcely enough food and water to survive the voyage ahead, he felt 'wonderfully supported' and sure that he would 'one day be able to account to [his] king and country for the misfortune'.[60] For, despite the costly failure of the expedition, he could be confident that the state would find evidence, first in his logbook and later in his published narratives, for the justice and humanity in his heart. His restored favour in the eyes of the Admiralty was testimony to the latter's faith in Bligh's character. Like Cook, he appeared to be a man of sympathy who had done his best to manage the raw passions of his crew members which had sought free expression in the 'uncivilized' South Pacific. His captain's heart was indeed, his superiors recognized, capable of exercising the kind of justice necessary not just to preserving social order on board ship, but also to the expansion of the commercial world. The challenges that he, like Cook, faced from seamen who objected to the brutal conditions of their employment thus had to be identified and dismissed as the impulsive actions of narrow-minded men, who had unfortunately forgotten that social happiness demands deferral to one of superior feeling and greater foresight.

7
Conclusion: Global Commerce and Homelessness

Since the publication of Gilles Deleuze and Félix Guattari's *A Thousand Plateaus* in 1980, nomadism has, at least metaphorically, offered a means of rethinking subjectivity outside the dominant social and political structures of the West. Where the state manages its subjects in the process of demarcating and protecting private property and national territory, nomadism, in Deleuze and Guattari's terms, enacts a form of deterritorialization that represents an indirect form of resistance to the state. They characterize nomadic thought as 'rhizomorphous': that is, as offering multiple and heterogeneous forms of connection that are illegible to existing forms of social power. 'Beneath' language, in 'subterranean stems and flows'[1,] these 'rhizomes' evade the processes of interpretation and representation that make it possible, semiotically speaking, to demarcate differences between, for example, 'yours' and 'mine', or 'centre' and 'periphery'. In this somewhat nostalgic formulation, nomadism signifies a primitive time and place that pre-exists such dualisms.[2] But it also suggests the possibility of transgressing forms of authority exerted through territorial, social and linguistic boundaries and of thinking outside the vocabulary that belongs to violent histories of territorialization, outstepping, as Robert Young puts it, 'not only the discourse, but also the repressive geopolitics of colonialism.'[3]

This concept of nomadism has been useful to post-structuralists looking for a mode of political expression that is not managed by existing regimes of signification.[4] More specifically, it has provided the basis for rethinking questions of post-colonial identity, generating a cosmopolitan and coalitional vision of the relationships between formerly colonized subjects in place of the narrow nationalisms and ethnic particularisms that have given symbolic form to most anticolonial move-

ments.[5] Emphasizing how ethnographic study has traditionally concentrated on fixed communities, James Clifford points out that it needs
to focus on 'hybrid, cosmopolitan experiences as much as on rooted,
native ones'.[6] Similarly, in *The Black Atlantic*, Paul Gilroy suggests that
the political and cultural histories of Europe, America, Africa and the
Caribbean are not exclusively tied to the fortunes of modern national
states, but that these histories transcend national boundaries, unfold-
ing alongside, but not identically with, the accumulation of capital.
Gilroy's argument is particularly apposite here, since for him this
transnational and intercultural experience is most effectively imaged in
the ship, which he calls 'a living, micro-cultural, micro-political system
in motion'.[7] Sailors, he goes on to say, 'move to and fro between
nations, crossing borders in modern machines that were themselves
micro-systems of linguistic and political hybridity'.[8] They are emblematic of the 'rhizomorphic, fractal structure'[9] of what he calls the black
Atlantic. This transnational maritime community is also what Marcus
Rediker identifies as part of a rising international working class. Sailors,
Rediker argues, are internationalized through contact with other seafaring workers of different national, class and racial status from their
own.[10]

Yet while the term has been animated with a kind of anti-imperialist,
proletarian and generally anti-authoritarian energy, nomadism can still
seem less like an activist transnationalism or cosmopolitanism than
like a condition which precedes or which, in a utopian form, lies
beyond nationhood and Western notions of civility. Caren Kaplan has
argued that, as a persistently modernist formulation even in post-
structuralist and post-modern thinking, nomadism romanticizes exile
and replaces any investigation of the evolution of specific diasporic
communities with a 'generalized poetics of displacement'. Deleuze and
Guattari, she suggests, 'roam into realms of nostalgia, searching for a
way to detour Western civilization'.[11] In this book, I have attempted to
avoid romanticizing the willed and semi-willed homelessness of
eighteenth-century travellers while continuing to identify, as Gilroy
and Rediker do, the articulation of extra-national perspectives that
exercise some subversive agency in a world economy managed by
strong, usually imperial states. The very distinction between a settled and
civilized society and a wild, nomadic one, I have suggested, is invented
by a philosophical tradition that sees the growth of the state and the
expansion of commerce as part of the natural progress of societies. Yet
even as the creature of this tradition, the stateless traveller does have

the capacity to criticize the distinctions it puts in place and the vicious inequalities it has created.

The travellers I have looked at here ranged beyond the Atlantic, but in a sense their narratives put the idea of nomadism as a form of emancipatory politics to the test. Some of them do describe the kinds of alliances and affections that Gilroy refers to, which transcend national boundaries and ethnic differences. And these attachments, as we have seen in the case of the young Dampier, Singleton and the *Bounty* mutineers, represent a direct affront to the state. Other travellers, such as Gulliver and Rasselas (not outlaws but troubled observers), highlight the moral and epistemological fractures created by mercantilist globalism. They do so in defiance of the apologists for mercantilism, who insist not only on the urgency of increasing the nation's wealth, but also on the improving influence of commerce. These travellers challenge the ability of commerce to absorb seemingly unassimilable differences between peoples, climates and things into a single, intelligible, global space within which these differences can be compared, measured and valued against one another. In these respects, such travellers are radical outsiders to a modern globalism managed by powerful commercial states. Like Gilroy's sailors, they are at the centre of national-imperial undertakings, yet their needs and affections take them beyond these boundaries.

At the same time, like the 'primitive' peoples with whom they are so regularly compared, 'nationless' wanderers are also *creations* of commercial modernity, invented 'pre-civil' beings against whom the progress of civilized manners can be measured, positively or negatively. With the fiction of a state of nature from which human beings supposedly exit into properly governed societies and a regular (if sometimes corrupting) commerce, there comes the reality of a ranked assessment of different forms of affiliation. Those who are either incapable of organizing themselves into peaceful, commercial societies, or who actively turn their backs on such societies, fall lowest in the hierarchy. Even when the members of 'civilized' nations appear more savage than their primitive counterparts, as Johann and Georg Forster both suggest in their more Rousseauesque moments, the distinctions between advanced and backward peoples still remain in place. The differences between industrial and commercial and pre-industrial and pre-commercial regions of the globe appear determined by nature (and the forms of civil evolution it dictates), rather than constructed by imperial eyes and then exaggerated by the economic inequalities that global commerce creates. The possibility that the violent or asocial behaviour of so-called primitive peoples or renegade wanderers might express an active resistance to commercial imperialism or to the conditions of maritime life is often, therefore, obscured by a powerful historicization of culture: one that identifies the wandering life as the most primitive of the modes of subsistence and the most in need of correction through the benevolent influence of commerce.

The travellers and traveller-narrators who criticize naval discipline, such as James Morrison, and, in his 'better' moments, Roderick Random, or who point out the sheer human cost of economic expansion, such as Johnson's spectators, are still confined by these larger cultural histories. Morrison defends himself in part by distinguishing between Tahitian indolence and European industry, as Cook and Bligh had done. The moral impact of Random's outrage at the conduct of the generals during the Cartagena offensive is blunted by his own shaky moral status as nomadic picaro-hero. Johnson's cosmopolitan spectators are trapped in indecision as they contemplate the hardships of a savage life and the political and moral corruption of a civilized one. In none of these cases does the 'homelessness' of the traveller in itself provide the epistemological basis for criticizing imperial policy or the unequal distribution of happiness in a world economy. Instead, it is either a condition that the writer tries to distance himself from or else a state in which moral observations lack authority or certainty.

Nevertheless, the transformations that these travellers undergo – from maritime criminals into loyal subjects, from British subjects into renegades or asocial Gullivers, or from cosmopolitan spectators to befuddled participants in the stream of commercial life – do compromise the idea that commercial and social 'improvement' are inevitably twinned. Although one of the tasks that these travellers were formally or informally set was to gather data about the relationship between civility and commerce in different parts of the world, their own careers did not necessarily testify to the smooth evolution of civil communities and the connection between increasingly sophisticated modes of exchange and well-governed and therefore peaceful social relations. Even the narratives of reformation in which pirate 'savages' become merchants or men of science and confirm the proper hierarchy between savage and civilized nations, are not evidence of such evolution. They are in fact responses to the disciplinary pressure exercised by the state and its discursive alibis (ethnography, political science and so on), rather than evidence of the civilizing influence of commerce. Like the stories in which travellers sever their ties with home, these narratives demonstrate the pains which states must take to manage the subjects whom they send on imperial errands to places enormously distant and unfamiliar. And they also expose the fragility of the affective bonds that prevent civilized men from reverting to a more primitive state. Moreover, if the inherent civility of Europeans is cast in doubt during such journeys, then the supposedly equally inherent savagery of less commercial nations must also come under scrutiny. This is something that Cook and the Forsters are alerted to as they come to reflect both on the urgency of managing passions on board the ship and on the possibility that European voyages into the Pacific have introduced little other than moral corruption and disease to its 'uncivilized' peoples.

What these narratives of severance from home reveal, then, is not quite a radical epistemology unleashed by the condition of statelessness. Instead they dramatize how the conditions and circumstances of sea travel belie the principle that settled communities and social happiness arise from the development and expansion of commerce. These stories are not without use in our present age, when the role of the state in the global economy appears, in many ways, to be diminishing, for they highlight the role that major powers played in an earlier era of globalization, both in the management of increasingly mobile subjects and in the movement of capital between 'developed' and 'underdeveloped' regions of the world. Clearly, powerful states have not yet relinquished such responsibilities. Neither have they abandoned the rhetorical identification of their own economic and security interests with those of 'the earth' or humankind as a whole. These fictions are challenged in the stories told by the 'uncivil' and the homeless: stories which are less expressions of emancipatory transnational identities, than descriptions of the isolation and impoverishment augmented, rather than diminished, by commercial growth.

Notes

Introduction: Commerce, Society and the Sea Voyage

1 Recent studies include Srinivas Aravamudan, *Tropicopolitans: Colonialism and Agency, 1688–1804* (Durham, NC, and London: Duke University Press,1999); Laura Brown, *Ends of Empire: Women and Ideology in Early Eighteenth-Century England* (Ithaca, NY: Cornell University Press, 1993); Philip Edwards, *The Story of the Voyage: Sea Narratives in Eighteenth- Century England* (Cambridge: Cambridge University Press, 1994); Jonathan Lamb, 'Minute Particulars and the Representation of South Pacific Discovery', *Eighteenth-Century Studies*, 28:3 (1995), 281–94; Peter Linebaugh and Marcus Rediker, *The Many-Headed Hydra: Sailors, Slaves, Commoners, and the Hidden History of the Revolutionary Atlantic* (Boston, MA: Beacon Press, 2000); Mary Louise Pratt, *Imperial Eyes: Travel Writing and Transculturation* (London and New York: Routledge, 1992); Rediker, *Between the Devil and the Deep Blue Sea: Merchant Seamen, Pirates, and the Anglo-American Maritime World, 1700–1750* (Cambridge: Cambridge University Press, 1987).
2 Paul Gilroy, *The Black Atlantic: Modernity and Double-Consciousness* (Cambridge, MA: Harvard University Press, 1993), 4.
3 See Pratt (1992), 38–68.
4 Linebaugh and Rediker (2000), 144.
5 George E. Marcus and Michael M. Fischer, *Anthropology as Cultural Critique: An Experimental Moment in the Human Sciences*, 2nd edn (Chicago, IL and London: University of Chicago Press, 1999), xv–xxxiv.
6 James Clifford, 'Introduction: Partial Truths', in James Clifford and George E. Marcus (eds), *Writing Culture: The Poetics and Politics of Ethnography* (Berkeley, CA: University of California Press, 1986), 1–26.
7 This is not to argue that international trade is a new phenomenon in this period, but rather that the circulation of commodities on a global scale in the seventeenth and eighteenth centuries increasingly involved the creation of peripheries, in which the social relations of production were determined by the service that (primarily) colonial economies paid to the core economies. This is what Alan Smith has called 'the creation of the incipient first world economy'. See Smith, *Creating a World Economy: Merchant Capital, Colonialism and World Trade* (Boulder, CO: Westview Press, 1991), 124. On this subject, see also Immanuel Wallerstein, *The Modern World System II: Mercantilism and the Consolidation of the European World Economy, 1600–1750* (New York: Academic Press, 1974); David Hancock, *Citizens of the World: London Merchants and the Integration of the British Atlantic Community, 1735–1785* (Cambridge: Cambridge University Press, 1995). Fernand Braudel argues that there have always been world economies, organized around urban centres and linking individual areas in an economic hierarchy. In modern times, however, the inequalities created by an internal division of labour became more exaggerated and 'the primacy of

economics became more and more overwhelming'. See Braudel, *The Perspective of the World* (vol. 3 of *Civilization and Capitalism: 15ᵗʰ to 18ᵗʰ Century*), trans. Siân Reynolds (Berkeley, CA: University of California Press, 1992), 47. Also countering the idea that a world system only emerged between the sixteenth and eighteenth centuries, Elizabeth Fox-Genovese and Eugene Genovese have argued that the creation of a global market through merchant capital played a very specific and limited role in the rise of capitalism. Firmly tied to pre-capitalist labour systems, merchant capital at once assisted the capitalist mode of production by stimulating industry, organizing labour and centralizing profits from various economic activities, and yet at the same time it re-generated feudal relations of production in the slave trade and the slave-plantation economies of the Americas. See Fox-Genovese and Genovese, *Fruits of Merchant Capital: Slavery and Bourgeois Property in the Rise and Expansion of Capitalism* (Oxford: Oxford University Press, 1983), 3–26.

8 Eric J. Leed, *The Mind of the Traveler: From Gilgamesh to Global Tourism* (New York: Basic Books, 1991), 17.

9 Ibid., 72.

10 See James Clifford, *Routes: Travel and Translation in the Late Twentieth Century* (Cambridge, MA: Harvard University Press, 1997), 11.

11 The later Middle Ages saw a movement towards the development of a national economy with the development of occupational and regional specialization and the expansion of international trade, especially the exportation of wool. See Richard H. Britnell, *The Commercialisation of English Society 1000–1500* (Manchester and New York: Manchester University Press, 1996); Jenny Kermode, *Medieval Merchants: York, Beverley and Hull in the Later Middle Ages* (Cambridge: Cambridge University Press, 1998). State regulation of trade, including the enforcement of a standard of weights and measures, was also a feature of the relationships between government and merchants in the fourteenth and fifteenth centuries (Kermode (1998), 191–7; Britnell (1996), 90). Advocacy of such regulation featured in some sixteenth-century 'mercantilist' views. Other writers, however, stressed the independence of the merchant from the sovereign, and argued that the state should not interfere with the rate of exchange. On the differing views of Mun, Misselden, and de Malynes, see the 'Mercantilism and global commerce' section later in Chapter 1.

12 Richard Hakluyt, *The Principal Navigations, Voyages, Traffiques and Discoveries of the English Nation*, 12 vols (Glasgow: James MacLehose & Sons, 1903), 1:xxxi.

13 Richard Helgerson, *Forms of Nationhood: The Elizabethan Writing of England* (Chicago, IL: University of Chicago Press, 1992), 149–192. See also Emily C. Bartels, 'Imperialist Beginnings: Richard Hakluyt and the Construction of Africa', *Criticism*, 34:4 (1992), 517–38; David Armitage, 'From Richard Hakluyt to William Robertson,' in Karen Ordahl Kupperman (ed.), *America in European Consciousness, 1493–1750* (Chapel Hill, NC, and London: University of North Carolina Press, 1995), 52–78; James A. Williamson, 'Richard Hakluyt', in Edward Lynam (ed.), *Richard Hakluyt and his Successors* (London: The Hakluyt Society, 1946), 9–46.

14 Samuel Purchas, *Hakluytus Posthumus; Or, Purchas His Pilgrimes*, 20 vols (Glasgow: James MacLehose & Sons, 1905), 1:xxxix.

15 Sir Walter Ralegh, *The Discoverie of the large and bewtiful Empire of Guiana* (London: Argonaut Press, 1928), 10.

16 *Ibid.*, 62–3.

17 *Principal Navigations,* 8:349.

18 On the rhetorical force of taxonomy in Harriot's text see Mary C. Fuller, *Voyages in Print: English Travel to America, 1576–1624* (Cambridge: Cambridge University Press, 1995), 38–54.

19 See Christopher Hill, *Intellectual Origins of the English Revolution* (Oxford: Clarendon Press, 1965), 14–84.

20 Francis Bacon, 'Novum Organum', *Works of Francis Bacon*, edited by J. Spedding, R.L. Ellis and D.H. Heath, 15 vols (Boston, MA: Houghton Mifflin, 1860–2), 1:117.

21 Thomas Sprat, *The History of the Royal Society of London for the Improving of Natural Knowledge* (London, 1702), 20.

22 Ibid., 20.

23 Mary Poovey, *A History of the Modern Fact: Problems of Knowledge in the Sciences of Wealth and Society* (Chicago, IL: University of Chicago Press, 1998).

24 Samuel Pufendorf, *Of the Law of Nature and Nations*, trans. Basil Kennet, 3rd edn (London, 1717), 4.

25 Although this issue is not central to my argument here, it is important to note that Pufendorf sees human beings as naturally social. The state does not enforce sociality, as it does for Hobbes, but rather emerges as an answer to the problem of the socio-economic development that brings members of a society into increasingly competitive and potentially violent relations. For a recent analysis of the difference between Pufendorf and Hobbes on the state of nature and the significance of this difference for interstate relations in particular see Richard Tuck, *The Rights of War and Peace: Political Thought and the International Order from Grotius to Kant* (Oxford: Clarendon Press, 1999), 140–152.

26 On the historicization of material culture and the development of 'social theory' in the seventeenth and eighteenth centuries see Ronald L. Meek, *Social Science and the Ignoble Savage* (Cambridge: Cambridge University Press, 1976); Christopher J. Berry, *Social Theory of the Scottish Enlightenment* (Edinburgh: Edinburgh University Press, 1997); Richard Olson, *The Emergence of the Social Sciences 1642–1792* (New York: Twayne, 1993).

27 Henry Home, Lord Kames, *Sketches of the history of Man*, 2 vols (Edinburgh, 1774), 1:439.

28 Adam Smith, *An Inquiry into the Nature and Causes of the Wealth of Nations*, ed. Edwin Cannan, 2 vols (Chicago, IL: University of Chicago Press, 1976), 1:19.

29 See Lamb, 'Eye-Witnessing in the South Seas', *The Eighteenth-Century: Theory and Interpretation* 38:3 (Fall 1997), 201–12.

30 Michel Foucault, *The Archeology of Knowledge*, trans. A.M. Sheridan Smith (London: Tavistock, 1972), 32–3.

31 Stephen Greenblatt, *Marvelous Possessions: The Wonder of the New World* (Chicago, IL: University of Chicago Press, 1991), 26–85.

32 Lorraine Daston and Katharine Park, *Wonders and the Order of Nature 1150–1750* (New York: Zone Books, 1998), 216.

33 Ibid., 329–64.

34 On the history of the South Argentinian 'giants' and of the false topography of the Mississippi River region see Percy C. Adams, *Travellers and Travel Liars, 1600–1800* (Berkeley and Los Angeles, CA: University of California Press, 1962). On the problem of distinguishing fact from fiction in travel literature and on the character of the eye-witness see Neil Rennie, *Far-Fetched Facts: The Literature of Travel and the Idea of the South Seas* (Oxford: Clarendon Press, 1995).

35 David Hume, *Enquiries Concerning Human Understanding and Concerning the Principles of Morals*, ed. L.A. Selby-Bigge, 3rd edn (Oxford: Clarendon Press, 1975), 83. Although, for Hume, the process of delineating general rules is always clouded by uncertainty, the uniformity of human passions makes it possible to ascertain general truths about human nature despite the unpredictable influence of immediate environmental factors. For a more thorough analysis of this passage see Berry (1997), 68–9.

36 John Millar, *Observations Concerning the Distinction of Ranks in Society* (London, 1771), xii.

37 Ibid., i–iii.

38 Dugald Stewart, *Essays on Philosophical Subjects by the Late Adam Smith* (Dublin, 1795), lii.

39 Hugo Grotius, *The Rights of War and Peace*, incuding the Law of Nature and of Nations. trans. and ed. by Rev. A.C. Campbell, 3 vols (London, 1814); Pufendorf, *Law of Nature and Nations*; John Locke, *Two Treatises of Government*, ed. Peter Laslett (Cambridge: Cambridge University Press, 1988).

40 Thomas Hobbes, *Leviathan*, ed. Richard Tuck (Cambridge: Cambridge University Press, 1996), 117–254.

41 Charles de Secondat Montesquieu (Baron de), *The Spirit of the Laws*, trans. and ed. by Anne M. Cohler, Basia Carolyn Miller, and Harold Samuel Stone (Cambridge: Cambridge University Press, 1989), 339.

42 See 'Of the Origin of Government', in *David Hume: Essays Moral Political and Literary*, ed. Eugene F. Miller, Rev. ed. (Indianapolis, IN: Liberty Classics, 1987), 37–41.

43 See Kames (1774), 1:395–407; Millar (1774), 153–92, Smith, *Lectures on Jurisprudence*, edited by R.L. Meek, D.D. Raphael and P.G. Stein (Oxford: Clarendon Press, 1978), 5–140.

44 Hannah Arendt, *The Human Condition* (Chicago, IL: University of Chicago Press, 1958).

45 See J.G.A. Pocock, *Virtue, Commerce and History* (Cambridge: Cambridge University Press, 1983), 49. On the significance of the passions in the sciences of statecraft and political economy see also Albert O. Hirschman, *The Passions and the Interests: Political Arguments for Capitalism before its Triumph* (Princeton, N.J.: Princeton University Press, 1977).

46 Abbé Raynal, *A Philosophical and Political History of the Settlements and Trade of the Europeans in the East and West Indies* [1798], trans. J.O. Justamond, 6 vols (New York: Negro Universities Press, 1969), 6: 489–90. On Diderot's contributions and for a discussion of their commentary on the traveler's incivility see Anthony Pagden, *Lords of all the World: Ideologies of Empire in Spain, Britain and France c.1500–c.1800* (New Haven, CT, and London: Yale University Press, 1995), 163–8.

47 Adam Ferguson, *An Essay on the History of Civil Society* [1767], Duncan Forbes (Edinburgh: Edinburgh University Press, 1966), 221.

48 David Hume, 'Of the Rise and Progress of the Arts and Sciences', *Essays (1987)*, 112–13.
49 'The Skeptic', ibid., 159.
50 'Of the Standard of Taste', ibid., 239.
51 'Of the Rise and Progress of the Arts and Sciences', ibid., 124.
52 Terence Hutchison, *Before Adam Smith: The Emergence of Political Economy 1622–1776* (Oxford: Basil Blackwell, 1988); Lars Magnusson, *Mercantilism: The Shaping of an Economic Language* (London and New York: Routledge, 1994). See also Joyce Appleby, *Economic Thought and Ideology in Seventeenth-Century England* (Princeton, NJ: Princeton University Press, 1978), 24–51; Jonathan Gil Harris, 'The Canker of England's Commonwealth: Gerard de Malynes and the Origins of Economic Pathology,' *Textual Practice* 13:2 1999) 311–27.
53 Richard C. Wiles, 'Mercantilism and the Idea of Progress,' *Eighteenth-Century Studies* 8:1 (1974), 56–74.
54 Edward Misselden, *Free Trade, or the Means to make Trade Florish* (London, 1622).
55 Thomas Mun, *A Discourse of Trade from England unto the East-Indies* [1621] (New York: The Facsimile Text Society, 1930).
56 Gerald de Malynes, *The Maintenance of Free Trade* (London, 1622).
57 Josiah Child, *A New Discourse of Trade* [1668] (Glasgow, 1751).
58 Charles Davenant, 'An Essay upon the Balance of Power', in *Essays* (London, 1701).
59 John Locke, *Some Considerations Concerning Raising the Value of Money* (London, 1696), 9. Quoted in Magnusson (1994), 129.
60 William Petty, *Political Arithmetick* (London, 1791) (see title page).
61 William Appleman Williams, *The Contours of American History* (New York: W. W. Norton, 1988), 27–74.
62 See, for example, *An Essay on the Increase and Decline of Trade in London and the Outports* (London, 1749); Malchy Postlethwayt, *Britain's Commercial Interest Explained and Improved* (London, 1757), 32–6; John Campbell, *A Political Survey of Britain*, 2 vols (London, 1774), 1:5; *Candid and Impartial Considerations on the Nature of the Sugar Trade of the British and French Islands in the West Indies* (London, 1763), 3; Adam Anderson, *An Historical and Chronological Deduction of the Origin of Commerce* (London, 1764), 14; Richard Rolt, *A New Dictionary of Trade and Commerce*, 2nd edn (London, 1761), iv.
63 Postlethwayt (1757), 53 (1764); Anderson, 38; *Candid and Impartial Considerations*, (1763) 30. See also Josiah Tucker, *A Brief on the Advantages and Disadvantages which respectively attend France and Great Britain with regard to Trade*, 4th edn (Glasgow, 1756), 8.
64 Tucker (1756), 45.
65 Hume *Essays (1988)*, 288. On Hume's residually mercantilist positions see Hutchison (1988), 204–5.
66 See Williams, 70–1.
67 Bernard Mandeville, *The Fable of the Bees; Or, Private Vices made Public Benefits*, 2 vols (London, 1724), 1:428.
68 Eli F. Heckscher, *Mercantilism*, trans. Mendel Shapiro, 2nd edn, 2 vols (London: Allen & Unwin; New York: the Macmillan Company), 2:316–24.
69 A considerable amount of important excavatory work has been done recently on non-European, women, and working-class travellers. See for

example, Elizabeth Bohls, *Women Travel Writers and the Language of Aesthetics, 1718–1818* (Cambridge: Cambridge University Press, 1995); Aravamudan, *(1999)*; Karen Lawrence, *Penelope Voyages: Women and Travel in the British Literary Tradition* (Ithaca, NY: Cornell University Press, 1994); Rediker (1987); Edwards, *(1994).*
70 Pierre Bourdieu, *Field of Cultural Production: Essays on Art and Literature,* ed. Randal Johnson (New York: Columbia University Press, 1993).
71 Raymond Williams, *Culture and Society 1780–1950* (London: Chatto & Windus, 1958), xiii–xx.

2   Buccaneer Ethnography: Nature, Culture and the State

1 Pufendorf, *Of the Law of Nature and Nations,* trans. Basil Kennet, 3rd edn (London, 1717), 3.
2 Here I am indebted to Mary Louise Pratt's notion of a 'contact zone.' The term 'contact,' for Pratt, 'attempt[s] to invoke the spatial and temporal co-presence of subjects previously separated by geographic and historical disjunctures,' and in so doing foregrounds the 'improvisational' and 'interactive' dimensions of colonial encounters. See Pratt, *Imperial Eyes: Travel Writing and Transculturion* (London and New York: Routledge, 1992), 7. Rather different accounts of the epistemological character of colonial contact in the New World are offered by Stephen Greenblatt and Peter Hulme. Greenblatt sees acts of representation and interpretation as enabling European spectators of American marvels to transform their confusion and curiosity into the language of sovereign possession. Hulme similarly argues that the experience of contact in the Caribbean is organized by ethnographic typologies and legal formalisms which discursively eradicate the cultures of the indigenous peoples. See Greenblatt, *Marvelous Possessions: The Wonder of the New World* (Chicago, IL: University of Chicago Press, 1991) sp. 1–25; Hulme, *Colonial Encounters: Europe and the Native Caribbean 1492–1797* (London: Methuen, 1986).
3 See above, p. 3.
4 Hobbes, *Leviathan,* ed. Richard Tuck (Cambridge: Cambridge University Press, 1996), 11.
5 Francis Bacon, 'The Advancement of Learning,' *Works of Francis Bacon,* edited by J. Spedding, R.L. Ellis, and D.H. Heath, 7 vols (London: Longmans, 1876), 2:474.
6 Julie Solomon has shown that Bacon demonstrates a specifically mercantilist relationship between the new science and the consolidation of royal power. His emphasis on both the gathering and coordination of knowledge and the monarch's neutralization of the private, interested nature of this knowledge, she suggests, makes Bacon a kind of mediating figure between king and merchant. See Solomon, *Objectivity in the Making: Francis Bacon and the Politics of Inquiry* (Baltimore, MD: The Johns Hopkins University Press, 1998), 62–102.
7 *Leviathan (1996),* 89.
8 See Eli, F. Heckscher, *Mercantilism,* trans. Mendel Shapiro, 2nd edn, 2 vols (London: Allen & Unwin, 1935 new york Macmillan Company, 1955)

1: 442–74. Of course the joint-stock companies were also granted considerable political power where they administered territories. The devolution of sovereignty through the Companies is beyond the scope of my investigation here, particularly since at this point they are in fact the means by which the state extended its influence into various regions of the globe.

9 Lieutenant Governor Molesworth to William Blathwayt, 8 August 1687, Great Britain, Public Record Office, *Calendar of State Papers, Colonial Series, America and the West Indies* (1685–8), edited by J.W. Fortescue (London, 1899), no. 1382.

10 On this topic see Janice E. Thomson, *Mercenaries, Pirates and Sovereigns: State Building and Extraterritorial Violence in Early Modern Europe* (Princeton, NJ: Princeton University Press, 1994), 7–22. Thomson argues that the elimination of non-state violence from the arena of political activity is the direct effect of the increased wealth of European states, enabling them to abandon the international market of violence and sponsor all legal acts of aggression themselves. On changes in the state's attitude towards privateering and/or piracy see also David Cordingly, *Under the Black Flag: The Romance and the Reality of Life Among the Pirates* (New York: Random House, 1995); Robert C. Ritchie, *Captain Kidd and the War Against the Pirates* (Cambridge, MA: Harvard University Press, 1986), 148–9; James G. Lydon, *Pirates, Privateers, and Profits* (Upper Saddle River, NJ: The Gregg Press, 1970); C.M. Senior, *A Nation of Pirates: English Piracy in its Heyday* (New York: Crane, Russak, 1976); Neville Williams, *The Sea Dogs: Privateers, Plunder and Piracy in the Elizabethan Age* (New York: Macmillan, 1975); David Delison Hebb, *Piracy and the English Government, 1616–1642* (Aldershot: Scolar Press, 1994).

11 See Cordingly (1995), 42–55; Ritchie (1986), 1–26; C.H. Haring, *The Buccaneers in the West Indies in the Seventeenth Century* (London: Methuen, 1910), 200–31.

12 A Narrative of Sir Thomas Modyford, 23 August 1669, Great Britain, Public Record Office, *Calendar of State Papers, Colonial Series, America and the West Indies* (1669–74), edited by Noel Sainsbury (London, 1896), no. 103.

13 Petition of Chas Modyford on behalf of Sir Thomas Modyford and the planters and traders of Jamaica to the King, 28 September, 1670, ibid., no. 275.

14 Ritchie (1986), 148–50; Haring (1910), 198–99.

15 Sir Henry Morgan to the Earl of Sunderland, 1 February, 1681, Great Britain, Public Record Office, *Calendar of State Papers* (1681-1685), edited by J.W. Fortescue (London, 1898), no. 16.

16 Governor Lynch to H. Slingesby, Secretary to the Council for Plantations, 5 November, 1672, *Calendar of State Papers* (1669–74), no. 954.

17 *A Complete Collection of State Trials and Proceedings for High Treason and Other Crimes and Misdemeanors, from the Reign of King Richard II to the End of King George I*, 21 vols (London, 1816),12:378.

18 Ibid., 13:392.

19 Ibid.,15:457.

20 *The Tryal of Captain Thomas Green and his Crew before the High Court of Admiralty of Scotland and the Assessors Appointed by the Lords of the Privy Council for Piracy, Robbery and Murder* (Edinburgh, 1705), 34. Green was being tried for acts of piracy against Scottish shipping. The larger context for the trial was the commercial rivalry with England immediately prior to Union.

21 See Haring (1910), 69.
22 A.O. Exquemelin, *The Buccaneers of America*, trans. Alexis Brown (Harmondsworth: Penguin, 1969), 107. On the history of the buccaneer communities see also Haring (1910); Peter Bradley, *The Lure of Peru: Maritime Intrusion into the South Sea, 1598–1701* (New York: St. Martin's Press, 1989), 103-84.
23 Sir Thomas Lynch to Secretary Sir Leoline Jenkins, 26 July, 1681, *Calendar of State Papers* (1681-5), no. 1163.
24 Marcus Rediker and Peter Linebaugh have shown how piracy operated as a form of radical internationalism that opposed the authority of the state and how pirate communities provided democratic alternatives to the oppressive conditions of service in the navy or aboard merchant ships. In *Between the Devil and the Deep Blue Sea: Merchant Seamen, Pirates, and the Anglo- American Maritime World*, 1700–1750 (Cambridge: Cambridge University Press, 1987), Rediker describes how these conditions influenced the conversion of seamen to piracy. On the transnational, multi-racial and democratic character of working-class maritime communities generally see Linebaugh and Rediker, *The Many-Headed Hydra: Sailors, Slaves, Commoners, and the Hidden History of the Revolutionary Atlantic* (Boston, MA: Beacon Press, 2000); Linebaugh, *The London Hanged: Crime and Civil Society in the Eighteenth Century* (Cambridge: Cambridge University Press, 1992), 123–138.
25 Kemp and Lloyd, (1960), 78.
26 See Joseph C. Shipman, *William Dampier: Seaman-Scientist*, (Lawrence, KS: University of Kansas Libraries, 1962), 9–23. Clennell Wilkinson's older and more lengthy biography of Dampier suggests that the latter generally had a greater reputation as a scientist than as a buccaneer. See Wilkinson, *William Dampier* (London: John Lane The Bodley Head, 1929), 131–53.
27 *Dampier's Voyages*, ed. John Masefield, 2 vols (London, 1906), 1:242. All further references cited in the text.
28 There was some debate among his contemporaries about how much editorial assistance Dampier received when he came to revise the journal for publication. Philip Edwards points out, however, that most of the additions made for the published journal were based on eye-witness material. Edwards makes some insightful comparisons between the manuscript and the printed text that show him strategically omitting some episodes and adding others that highlight his spiritual as well as his natural-scientific credentials. See Edwards, *The Story of the Voyage: Sea Narratives in Eighteenth-Century England* (Cambridge: Cambridge University Press 1994), 17–46.
29 Sloane MS 3236, British Library, f.29v. All further references cited in the text.
30 In the original (manuscript) description of the inhabitants of Guam, for example, Dampier says of these only that 'in general [they] are well limbed people and strong bodyd and very ingenious in building' and provides a description of their houses and canoes (MS f.186v). In the journal, however, we learn that:

> The natives of this island are strong bodied, large limb'd and well shaped. They are copper-coloured, like other Indians: Their hair is black and long, their eyes meanly proportioned; they have pretty high noses; their lips are pretty full, and their teeth indifferent white. They are long visaged and stern of countenace; yet we found them to be affable and courteous.

He then offers a much more detailed account of their engineering and building of boats and houses: See *Voyages,* 1:308.

31 See A.K. Smith, *Creating a World Economy: Merchant Capital, Colonialism and World Trade* (Boulder, Co.: Westview Press, 1991), 182–3.

32 See Anton Gill, *The Devil's Mariner: A Life of William Dampier, Pirate and Explorer 1651–1715* (London: Michael Joseph, 1997), 260–1. Other useful biographical material on Dampier can be found in Leslie R. Marchant, *An Island Unto Itself: William Dampier and New Holland* (Carlisle, Western Australia: Hesperian Press, 1988) and Christopher Lloyd, *William Dampier* (Hamden, CT: Archon Books, 1966).

33 See Gill (1997), 237; Marchant (1998),16; Lloyd (1966), 69–71.

3 International Trade and Individual Enterprise: Defoe's Maritime Adventurers

1 Thomas Mun, *England's Treasure by Foreign Trade* (London, 1664), 11.

2 Defoe, *Reflection on the Prohibition Act* (London, 1708). Beginning on 23 May 1713, Defoe began to publish arguments in favour of the commercial treaty in his journal, the *Mercator.* As Maximillian Novak has pointed out, however, the balance of trade with France weighed heavily against England during this period. What Defoe sought was a trade in which England could regain the advantage. See Novak, *Economics and the Fiction of Daniel Defoe* (Berkeley, CA: University of California Press 1962), 23–4.

3 Defoe, *A Plan of the English Commerce* (1728; reprinted, Oxford: Basil Blackwell, 1928), 10. On Defoe's mercantilism see especially Novak (1962); Thomas Keith Meier *Defoe and the Defense of Commerce* (University of Victoria: English Literary Studies, 1987); Geoffrey M. Sill, *Defoe and the Idea of Fiction 1713–1719* (Newark, DE: University of Delaware Press, 1983), 29–55.

4 See Novak (1962), 1–31; Manuel Schonhorn, *Defoe's Politics: Parliament, Power, Kingship and Robinson Crusoe* (Cambridge: Cambridge University Press, 1991), 9–19.

5 *Defoe (1728),* 34.

6 Although the idea of a home country as a site of affective belonging is important to Defoe, I use the concept of national loyalty in this instance to describe economic loyalty to the interests of the state. As Heckscher has pointed out, the unifying entity to which economic elements are responding in the seventeenth and early eighteenth centuries is not a nation unified by a common culture, but a *state.* See Heckscher, *Mercantilism,* trans. Mendel Shapiro 2nd edn., 2 vols (London: Allen & Unwin, 1935; New York: The Macmillan Company, 1955) 2: 13–16.

7 Charles Davenant, *Essay on the East India Trade* (London, 1696). Cited in Henry William Spiegel, *The Growth of Economic Thought* (Durham, NC: Duke University Press, 1991), 139.

8 Defoe, *The Best of Defoe's Review*, edited by William L. Payne (New York: Columbia University Press, 1951), Thursday,16 October 1707.

9 *Review,* Tuesday, 1 May, 1711. Emphasis in original.

10 Isaac Kramnick, *Republicanism and Bourgeois Radicalism: Political Ideology in Eighteenth-Century England and America* (Ithaca, NY: Cornell University Press, 1990), 13.

194 *Notes*

11 Ian Watt, *The Rise of the Novel* (Berkeley, CA: University of California Press, 1965), 60–92.
12 Michael McKeon, *The Origins of the English Novel 1600–1740* (Baltimore, MD: The Johns Hopkins University Press, 1987), 315-37.
13 Karl Marx, *Grundrisse: Foundations of the Critique of Political Economy*, trans. Martin Nicolaus (London: Allen Lane and New Left Review, 1973), 83.
14 Karl Marx, *Capital*, trans. Ben Fowkes, 3 vols (Harmondswort: Penguin, 1990), 1:170.
15 Defoe, *The Life and Strange Surprising Adventures of Robinson Crusoe, Of York, Mariner* (London: Oxford University Press, 1972), 82. All further references are cited in the text.
16 Peter Hulme, *Colonial Encounters: Europe and the Native Caribbean 1492–1797 (London and New York: Methuen*, 1986), 175–224.
17 See Schonhorn (1991), Novak (1962); Carol Kay, *Political Constructions: Defoe, Richardson and Sterne in Relation to Hobbes, Hume and Burke* (Ithaca, NY: Cornell University Press, 1988), 71. A different political reading of *Robinson Crusoe* has been offered recently by Ilse Vickers. She argues that Crusoe's cataloguing of everything he finds marks him as a good Baconian, and she suggests that the novel can be read as an allegory of the advancement of modern learning and the relationship between government and science. See Vickers, *Defoe and the New Sciences* (Cambridge: Cambridge University Press, 1996), 4–18.
18 Michael Seidel has pointed out that *Robinson Crusoe* follows the narrative pattern of the *Odyssey* as it 'root[s] out the lust for wandering and for adventure and instill[s] the desire for permanent settlement'. See Seidel, *Robinson Crusoe: Island Myths and the Novel* (Boston, MA: Twayne,1991), 38.
19 John Locke, *Two Treatises of Government*, ed. Peter Laslett (Cambridge: Cambridge University Press, 1988), 268.
20 *Jure Divino* (London, 1706), 2:16.
21 On the relationship of Locke's principles of government to English colonization of North America see Barbara Arneil, *John Locke and America: The Defence of English Colonialism* (Oxford: Clarendon Press,1996); James Tully, *An Approach to Political Philosophy: Locke in Contexts* (Cambridge: Cambridge University Press, 1993); Anna Neill, From Contact to Contract: Colonial Enclosure and Civil Identity in Eighteenth-Century Political Literature (PhD, Cornell University, 1995), 61–78.
22 *Party Tyranny, Or An Occasional Bill in Miniature* (London, 1705), 2.
23 *Locke (1988)*, 309.
24 McKeon (1987), 330.
25 See for example *Review*, Thursday, 19 August, 1708. Defoe describes the War of the Spanish Succession as revealing 'the ambition and unbounded pride of usurping monarchs' and destructive of the health and prosperity of their nations. See also his arguments in favour of a Treaty of Commerce with France in *Mercator: Or Commerce Retrieved* (London,1713) no. 67, Saturday, 24 October to Tuesday 27 October, 1713.
26 Hugo Grotius, *The Rights of War and Peace, including the Law of Nature and of Nations*, trans. and ed. Rev. A. C. Campbell, 3 vols (London, 1814) 3:39.
27 Hugo Grotius, *The Freedom of the Seas; or the Right that Belongs to the Dutch to Take Part in the East India Trade*, trans. Ralph Van Deman Magoffin (New York, 1916), 11.

28 Defoe, *The Complete English Tradesman* (Manila: Beverly Hills, CA: Historical Conservation Society, 1989), 16.

29 Defoe, *The Farther Adventures of Robinson Crusoe* (London, 1719), 1. All further references are cited in the text.

30 For an account of the already textualized conditions of contact that are revealed in *The Farther Adventures* see Norman Sims, 'On the Fringes: Translation and Pseudo-Translation in Intercultural Encounters', in *Council on National Literatures: World Report*, New Series: 1 (1987) 13–27.

31 Daniel Defoe, *The Life, Adventures, and Pyracies of the Famous Captain Singleton* (Oxford: Oxford University Press, 1990), 2. All further references are cited in the text.

32 *Captain Singleton*, like *Robinson Crusoe*, has been read as an allegory of individualism. See John Richetti, *Popular Fiction Before Richardson* (Oxford: Clarendon Press, 1969), 75–87. Paula Backscheider's more recent analysis stresses Singleton's alienation from the structures of socialization that produce good citizens and the way that Defoe uses the figure of the pirate to represent the 'desolate estrangement' of formal severance from one's place of birth. See Backscheider, *Daniel Defoe: Ambition and Innovation* (Lexington, KY: The University Press of Kentucky, 1986). See also Joel Baer, 'The Complicated Plot of Piracy': Aspects of English Criminal Law and the Image of the Pirate in Defoe,' in Roger D. Lund (ed.) *Critical Essays on Daniel Defoe*, (New York: Simon & Schuster and Macmillan, 1997), 62.

33 On the possible source this character provided for Conrad's *Heart of Darkness* see Michael Seidel, 'Defoe in Conrad's Africa', *Conradiana: A Journal of Joseph Conrad Studies*, 17:2 (1985) 145–6.

34 In fact European trade in West Africa for gold and other products had been well established since the Middle Ages. See Eric R. Wolf, *Europe and the People without History* (Berkeley, CA: University of California Press, 1982), 39–40.

4 Swift and the Geographers: Race, Space and Merchant Capital in *Gulliver's Travels*

1 Jonathan Swift, 'On Poetry: A Rhapsody,' *Jonathan Swift: The Complete Poems*, ed. Pat Rogers (Harmondworth: Penguin, 1983), 522–36, ll. 179–82.

2 Swift's satires are generally read as anti-colonial. Claude Rawson has proposed, however, that *Gulliver's Travels* provokes genuine disgust at the 'savagery' of Africans or Irish Catholics in order to create the satiric vehicle for a generalized misanthropy. See Rawson, *Order from Confusion Sprung: Studies in Eighteenth-Century Literature from Swift to Cowper* (London: George Allen & Unwin, 1985), 68–105. In a related argument, Bruce McLeod suggests that imperial geography is not necessarily a target of satiric invective in Swift's work and that he may, in fact, be identifying geography as an instrument of the civilizing mission. McLeod argues that Swift uses the language of anti-imperialism, not to defend the integrity of primitive cultures, but rather as a means of distinguishing the English model of colonialism from that of its (Catholic) commercial competitors, France and Spain. See McLeod, *The Geography of Empire in English Literature, 1580–1745* (Cambridge: Cambridge University Press, 1999).

3 See Carole Fabricant, *Swift's Landscape* (Baltimore, MA: The Johns Hopkins University Press, 1982); Thomas Metscher, 'The Radicalism of Swift:

Gulliver's Travels and the Irish Point of View', *in Studies in Anglo-Irish Literature* (Bonn: Bouvier Verlag Herbert Grundmann, 1982), 13–22.

4 Mikhail Bakhtin, *Rabelais and his World*, trans. Helene Iswolsky (Bloomington, IN: Indiana University Press, 1984).

5 My discussion of Swift's texts uses race as a category of difference constructed by theories of cultural 'evolution' and 'degeneration' that belong to seventeenth- and eighteenth-century natural-scientific thought. Such theories, for whom the best-known representative is perhaps George Louis Leclerc Buffon (who attributed both physical and cultural differences to the effects of climate), often suggest that the character of a people is inscribed on the bodies of its individual members. In other words, race in this context is not quite the invention of biological science that it becomes in the nineteenth century: a myth that heritable characteristics divide human beings naturally into distinct groups. While 'race' is in some ways an anachronistic term here, I am using it to describe an enlightenment categorization of the manners, more or less 'advanced', 'backward', or 'degenerated', of particular peoples that eighteenth-century Europeans often saw expressed in the shape as well as in the erotic inclinations of (usually) non-European bodies. The studies of the history of 'race' in the European imagination and its relationship to ideas about nation and culture that I have found most useful include: Kwame Antony Appiah, *In My Father's House: Africa in the Philosophy of Culture* (New York: Oxford University Press, 1992); Henry Louis Gates, Jr, 'Writing "Race" and the Difference it Makes,' in *'Race,' Writing and Difference* (Chicago, IL: University of Chicago Press, 1985), 1–20; Paul Gilroy, *The Black Atlantic: Moderenity and Double-Consciousness (Cambridge, MA: Harvard University Press, 1993)*; Anne McClintock, *Imperial Leather: Race, Gender and Sexuality in the Colonial Conquest* (New York: Routledge, 1995).

6 Useful accounts of the emergence of the science of geography include those of Lesley B. Cormack, 'Good Fences Make Good Neighbours: Geography as Self-Definition in Early Modern England', *Isis*, 82 (1991), 639–61; David N. Livingstone, *The Geographical Tradition: Episodes in the History of a Contested Enterprise* (Oxford: Basil Blackwell, 1993); D.R. Stoddard, *On Geography and its History* (Oxford: Basil Blackwell, 1986); Margarita Bowen, *Empiricism and Geographical Thought* (Cambridge: Cambridge University Press, 1981); Roy Porter, 'The Terraqueous Globe', in G.S. Rousseau and Roy Porter (eds), *The Ferment of Knowledge: Studies in the Historiography of Eighteenth-Century Science*, (Cambridge: Cambridge University Press, 1980), 285–324.

7 Jerry Brotton, *Trading Territories: Mapping the Early Modern World* (Ithaca, NY: Cornell University Press, 1998), 42–5.

8 Although increasingly maps were commissioned by merchants and landed gentry during the sixteenth and seventeenth centuries, the Crown continued to sponsor map production either through direct commission (where the defence or administration of the realm was concerned) or through involvement with charter companies and investors. See Peter Barber, 'England II: Monarchs, Ministers and Maps 1550–1625', in David Buisseret (ed.), *Monarchs, Ministers and Maps: The Emergence of Cartography as a Tool of Government in Early Modern Europe* (Chicago, IL: University of Chicago Press, 1992), 58–60.

9   On English colonialism and mapmaking see Jeannette A. Black, 'Mapping the English Colonies in North America: The Beginnings', in Norman J.W. Thrower (ed.), *The Compleat Plattmaker: Essays on Chart, Map and Globe Making in England in the Seventeenth and Eighteenth Centuries* (Berkeley, CA: University of California Press), 101–126 (see esp. 103–4); Geoff King, *Mapping Reality: An Exploration of Cultural Geographies* (New York: St Martin's Press, 1996), esp. ch. 1, 'The Map that Precedes the Territory', 1–17; R.V. Tooley, *Maps and Map-makers* (London: B.T. Batsford, 1987), esp. 47–79. On mapping and empire in Elizabethan England specifically see also Lesley B. Cormack, 'The Fashioning of an Empire: Geography and the State in Elizabethan England,' in Anne Godlewska and Neil Smith (eds), *Geography and Empire* (Oxford: Basil Blackwell, 1994), 15–30; Barber, 57–98.

10 This point is made by J.B. Harley, 'Silences and Secrecy: The Hidden Agenda of Cartography in Early Modern Europe', *Imago Mundi*, 40 (1988), 57–76.

11 See William Cunningham, *The Cosmographical Glasse* (London, 1559); John Dee, 'Mathematical Preface' to the first English translation of Euclid's *Elements of Geometrie* [1570], cited by Livingstone (1993), 75–6.

12 Matthew Edney has cautioned that introductions to atlases and other carto-graphical texts have tended to emphasize the 'progressive' history of the science. Such teleologies, he warns, belong to a Whiggish model of history. Instead, he suggests, different cartographic modes should be seen as interrelated and historically overlapping. See Edney, 'Cartography without "Progress": Reinterpreting the Nature and Historical Development of Mapmaking,' *Geographia*, 30: 3 (Autumn 1993), 54–68. Jerry Brotton also argues that Ptolemaic models were integrated with new geographical discoveries rather than discarded as outmoded. See Brotton (1998), 35–42.

13 See, for example, Sebastian Munster's 1540 edition. Ptolemy's treatise offered directions for map projection, the division of a world map into multiple separate maps, and the coordinates of latitude and longitude: Munster, *Geographia*, facsimile edn (Amsterdam: Theatrum Orbis Terrarum, 1946).

14 Abraham Ortelius, *Theatrum Orbis Terrarum* [1570], facsimile edn (Amsterdam: Meridian, 1964); Gerhardus Mercator, *A Geographical Description of the Whole World* [1636], facsimile edn (Amsterdam: Theatrum Orbis Terrarum, 1948); Johan Blaeu, *Le Grand Atlas* [1663], facsimile edn (Amsterdam: Theatrum Orbis Terrarum, 1967).

15 See James R. Akerman, 'The Structuring of Political Territory in Early Printed Atlases', *Imago Mundi*, 47 (1995), 138–54. Akerman discusses the importance of the appearance of graded boundary lines in the context of a shift from territory ruled by dynastic influence to the emergence of powerful sovereign states in Europe in the mid seventeenth century. On the history of atlas publication see Lee Bagrow and R.A. Skelton, *History of Cartography* (Chicago, IL: Precedent, 1966), 179–89.

16 J.B. Harley has pointed out that the 'epistemological silences' of mapmaking in early modern Europe were not only concerned with the protection of state power and the organization of military intelligence but that they were also a feature of 'a second theatre of geographical activity – that of commerce and the rise of monopoly capitalism.' See Harley (1998), 61.

17 On cartographic history and 'enlightenment singularity' see Edney (1993), 62.

18 These become more and more popular over the course of the eighteenth century. Barbara McCorkle has calculated that more than 400 geographical works were published in the eighteenth century. See McCorkle, 'The Maps of Patrick Gordon's *Geography Anatomiz'd*: An Eighteenth-Century Success Story', *The Map Collector*, 66 (1994), 10–15.

19 See O.F.G. Sitwell, *Four Centuries of Special Geography: An annotated guide to books that purport to describe all the countries in the world published before 1888* (Vancouver: University of British Columbia Press, 1993).

20 McCorkle (1994), 14.

21 Patrick Gordon, *Geography Anatomiz'd: Or A Geographical Grammar* (London, 1741), [B6r.].

22 Immanuel Wallerstein has pointed out that, although mercantilist principles focus on the movement of bullion and a balance of trade, to suggest that they are purely concerned with economic competition between states is to ignore their investment in the overall increased efficiency in the global sphere of production. The economic strength and 'productive superiority' of a state depends on its ability to produce goods so efficiently that they can be competitive even in other core states. See Wallerstein, *The Modern World System II*: Mercantilism and the Consolidation of the European World Economy 1600–1750 (New York: Academic Press, 1974), 37–40.

23 Henri Lefebvre, *The Production of Space,* trans. Donald Nicolson Smith (Oxford: Basil Blackwell, 1991), 27–36.

24 Harley, 66. See also David Harvey, 'From space to place and back again: Reflections on the condition of postmodernity,' in Jon Bird, Barry Curtis, Tim Putnam, George Robertson and Lisa Tickner (eds), *Mapping the Futures: Local Cultures, Global Change* (London: Routledge, 1993), 3–29.

25 John Senex, *A New General Atlas of the World* (London, 1721), [A3r.]. The preface (unpaginated) is probably written by the publisher.

26 I am borrowing the concept of a 'rational comparison' and reconciliation of different sources of information' in eighteenth-century epistemology from Matthew Edney. See his *Mapping an Empire: The Geographical Construction of British India 1765–1843* (Chicago, IL: University of Chicago Press, 1997), 26.

27 Herman Moll, *Thesaurus Geographicus* (London, 1695), [A2r.].

28 Moll, *A System of Geography: or, a New and Accurate Description of the Earth in all its Empires, Kingdoms and States* (London, 1701), [A1r.].

29 Robert Morden, *Geography Rectified: Or a Description of the World* (London, 1688), 261.

30 Moll, *The Compleat Geographer: or, the Chorography and Topography of all the known Parts of the Earth* (London, 1709), [B1r.]. Although both *A System of Geography* and *The Compleat Geographer* have new introductions to geography and earth science, these are otherwise new editions of *Thesaurus Geographicus*.

31 Moll, *A View of the Coasts, Countries and Islands within the Limits of the South Sea Company* (London, 1711), A2v.

32 *Ibid.,* 1.

33 This point is made by Dennis Reinhartz. See his *The Cartographer and the Literati – Herman Moll and his Intellectual Circle* (Lewiston, NY: Edwin Mellen Press, 1997), 44.

34 Moll, 'A New and Correct Map of the Whole World', *The World Described* (London, 1758), plate 1.

35   See Burton J. Fisherman, 'Defoe, Herman Moll and the Geography of South America,' *Huntington Library Quarterly*, 36:3 (1973), 227–38. Fisherman argues that Defoe's *A New Voyage Round the World* (1724), which dramatized the proposed exploration and colonization of minimally charted areas of South America, drew on several of Moll's maps, particularly the 'Kingdom of Chile' in *The Complete Geographer*.

36   Edward Godfrey Cox, *A Reference Guide to the Literature of Travel*, 2 vols. (Seattle, WA: University of Washington, 1938), 2:389.

37   *Atlas Maritimus and Commercialis; Or A General View of the World so far as it relates to Trade and Navigation* (London, 1728), ii.

38   Awnsham Churchill and John Churchill, *A Collection of Voyages*, 4 vols (London, 1704), 1:lxxiii.

39   Gordon, (1741), [B6v].

40   Thomas Salmon, *Modern History: Or the Present State of All Nations*, 3 vols (London, 1744–6), 1: v.

41   This is the earliest known map of postal routes in North America. See R.D. Harris, 'The Beaver Map', *P.S.: A Postal Quarterly*, 4 (1977), 11–19.

42   *Senex, A Map of North America Corrected from the Observations Communicated to the Royal Society at London and the Royal Academy at Paris*, 1710.

43   *Senex, A New General Atlas*, 1.

44   Baron de Lahontan, *New Voyages to North America*, 2 vols (London, 1703), vol. 1, plate 1B.

45   See Salmon (1744–6), 3:129.

46   These terms are taken here from Gordon's *Geography Anatomiz'd* (see the category of 'manners' under the description of each country.) However, they are descriptive terms typical to the accounts of the manners of isolated peoples in the special geographies.

47   For recent studies of the unstable national identity of the explorerer/colonizer in *Gulliver's Travels* see Michael Seidel, 'Strange Dispositions: Swift's *Gulliver's Travels*', in Frank Palmeri (ed.) *Critical Essays on Jonathan Swift* (New York: G. K. Hall & Co., 1993), 75–89; Clement Hawes, 'Three Times Around the Globe: Gulliver and Colonial Discourse', *Cultural Critique,*18 (Spring 1991) 187–214; Howard Erskine-Hill, *Gulliver's Travels* (Cambridge: Cambridge University Press, 1993); Laura Brown, 'Reading Race and Gender: Jonathan Swift', *Eighteenth-Century Studies* 23:4 (1990) 425–43.

48   This topic has been touched on in an essay by Karin Johannisson, 'Society in Numbers: The Debate over Quantification in Eighteenth-Century Political Economy', in *The Quantifying Spirit in the Eighteenth Century*, Tore Frangsmyr, J.L. Heilron, and Robin E. Rider (Berkeley, CA: University of California Press, 1990), 343–61. Johannisson points out that some of Swift's satire is aimed at political arithmetic and the way in which state power is invested in popular faith in mathematical truths. Also useful on *Gulliver's Travels* and the human object of mathematical investigation is Christopher Fox, 'How to Prepare a Noble Savage: The Spectacle of Human Science', in Christopher Fox, Roy Porter and Robert Wokler (eds) *Inventing Human Science: Eighteenth-Century Domains* (Berkeley, CA: University of California Press, 1995), 1–30.

49   For a discussion of the way in which Swift has been 'adopted' as an Irish patriot both by his contemporaries (particularly readers of the *Drapier's Letters*) and by later nationalist writers see Robert Mahoney, *Jonathan Swift: The Irish Identity* (New Haven, CT: Yale University Press, 1995); A. Norman

Jeffares, 'Swift: Anatomy of an Anti-Colonialist', in Okifumi Komesu and Masaru Sekine (eds) *Irish Writers and Politics* (Savage, Maryland: Barnes & Noble, 1990), 36–46. Joel Reed argues that the spectacle of the Irish poor in Swift's writing is an expression of the desire to assert the difference between Anglo-Irish and Irish Catholic: see Reed, 'Monstrous Knowledge: Representing the National Body in Eighteenth-Century Ireland,' in *Defects: Engendering the Modern Body* Helen Deutsch and Felicity Nussbaum (eds), (Ann Arbor, MI: University of Michigan Press, 2000), 154–176.

50 *The Works of Jonathan Swift,* ed. Walter Scott, 2nd edn, in 19 vols (Edinburgh, 1824), 7:99.

51 *Gulliver's Travels and Other Writings,* ed. Louis A. Landa (Boston, MA: Houghton Mifflin, 1960), 443. All further references are cited in the text.

52 On the complex use of the figure of the cannibal to represent both consuming colonizer and barbarous colonized see Claude Rawson, '"Indians" and Irish: Montaigne, Swift and the Cannibal Question', *Modern Language Quarterly*, 53:3 (1992), 299–363. The question of how Swift's anti colonial views get expressed through a depiction of the racialized and gendered body has been addressed by Laura Brown. See Brown, *Ends of Empire: Women and Ideology in Early Eighteenth-Century England* (Ithaca, NY: Cornell University Press), 170–200.

53 See Frederick Bracher, 'The Maps in *Gulliver's Travels*', *The Huntington Library Quarterly*, 8:1 (1944–5), 59–74.

54 John Robert Moore has already argued that absurd geographical calculations in *Gulliver's Travels* demonstrate Swift's conviction that geography is false learning. Despite their popularity at the time, Swift had only two atlases in his library, the latest published in 1686. See Moore, 'The Geography of *Gulliver's Travels*', *Journal of English and Germanic Philology*, 40 (1941), 214–28.

55 Bracher (1944–5), 67.

56 In particular, eighteenth-century natural historical accounts of the 'Hottentots' routinely ascribe physical characteristics to 'degenerate' cultural practices including the habits of child rearing. Such accounts invariably also involve a sexualization of the bodies of the people described. Daniel Beeckman's *A Voyage to and from the Island of Borneo* (London, 1718) describes the women as 'having long flabby breasts, odiously dangling down to their waists which they can toss over their shoulders for their children to suck, whom they generally carry on their backs'. Quoted by Hawes (1991), 193. Hawes points out that this same account of breast feeding on the mother's back appears in Charles White's 1797 *Account of the Regular Gradation in Man and in Different Animals and Vegetables*. He suggests that it should be compared with another passage in the same text in which the features of the European are presented as a sign of racial superiority. Similar racist topoi are used by Mary Wollstonecraft in *A Vindication of the Rights of Woman*. Having taken Gulliver's description at face value she asks: 'who that has read Dean Swift's disgusting description of the Yahoos ... can avoid seeing the futility of degrading the passions, or making man rest in contentment?' It is then no surprise that she accepts the findings of contemporary travellers and natural historians that African men are enervated by the practice of polygamy and that therefore their societies are altogether lest robust and more 'degenerate' than they might be. See Wollstonecraft, *Vindication* (Harmondsworth: Penguin, 1992), 166, 218.

5 *Roderick Random, Rasselas* and the Currents of Fancy

1 Johnson, *The Rambler*, no. 4, (31 March 1750). *Yale Edition of the Works of Samuel Johnson*, edited by W.J. Bate and Albrecht B. Strauss, 16 vols (New Haven, CT: Yale University Press, 1969), 3:19–25.

2 Smollett sometimes contrasts this robust modern citizen with the effete and overly adorned body of the aristocrat whose weakened body and taste for the foreign and frivolous are responsible for the dissension and corruption in the nation. See Terence Bowers, 'Reconstituting the National Body in Smollett's Travels through France and Italy', *Eighteenth-Century Life*, 21:1 (1997), 1–25. On contemporary English attitudes to national identity and its characteristics see Paul Langford, *Englishness Identified: Manners and Character 1650–1850* (Oxford: Oxford University Press, 2000).

3 Onno Zwier van Haren and John Campbell, *The Sentiments of a Dutch Patriot, Being the Speech of **** (London, 1746), i.

4 Ibid., v.

5 *A Letter to a Member of Parliament Concerning the Present State of Affairs at Home and Abroad* (London, 1740), 51.

6 See *Observations on the Present Convention with Spain* (London 1739); *Observations Arising from the Declaration of War against Spain* (London, 1739); *A Dissertation on the Present Conjuncture particularly with Regard to Trade* (London, 1739); *The Grand Question whether War or no War with Spain* (London, 1739); *A Review of all that hath pass'd between the Courts of Great Britain and Spain* (London, 1739); *A Reply to the Pamphlet entitled Popular Prejudice against the Convention with Spain* (London, 1740).

7 A number of recent studies have examined the impact of popular politics on public policy in mid eighteenth-century Britain. See Kathleen Wilson, *The Sense of the People: Politics, Culture and Imperialism in England, 1715–1785* (Cambridge: Cambridge University Press, 1995); H.T. Dickinson, *The Politics of the People in Eighteenth-Century Britain* (London: St Martin's Press, 1995); Paul Langford, *A Polite and Commercial People: England 1727–1783* (Oxford: Clarendon Press, 1989). Jeremy Black has suggested that the emphasis such studies place on the influence of urban public culture may obscure the nature of extra-Parliamentary activity in rural areas which did not necessarily concord with that of the towns. See Black, 'Introduction: An Age of Political Stability?', in Jeremy Black (ed.), *Britain in the Age of Walpole*, (London: Macmillan, 1984), 1–22.

8 I use the term 'popular' or 'the people' here in the sense that Wilson does. The 'people', she points out, refers not simply to a plebian opposition to patrician authority and government, but also to an extra-Parliamentary urban political culture in which citizens' interests achieved a voice that was influential on official opposition politics. Wilson's argument is that the 'people' are active in political culture; they are not a subpolitical and passion-driven 'mob'. See Wilson (1995), 3–27.

9 *The Operations of the War for the first Twelve Months Examined and Accounted for* (London, 1740), 17.

10 Lord Lyttleton, *Considerations upon the Present State of Affairs at Home and Abroad* (London, 1739); *Popular Prejudices against the Convention and Treaty with Spain examined and answered* (London, 1739); *Reflections on the Welfare and Prosperity of Great Britain in the Present Crisis* (London, 1742).

11 Wilson (1995), 153.
12 *A Fifth Letter to the People of England on M—Influence and Management of the National Treasure* (London, 1756), 10.
13 Dickinson links the food riots that coincided with the early defeats with popular patriotism. Although the riots were directed principally at unscrupulous millers and dealers who deliberately drove up the price of grain at a time of scarcity, they can also be connected to broader patterns of political agitation that argued profit should be subordinated to the national interest. See Dickinson (1995), 125–60.
14 Wilson, 195.
15 *The Briton*, no. 17 (18 September, 1762), in O.M. Brack Jr and Byron Gassman (eds), *Poems, Plays and The Briton: Tobias Smollett* (Athens, GA, and London: University of Georgia Press, 1993), 324.
16 *The Critical Review*, ed. Tobias Smollett, 1:19 (April 1756), 266.
17 See Christopher J. Berry, *The Idea of Luxury: A Conceptual and Historical Investigation* (Cambridge: Cambridge University Press, 1994); Maxine Berg, 'New Commodities, Luxuries and their Consumers in Eighteenth-Century England', in Maxine Beg and Helen Clifford (eds), *Consumers and Luxury: Consumer Culture in Europe 1650–1850*, (Manchester and New York: Manchester University Press, 1999), 63–87; John Sekora, *Luxury: The Concept in Western Thought, Eden to Smollett* (Baltimore, MA: The Johns Hopkins University Press, 1977).
18 Ibid., 2:1 (August 1756), 1.
19 Ibid., 2:3 (September 1756), 44. In the early years of the war, Smollett supported Pitt. By 1762, however, when French power had been contained in both North America and India, he opposed Pitt's pursuit of the war and the German alliance. See Robert Spector, *Political Controversy: A Study in Eighteenth-Century Propaganda* (New York: Greenwood Press, 1992), 7–9; Robin Fabel, 'The Patriotic Briton: Tobias Smollett and English Politics 1756–1771,' *Eighteenth-Century Studies*, 8:1 (1974), 100–14.
20 See 'Review of *A Complete History of England*,' in *The Critical Review*, 5:1 (Feb. 1758), 1.
21 *Critical Review*, 3:4 (April 1757), 339.
22 Ibid., 2:2 (August 1756), 440.
23 Ibid., 4:1 (July 1757), 23.
24 *The Briton*, no. 6, 266.
25 Ibid., 266.
26 Ibid., no. 1, 241.
27 Ibid., no. 6, 266
28 Ibid., no. 16, 320.
29 *Roderick Random* (London: J.M. Dent, 1964), 379. All further references are cited in the text.
30 *The Briton*, no. 17, 324.
31 Ibid., no. 6, 266.
32 Ibid., no. 16, 324.
33 Smollett, *The Present State of All Nations*, 8 vols (London, 1768–9), 8:237.
34 Bowers argues that Scottishness in Smollett's writing becomes the basis for a revitalized body politic. See Bower (1997), 9.

35 Tobias Smollett, *A Compendium of Authentic and Entertaining Voyages*, 7 vols (London, 1766), 6:342.

36 Smollett, *The Complete History of England*, 11 vols (London, 1760), 11:304.

37 See for example David Hume, 'Of National Characters', note 10, where he argues that black Africans are naturally inferior to white Europeans: David Hume: *Essays Moral Political and Literacy*, ed. Eugene F. Miller, rev. edn (Indianapolis, IN: Liberty Classics, 1987), 208.

38 *Bate and Strauss (1969)*, 4: 105.

39 This point has recently been made in studies of Johnson's political career. See John Cannon, *Samuel Johnson and the Politics of Hanoverian England* (Oxford: Clarendon Press, 1994); Robert Folkenflik, 'Johnson's Politics',Greg Clingham (ed.), in *The Cambridge Companion to Samuel Johnson* (Cambridge: Cambridge University Press, 1997), 102–113. Both of these studies are indebted to Donald Greene's older *The Politics of Samuel Johnson*, the second edition of which was published in 1990 with a new introduction outlining how the view of Johnson as a reactionary Tory inherited from Boswell ignores the flexibility and variety in his political thinking. See Greene, *The Politics of Samuel Johnson*, 2nd edn (Athens, GA, and London: The University of Georgia Press, 1990). An opposing argument has recently been made by J.C.D. Clark that Johnson was a Jacobite and a non-juror. See Clark, *Samuel Johnson: Literature, Religion and English Cultural Politics from the Restoration to Romanticism* (Cambridge: Cambridge University Press, 1994).

40 *A Review of The Conduct of the Ministry Impartially Examined* (1756), *Works*, 10, ed. Donald J. Greene (1977), 252–60; 'Observations', in *The Universal Chronicle* (1758), ibid., 10: 272–3; and 'Speech on the Rochefort Expedition' (1757), ibid., 10:262–5.

41 Ibid., 10:318.

42 See, for example, 'Observations on the Present State of Affairs' and 'Speech on the Rochefort Expedition'.

43 Christopher Smart, Oliver Goldsmith and Samuel Johnson, *The World Displayed; Or a Curious Collection of Voyages and Travels, Selected and Compiled from the Writers of all Nations*, 8 vols (Philadelphia, PA: 1795), 1:11.

44 See *London: A Poem, Works*, 6, ed. E.L. McAdam, Jr (New Haven, CT: Yale University Press, 1964), 47–61, l. 178.

45 Ibid. ll. 190–1.

46 *The Adventurer*, no. 67, *Works*, 2, ed. W.J. Bate, John M. Bullit and L.F. Powell (New Haven, CT: Yale University Press, 1963), 384.

47 On the epistemological significance of the figure of the crowd in Johnson's writing see Thomas Reinert, *Regulating Confusion: Samuel Johnson and the Crowd* (Durham, NC, and London: Duke University Press, 1996).

48 *The Rambler*, no.4, *Works*, ed. Bate and Strauss (1969), 3:19.

49 Katie Trumpener has argued that enlightenment calculation is confounded by the appropriation of local, nationalist literary tropes into the enlightenment generalities of *Journey to the Western Isles of Scotland*. See Trumpener, *Bardic Nationalism: The Romantic Novel and the British Empire* (Princeton, NJ: Princeton University Press, 1997), 67–127. On Johnson's recognition of the relationship between the cosmopolitan, but necessarily imperial, gaze and cultural and material poverty in the Highlands see

John Wiltshire, '"From China to Peru": Johnson in the Traveled World', in Greg Clingham (ed.), *The Cambridge Companion to Samuel Johnson* (Cambridge: Cambridge University Press, 1997), 209–23.

50 *Works*, 16, ed. Gwin J. Kolb (New Haven, CT: Yale University Press, 1990), 112. All further references are cited in the text.

6 South Seas Trade and the Character of Captains

1 *Mutiny on the Bounty* (Lewis Milestone, Metro-Goldwyn-Mayer, USA, 1962).
2 See David MacKay, *In the Wake of Cook: Exploration Science and Empire, 1780–1801* (London: Croom Helm, 1985); John Gascoigne, *Science in the Service of Empire: Joseph Banks, the British State and the Uses of Science in the Age of Revolution* (Cambridge: Cambridge University Press, 1998) and his earlier *Joseph Banks and the English Enlightenment: Useful Knowledge and Polite Culture* (Cambridge: Cambridge University Press, 1994); Nigel Rigby, 'The Politics and Pragmatics of Seaborne Plant Transportation, 1769–1805,' in Margarette Lincoln (ed.), *European Voyages to the Southern Ocean in the Eighteenth Century* (London: Boydell Press, 1998), 183–198; David Philip Miller and Peter Hans Reill (eds), *Visions of Empire: Voyages, Botany and Representations of Nature*, (Cambridge: Cambridge University Press, 1996).
3 *The Endeavour Journal of Joseph Banks, 1768–1771*, ed. J.C. Beaglehole, 2 vols (Sydney: Angus & Robertson, 1963), 2:10; 2:265.
4 Georg Forster, *A Voyage Round the World in his Britannic Majesty's Sloop, Resolution, Commanded by Captain James Cook*, 2 vols (London, 1777),1:216. All further references are cited in the text.
5 Anthony Ashley Cooper, Earl of Shaftesbury, *Characteristicks of Men, Manners, Opinions, Times*, 3rd edn, 3 vols (London, 1723), 2:35.
6 Ibid., 2:30.
7 David Hume, *Treatise of Human Nature*, ed. L.A. Selby-Bigge (Oxford: Clarendon Press, 1928), 457–8.
8 Adam Smith, *The Theory of Moral Sentiments*, ed. D.D. Raphael and A.L. MacFie (Oxford: Clarendon Press, 1976), 152.
9 Ibid., 137.
10 Thomas L. Haskell, 'Capitalism and the Origins of the Humanitarian Sensibility', *American Historical Review*, 90:2 (1985), 339–61 and 90:3 (1985), 547–66.
11 Ibid., 562.
12 Adam Smith, *An Enquiry into the Nature and Cause of The Wealth of Nations*, ed. Edwin Cannan (Chicago, IL: University of Chicago Press, 1976) 1:17.
13 The identification of Smith with *laissez-faire* economics ignores the residual mercantilist principles that he continues to uphold in some parts of *The Wealth of Nations*. His political economy was as focused on the accumulation of national wealth as it was on the deregulation of trade. While he condemned the colonial system that had stunted the growth of both metropolitan and colonial economies with protectionist legislation, he did recognize the importance of colonies to the development of national wealth and power. He also made an exception to the arguments about degregulation by supporting the Navigation Acts. Neomercantilism in the style of Adam

Smith, as John Crowley has argued, 'combined economic liberalism with economic nationalism'. See Crowley, 'Neomercantilism and *The Wealth of Nations*', *The Historical Journal* 33:2 (1990), 339–60.

14 Commentating on the relevance of *The Wealth of Nations* to Pacific voyage narratives, Bernard Smith suggests that Cook acted as the (paradoxically) intervening 'God' figure, or 'invisible hand': he stepped in to enforce the laws of a free-market economy that were supposedly regulated by nature. See Smith, *Imagining the Pacific: In the Wake of the Cook Voyages* (New Haven, CT, and London: Yale University Press, 1992), 209.

15 *The Adventures and Vicissitudes of Captain Cook, Mariner* (London: E. Harrison, 1870); Daniel J. Carrison, *Captain Cook: Genius Afloat* (London and New York: Franklin Watts, 1967).

16 Carrison (1967), 170.

17 J.C. Beaglehole, *The Life of Captain James Cook* (Stanford, CA: Stanford University Press, 1974), 698.

18 Ibid., 698.

19 Anna Seward, *Elegy on Captain Cook* (London: J. Dodsley, 1781), ll. 35, 41, 43, 267.

20 *A Catalogue of the different specimens of cloth collected in the three voyages of Captain Cook to the Southern Hemisphere* (London: Alexander Shaw, 1787), [A1r.].

21 *The Voyage of the Resolution and Discovery*, volume 3 of *The Journals of Captain James Cook on his Voyages of Discovery*, ed. J.C. Beaglehole (Cambridge: Cambridge University Press, 1967), 568.

22 George Gilbert, *Captain Cook's Final Voyage*, ed. Christine Holmes (Honolulu: University Press of Hawaii, 1982), 108.

23 *Zimmermann's Captain Cook: An Account of the 3rd Voyage of Captain Cook around the world, 1776–1780*, ed. F.W. Howay and trans. Elsa Michaels and Cecil French (Toronto: The Ryerson Press, 1930), 102.

24 Gilbert (1982), 106.

25 William Ellis, *An Authentic Narrative of a voyage performed by Captain Cook in His Majesty's Ships Resolution and Discovery*, 2 vols (London: G. Robinson, 1782),1:148.

26 Zimmerman (1930), 59. Another member of the crew omits the mutilation in his account of this incident. See John Rickman, *An Authentic Narrative of a Voyage Performed by Captain Cook and Captain Clerke inn his Majesty's Ships Resolution and Discovery*, 2 vols (Altenburg: Gottlob Emanuel Richter, 1788), 1:91.

27 Zimmermann (1930), 114.

28 A rather different 'heroicization' of Cook has recently become a subject of debate in postcolonial criticism. Gananath Obeyesekere has objected to Marshall Sahlins's structuralist account of native Hawaiian reactions to Cook. Sahlins argues that Cook was killed because the Hawaiians believed him to be the God Lono appearing to them at a particular moment in the sacred calendar when he was supposed to be most vulnerable. Obeyesekere accuses Sahlins of the kind of 'European mythmaking' that sees traditional cultures as entirely static. Sahlins, he suggests, is insensitive to the capacity for reflection and narrative flexibility that enables cultural beliefs to adapt to historical circumstances. Sahlins counters by saying that Obeyesekere

buys into a neo-Enlightenment set of values which privileges Western rationality and scepticism. See Obeyesekere, *The Apotheosis of Captain Cook: European Mythmaking in the Pacific* (Princeton, NJ: Princeton University Press, 1992); '"British Cannibals": Contemplation of an Event in the Death and Resurrection of James Cook, Explorer', in Kwame Anthony Appiah and Henry Louis Gates (eds), *Identities* (Chicago, IL, and London: University of Chicago Press, 1995), 7–31; Sahlins, *How 'Natives' Think: About Captain Cook, For Example* (Chicago, IL and London: University of Chicago Press, 1995), esp. 1–15.

29 David Samwell, *A Narrative of the Death of Captain James Cook* (London: G.G.J. and J. Robinson, 1786), 27. Bernard Smith has also shown that Cook constructed himself as a man of peace through the visual record of, in particular, his third voyage. See Smith (1992), 193–224.

30 George Anderson, *A New, Authentic and Complete Collection of Voyages Round the World* (London: Alex Hogg, 1784), iii.

31 Francis Bacon, *Works of Francis Bacon*, ed. J. Spedding, R.L. Ellis and D.D. Heath, 7 vols (London: Longmans, 1876), 3:294.

32 Georg Forster, *A Letter to the Right Honorable Earl of Sandwich, First Lord Commissioner of the Board of Admiralty* (London: G. Robinson, 1778), 15.

33 William Wales, *Remarks on Mr. Forster's Account of Captain Cook's Last Voyage Round the World* (London: J. Nourse, 1778), 89.

34 Quoted in Wales (1778), 26.

35 Johann Forster, *The Resolution Journal of Johann Reinhold Forster, 1772–1775*, ed. Michael E. Hoare, 4 vols (London: Hakluyt Society, 1982), 2:188.

36 Ibid., 4:710.

37 John Hawkesworth's rewriting of Cook's journal of his first voyage often plays up such scenes of arbitration, having the latter, for instance, reflect on the illegality of firing on Tahitian thieves where, in his own journal, Cook merely reflects on the likely consequences of doing so. See Hawkesworth, *An Account of the Voyages undertaken by the order of His Present Majesty for making Discoveries in the Southern Hemisphere*, 3 vols (London, 1773), 1:148; Cook, 1:101.

38 James Cook, *The Journals of Captain James Cook on his Voyages of Discovery*, ed. J.C. Beaglehole, 4 vols (Cambridge: Cambridge University Press, 1955), 1: 75 (hereafter referred to as *Voyages.*)

39 Georg Forster, (1777), 2:112. (hereafter referred to as *A Voyage*).

40 On the influence of Scottish Enlightenment philosophy on Forster's *Observations* see Nicholas Thomas, '"On the Varieties of the Human Species": Forster's Comparative Ethnology,' in *Observations Made During a Voyage Round the World*, edited by Nicholas Thomas, Harriet Guest, and Michael Dettelbach (Honolulu: University of Hawai'i Press, 1996), xxiii–xl. Hereafter referred to as *Observations*.

41 Jonathan Lamb has argued that, in such moments, the European observer is the subject not of enlightened knowledge, but of an unregulated free-floating intensity. See Lamb, 'Minute Particulars and the Representation of South Pacific Discovery', *Eighteenth-Century Studies*, 28:3 (1995), 288–92.

42 John Elliott, *Captain Cook's Second Voyage: The Journals of Lieutenants Elliott and Pickersgill*, ed. Christine Holmes (London: Caliban Books, 1984), 17.

43   Ibid., 34.

44   Johann Forster (1982), 2:314.

45   Ibid., 3: 427.

46   J.C. Beaglehole, *Captain Cook and Captain Bligh: The W.E. Collins Lecture* (Wellington: The Victoria University, 1967), 3.

47   William Bligh, *The Log of the Bounty*, ed. Owen Rutter 2 vols (London: Golden Cockerel Press, 1936–7), 1:393. All further references cited in the text.

48   Greg Denning, *Mr. Bligh's Bad Language: Passion, Power and Theatre on the Bounty* (Cambridge: Cambridge University Press, 1992), 62.

49   Ibid., 34–5.

50   Ibid., 34.

51   *The Voyage of the Bounty's Launch as related in William Bligh's Despatch to the Admiralty and the Journal of John Fryer*, ed. Owen Rutter (Golden Cockerel Press, 1934), 72.

52   James Morrison, *The Journals of James Morrison* (London: Golden Cockerel Press, 1935), 19.

53   'Remarks on Mr. Morrison's Journal', in Bligh, *Bligh's Voyage in the Resource* (London: Cockerel Press, 1937), 151.

54   'John Fryer's Journal', in *The Voyage of the Bounty's Launch* (1934), 48–79.

55   *Mutiny on the Bounty* (Frank Lloyd, Metro-Goldwyn-Mayer, USA, 1935).

56   *Log*, 2:223; *A Narrative of the Mutiny on Board His Majesty's Ship Bounty* (London: George Nicol, 1790), 9; *A Voyage to the South Seas*, ed. Geoffrey Ingleton (Adelaide: Griffin Press, 1975), 94. All further references are cited in the text.

57   *The Letters of Fletcher Christian*, ed. Stephen Walters (Guildford: Genesis 1984), 30.

58   *A Narrative (1790)*, 9.

59   'Letter to Sir Joseph Banks', Mitchell Library, Sydney, Australia (Safe 1/37), quoted in Gavin Kennedy, *Captain Bligh: The Man and his Mutinies* (London: Duckworth, 1989), 182.

60   *A Narrative* (1790), 9.

7   Conclusion: Global Commerce and Homelessness

1   Gilles Deleuze and Félix Guattari, *A Thousand Plateaus: Capitalism and Schizophrenia*, trans. Brian Massumi (Minneapolis, MN: University of Minnesota Press, 1987), 7.

2   Christopher Miller has made this point about the nostalgia of nomadology in *A Thousand Plateaus*. He also argues that such nostalgia has the function of 'attributing pre-conscious thoughts to natives that the Western [anthropologist] then makes explicit'. See Miller, 'The Postidentitarian Predicament in the Footnotes of *A Thousand Plateaus*: Nomadology, Anthropology and Authority', *Diacritics*, 23:3 (Fall 1993),16.

3   Robert J.C. Young, *Colonial Desire: Hybridity in Theory, Culture and Race* (London and New York: Routledge, 1995), 173.

4   For a recent example, see Rose Braidotti, *Nomadic Subjects* (New York: Columbia University Press, 1994).

5 Bruce Robbins has pointed out that such coalitional transnationalisms represent a departure from an older conception of cosmopolitanism as a mode of detachment (the privilege of an intellectual class whose sensibility transcends that of ethnic or national affiliation). This new understanding of cosmopolitanism as a radical politics is a feature of much post-colonial criticism. See Robbins, 'Actually Existing Cosmpolitanism', in Pheng Cheah and Bruce Robbins (eds) *Cosmopolitics: Thinking and Feeling beyond the Nation*, (Minneapolis, MN: University of Minnesota Press, 1988), 1–19.

6 James Clifford, *Routes: Travel and Translation in the Late Twentieth Century* (Cambridge, MA: Harvard University Press, 1997), 24.

7 Paul Gilroy, *The Black Atlantic: Modernity and Double-Consiousness* (Cambridge, MA: Harvard University Press, 1993), 4.

8 Ibid., 12.

9 Ibid., 4.

10 Marcus Rediker, *Between the Devil and the Deep Blue Sea: Merchant Seamen, Pirates, and the Anglo-American Maritime World, 1700–1750* (Cambridge: Cambridge University Press, 1987), 288–98.

11 Caren Kaplan, *Questions of Travel: Postmodern Discourses of Displacement* (Durham, NC, and London: Duke University Press, 1996), 88.

References

Adams, Percy C., *Travelers and Travel Liars, 1600–1800* (Berkeley and Los Angeles, CA: University of California Press, 1962).

The Adventures and Vicissitudes of Captain Cook, Mariner (London: E. Harrison, 1870).

Akerman, James R., 'The Structuring of Political Territory in Early Printed Atlases', *Imago Mundi*, 47 (1995), 138–54.

Anderson, Adam, *An Historical and Chronological Deduction of the Origin of Commerce* (London, 1764).

Anderson, George, *A New, Authentic and Complete Collection of Voyages Round the World* (London: Alex Hogg, 1784).

Appiah, Kwame Anthony, *In My Father's House: Africa in the Philosophy of Culture* (New York: Oxford University Press, 1992).

Appleby, Joyce, *Economic Thought and Ideology in Seventeenth-Century England* (Princeton, NJ: Princeton University Press, 1978).

Aravamudan, Srinivas, *Tropicopolitans: Colonialism and Agency, 1688–1804* (Durham, NC, and London: Duke University Press, 1999).

Arendt, Hannah, *The Human Condition* (Chicago, IL: University of Chicago Press, 1958).

Armitage, David, 'From Richard Hakluyt to William Robertson', in Karen Ordahl Kupperman (ed.), *America in European Consciousness, 1493–1750* (Chapel Hill, NC, and London: University of North Carolina Press, 1995), 52–78.

Arneil, Barbara, *John Locke and America: The Defence of English Colonialism* (Oxford: Clarendon Press, 1996).

Atlas Maritimus and Commercialis; Or A General View of the World so far as it relates to Trade and Navigation (London, 1728).

Backscheider, Paula, *Daniel Defoe: Ambition and Innovation* (Lexington, KY: The University Press of Kentucky, 1986).

Bacon, Francis, *Works*, ed. J. Spedding, R.L. Ellis and D.D. Heath, 15 vols (Boston, MA: Houghton-Mifflin,1860–2).

—— *Works of Francis Bacon*, ed. J. Spedding, R.L. Ellis and D.D. Heath, 7 vols (London: Longmans, 1876).

Baer, Joel, '"The Complicated Plot of Piracy": Aspects of English Criminal Law and the Image of the Pirate in Defoe', in Roger D. Lund (ed.), *Critical Essays on Daniel Defoe* (New York: Simon & Schuster Macmillan, 1997), 56–77.

Bagrow, Lee and R.A. Skelton, *History of Cartography* (Chicago, IL: Precedent, 1966).

Bakhtin, Mikhail, *Rabelais and his World*, trans. Helene Iswolsky (Bloomington, IN: Indiana University Press, 1984).

Banks, Joseph, *The Endeavour Journal of Joseph Banks, 1768–1771*, ed. J.C. Beaglehole, 2 vols (Sydney: Angus & Robertson, 1963).

Barber, Peter, 'England II: Monarchs, Ministers and Maps 1550–1625', in David Buisseret (ed.), *Monarchs, Ministers and Maps: The Emergence of Cartography as a Tool of Government in Early Modern Europe* (Chicago, IL: University of Chicago Press, 1992), 58–60.

209

Bartels, Emily C., 'Imperialist Beginnings: Richard Hakluyt and the Construction of Africa', *Criticism*, 34:4 (1992), 517–38.

Beaglehole, J.C., *Captain Cook and Captain Bligh: The W.E. Collins Lecture* (Wellington: The Victoria University, 1967).

—— *The Life of Captain James Cook* (Stanford, CA: Stanford University Press, 1974).

Beeckman, Daniel, *A Voyage to and from the Island of Borneo* (London, 1718).

Berg, Maxine, 'New Commodities, Luxuries and their Consumers in Eighteenth-Century England', in Maxine Berg and Helen Clifford (eds), *Consumers and Luxuries: Consumer Culture in Europe 1650–1850* (Manchester and New York: Manchester University Press, 1999), 63–87.

Berry, Christopher J., *The Idea of Luxury: A Conceptual and Historical Investigation* (Cambridge: Cambridge University Press, 1994).

—— *Social Theory of the Scottish Enlightenment* (Edinburgh: Edinburgh University Press, 1997).

Black, Jeanette A., 'Mapping the English Colonies in North America: The Beginnings', in Norman J.W. Thrower (ed.), *The Compleat Plattmaker: Essays on Chart, Map and Globe Making in England in the Seventeenth and Eighteenth Centuries* (Berkeley, CA: University of California Press), 101–26.

Black, Jeremy (ed.), *Britain in the Age of Walpole* (London: Macmillan, 1984).

Blaeu, Johan, *Le Grand Atlas* [1663]. Facsimile edn (Amsterdam: Theatrum Orbis Terrarum, 1967).

Bligh, William, *A Narrative of the Mutiny on Board His Majesty's Ship Bounty* (London: George Nicol, 1790).

—— *The Voyage of the Bounty's Launch as related in William Bligh's Despatch to the Admiralty and the Journal of John Fryer*, ed. Owen Rutter (Golden Cockerel Press, 1934), 72.

—— *The Log of the Bounty*, ed. Owen Rutter, 2 vols (London: Golden Cockerel Press, 1936–7).

—— *Bligh's Voyage in the Resource* (London: Cockerel Press, 1937).

—— *A Voyage to the South Seas*, ed. Geoffrey Ingleton (Adelaide: Griffin Press, 1975).

Bohls, Elizabeth, *Women Travel Writers and the Language of Aesthetics, 1718–1818* (Cambridge: Cambridge University Press, 1995).

Bourdieu, Pierre, *The Field of Cultural Production: Essays on Art and Literature*, ed. Randal Johnson (New York: Columbia University Press, 1993).

Bowen, Margarita, *Empiricism and Geographical Thought* (Cambridge: Cambridge University Press, 1981).

Bowers, Terence, 'Reconstituting the National Body in Smollett's Travels through France and Italy', *Eighteenth-Century Life*, 21:1 (1997), 1–25.

Bracher, Frederick, 'The Maps in *Gulliver's Travels*', *The Huntington Library Quarterly*, 8:1 (1944–5), 59–74.

Bradley, Peter, *The Lure of Peru: Maritime Intrusion into the South Sea, 1598–1701* (New York: St Martin's Press, 1989).

Braidotti, Rose, *Nomadic Subjects* (New York: Columbia University Press, 1994).

Braudel, Fernand, *The Perspective of the World* (volume 3 of *Civilization and Capitalism: 15th to 18th Century*), trans. Siân Reynolds (Berkeley, CA: University of California Press, 1992).

Britnell, Richard H., *The Commercialisation of English Society 1000–1500* (Manchester and New York: Manchester University Press, 1996).

Brotton, Jerry, *Trading Territories: Mapping the Early Modern World* (Ithaca, NY: Cornell University Press, 1998), 42–5.

Brown, Laura, 'Reading Race and Gender: Jonathan Swift', *Eighteenth-Century Studies*, 23:4 (1990), 425–43.

—— *Ends of Empire: Women and Ideology in Early Eighteenth-Century England* (Ithaca, NY: Cornell University Press, 1993).

Campbell, John, *A Political Survey of Britain*, 2 vols (London, 1774).

Candid and Impartial Considerations on the Nature of the Sugar Trade of the British and French Islands in the West Indies (London, 1763).

Cannon, John, *Samuel Johnson and the Politics of Hanoverian England* (Oxford: Clarendon Press, 1994).

Carrison, Daniel J., *Captain Cook: Genius Afloat* (London and New York: Franklin Watts, 1967).

A Catalogue of the different specimens of cloth collected in the three voyages of Captain Cook to the Southern Hemisphere (London: Alexander Shaw, 1787).

Cheah, Pheng and Bruce Robbins (eds), *Cosmopolitics: Thinking and Feeling Beyond the Nation* (Minneapolis, MN: University of Minnesota Press, 1998).

Child, Josiah, *A New Discourse of Trade* [1668], 5th edn (Glasgow, 1751).

Churchill, Awnsham and John Churchill, *A Collection of Voyages*, 4 vols (London, 1704).

Clark, J.C.D., *Samuel Johnson: Literature, Religion and English Cultural Politics from the Restoration to Romanticism* (Cambridge: Cambridge University Press, 1994).

Clifford, James and George E. Marcus (eds), *Writing Culture: The Poetics and Politics of Ethnography* (Berkeley, CA: University of California Press, 1986).

—— *Routes: Travel and Translation in the Late Twentieth Century* (Cambridge, MA: Harvard University Press, 1997).

A Complete Collection of State Trials and Proceedings for High Treason and Other Crimes and Misdemeanors, from the Reign of King Richard II to the End of King George I, 21 vols (London, 1816).

Cook, James, *The Journals of Captain James Cook on his Voyages of Discovery*, ed. J.C. Beaglehole, 4 vols, (Cambridge: Cambridge University Press, 1955–74).

Cordingly, David, *Under the Black Flag: The Romance and the Reality of Life Among the Pirates* (New York: Random House, 1995).

Cormack, Lesley B., 'Good Fences Make Good Neighbours: Geography as Self-Definition in Early Modern England', *Isis*, 82 (1991), 639–61.

—— 'The Fashioning of an Empire: Geography and the State in Elizabethan England', in Anne Godlewska and Neil Smith (eds), *Geography and Empire* (Oxford: Basil Blackwell, 1994), 15–30.

Cox, Edward Godfrey, *A Reference Guide to the Literature of Travel*, 2 vols (Seattle, WA: University of Washington, 1938).

Crowley, John, 'Neomercantilism and *The Wealth of Nations*', *The Historical Journal*, 33:2 (1990), 339–60.

Cunningham, William, *The Cosmographical Glasse* (London, 1559).

Dampier, William, *Dampier's Voyages*, ed. John Masefield, 2 vols (London, 1906).

—— Manuscript of the early version of *New Voyage Round the World*, Sloane MS 3236, British Library.

Daston, Lorraine and Katharine Park, *Wonders and the Order of Nature 1150–1750* (New York: Zone Books, 1998).

Davenant, Charles, *Essay on the East India Trade* (London, 1696).
—— 'An Essay upon the Balance of Power', in *Essays* (London, 1701).
Defoe, Daniel, *Party Tyranny, Or An Occasional Bill in Miniature* (London, 1705), 2.
—— *Jure Divino* (London, 1706).
—— *Reflection on the Prohibition Act* (London, 1708).
—— *Mercator: Or Commerce Retrieved* (London, 1713–).
—— *The Farther Adventures of Robinson Crusoe* (London, 1719).
—— *A Plan of the English Commerce* (1728; reprinted, Oxford: Basil Blackwell, 1928).
—— *The Best of Defoe's Review*, ed. William L. Payne (New York: Columbia University Press, 1951).
—— *The Life and Strange Surprising Adventures of Robinson Crusoe, Of York, Mariner* (London: Oxford University Press, 1972).
—— *The Complete English Tradesman* (Manila: Beverly Hills, Calif.: Historical Conservation Society, 1989).
—— *The Life, Adventures, and Pyracies of the Famous Captain Singleton* (Oxford: Oxford University Press, 1990).
Deleuze, Gilles and Félix Guattari, *A Thousand Plateaus: Capitalism and Schizophrenia*, trans. by Brian Massumi (Minneapolis, MN: University of Minnesota Press, 1987).
Denning, Greg, *Mr. Bligh's Bad Language: Passion, Power and Theatre on the Bounty* (Cambridge: Cambridge University Press, 1992).
Dickinson, H.T., *The Politics of the People in Eighteenth-Century Britain* (London: St Martin's Press, 1995).
A Dissertation on the Present Conjuncture particularly with Regard to Trade (London, 1739).
Edney, Matthew, 'Cartography without "Progress": Reinterpreting the Nature and Historical Development of Mapmaking', *Geographia*, 30:3 (Autumn 1993), 54–68.
—— *Mapping an Empire: The Geographical Construction of British India 1765–1843* (Chicago, IL: University of Chicago Press, 1997).
Edwards, Philip, *The Story of the Voyage: Sea Narratives in Eighteenth-Century England* (Cambridge: Cambridge University Press, 1994).
Elliott, John, *Captain Cook's Second Voyage: The Journals of Lieutenants Elliott and Pickersgill*, ed. Christine Holmes. (London: Caliban Books, 1984).
Ellis, William, *An Authentic Narrative of a voyage performed by Captain Cook in His Majesty's Ships Resolution and Discovery*, 2 vols (London: G. Robinson, 1782).
Erskine-Hill, Howard, *Gulliver's Travels* (Cambridge: Cambridge University Press, 1993).
An Essay on the Increase and Decline of Trade in London and the Outports (London, 1749).
Exquemelin, A.O., *The Buccaneers of America*, trans. Alexis Brown (Harmondsworth: Penguin, 1969).
Fabel, Robin, 'The Patriotic Briton: Tobias Smollett and English Politics 1756–1771', *Eighteenth-Century Studies*, 8:1 (1974), 100–14.
Fabricant, Carole, *Swift's Landscape* (Baltimore, MA: The Johns Hopkins University Press, 1982).
Ferguson, Adam, *An Essay on the History of Civil Society* [1767], ed. Duncan Forbes (Edinburgh: Edinburgh University Press, 1966).
A Fifth Letter to the People of England on M—l Influence and Management of the National Treasure (London, 1756).

Fisherman, Burton J., 'Defoe, Herman Moll and the Geography of South America', *Huntington Library Quarterly*, 36:3 (1973), 227–38.

Folkenflik, Robert, 'Johnson's Politics', in Greg Clingham (ed.), *The Cambridge Companion to Samuel Johnson* (Cambridge: Cambridge University Press, 1997).

Forster, Georg, *A Voyage Round the World in his Britannic Majesty's Sloop, Resolution, Commanded by Captain James Cook*, 2 vols (London, 1777).

—— *A Letter to the Right Honorable Earl of Sandwich, First Lord Commissioner of the Board of Admiralty* (London: G. Robinson, 1778).

Forster, Johann, *The Resolution Journal of Johann Reinhold Forster, 1772–1775*, ed. Michael E. Hoare, 4 vols (London: Hakluyt Society, 1982).

Foucault, Michel, *The Archeology of Knowledge*, trans. A.M. Sheridan Smith (London: Tavistock, 1972).

Fox, Christopher, 'How to Prepare a Noble Savage: The Spectacle of Human Science', in Christopher Fox, Roy Porter and Robert Wokler, (eds), *Inventing Human Science: Eighteenth-Century Domains* (Berkeley, CA: University of California Press, 1995), 1–30.

Fox-Genovese, Elizabeth and Eugene Genovese, *Fruits of Merchant Capital: Slavery and Bourgeois Property in the Rise and Expansion of Capitalism* (Oxford: Oxford University Press, 1983).

Fryer, John, 'Journal', in Bligh, *The Voyage of the Bounty's Launch as Related in William Bligh's Despatch to the Admiralty and the Journal of John Fryer*, ed. Owen Rutter (London: Cockerel Press, 1934), 48–79.

Fuller, Mary C., *Voyages in Print: English Travel to America, 1576–1624* (Cambridge: Cambridge University Press, 1995).

Gascoigne, John, *Joseph Banks and the English Enlightenment: Useful Knowledge and Polite Culture* (Cambridge: Cambridge University Press, 1994).

—— *Science in the Service of Empire: Joseph Banks, the British State and the Uses of Science in the Age of Revolution* (Cambridge: Cambridge University Press, 1998).

Gates, Henry Louis, Jr (ed.), *'Race', Writing and Difference* (Chicago, IL: University of Chicago Press, 1985).

Gilbert, George, *Captain Cook's Final Voyage*, ed. Christine Holmes (Honolulu: University Press of Hawaii, 1982).

Gill, Anton, *The Devil's Mariner: A Life of William Dampier, Pirate and Explorer 1651–1715* (London: Michael Joseph, 1997).

Gilroy, Paul, *The Black Atlantic: Modernity and Double-Consciousness* (Cambridge, MA: Harvard University Press, 1993).

Gordon, Patrick, *Geography Anatomiz'd: Or A Geographical Grammar* (London, 1741).

The Grand Question Whether War or no War with Spain (London, 1739).

Great Britain, Public Record Office. *Calendar of State Papers, Colonial Series, America and the West Indies* (1669–74), ed. Noel Sainsbury (London, 1896).

—— (1681–85), ed. J.W. Fortescue (London, 1898).

—— (1685–88), ed. J.W. Fortescue (London, 1899).

Greenblatt, Stephen, *Marvelous Possessions: The Wonder of the New World* (Chicago, IL: University of Chicago Press, 1991).

Greene, Donald, *The Politics of Samuel Johnson*, 2nd edn (Athens, GA, and London: The University of Georgia Press, 1990).

Grotius, Hugo, *The Rights of War and Peace Including the Law of Nature and of Nations*, trans. and ed. Rev. A.C. Campbell, 3 vols (London, 1814).

—— *The Freedom of the Seas; or the Right that Belongs to the Dutch to Take Part in the East India Trade*, trans. by Ralph Van Deman Magoffin (New York, 1916).

Hakluyt, Richard, *The Principal Navigations, Voyages, Traffiques and Discoveries of the English Nation*, 12 vols (Glasgow: James MacLehose & Sons, 1903).

Hancock, David, *Citizens of the World: London Merchants and the Integration of the British Atlantic Community, 1735–1785* (Cambridge: Cambridge University Press, 1995).

Haring, C.H., *The Buccaneers in the West Indies in the Seventeenth Century* (London: Methuen, 1910).

Harley, J.B., 'Silences and Secrecy: The Hidden Agenda of Cartography in Early Modern Europe', *Imago Mundi*, 40 (1988), 57–76.

Harris, Jonathan Gil, 'The Canker of England's Commonwealth: Gerard de Malynes and the Origins of Economic Pathology', *Textual Practice*, 13:2 (1999), 311–27.

Harris, R.D., 'The Beaver Map', *P.S.: A Postal Quarterly*, 4 (1977), 11–19.

Harvey, David, 'From space to place and back again: Reflections on the condition of postmodernity', in Jon Bird, Barry Curtis, Tim Putnam, George Robertson and Lisa Tickner (eds), *Mapping the Futures: Local Cultures, Global Change* (London: Routledge, 1993), 3–29.

Haskell, Thomas L., 'Capitalism and the Origins of the Humanitarian Sensibility', *American Historical Review*, 90:2 (1985), 339–61 and 90:3 (1985), 547–66.

Hawes, Clement, 'Three Times Around the Globe: Gulliver and Colonial Discourse', *Cultural Critique*, 18 (1991), 187–214.

Hawkesworth, John, *An Account of the Voyages undertaken by the order of His Present Majesty for making Discoveries in the Southern Hemisphere*, 3 vols (London, 1773).

Hebb, David Delison, *Piracy and the English Government, 1616–1642* (Aldershot: Scolar Press, 1994).

Heckscher, Eli F., *Mercantilism*. Trans. Mendel Shapiro. 2nd edn, 2 vols (London: Allen & Unwin, 1935; New York: Macmillan Company, 1955).

Helgerson, Richard, *Forms of Nationhood: The Elizabethan Writing of England* (Chicago, IL: University of Chicago Press, 1992).

Hill, Christopher, *Intellectual Origins of the English Revolution* (Oxford: Clarendon Press, 1965).

Hirschman, Albert O., *The Passions and the Interests: Political Arguments for Capitalism before its Triumph* (Princeton, NJ: Princeton University Press, 1977).

Hobbes, Thomas, *Leviathan*, ed. Richard Tuck (Cambridge: Cambridge University Press, 1996).

Hulme, Peter, *Colonial Encounters: Europe and the Native Caribbean 1492–1797* (London and New York: Methuen, 1986).

Hume, David, *Treatise of Human Nature*, ed. L.A. Selby-Bigge (Oxford: Clarendon Press, 1928).

—— *Enquiries Concerning Human Understanding and Concerning the Principles of Morals*, ed. L.A. Selby-Bigge, 3rd edn (Oxford: Clarendon Press, 1975).

—— *David Hume: Essays Moral Political and Literary*, ed. Eugene F. Milter, rev. edn (Indianapolis, IN: Liberty Classics, 1987).

Hutchison, Terence, *Before Adam Smith: The Emergence of Political Economy 1622–1776* (Oxford: Basil Blackwell, 1988).

Jeffares, Norman A., 'Swift: Anatomy of an Anti-Colonialist', in Okifumi Komesu and Masaru Sekine (eds), *Irish Writers and Politics* (Savage, MD: Barnes & Noble, 1990), 36–46.

Johannisson, Karin, 'Society in Numbers: The Debate over Quantification in Eighteenth-Century Political Economy', in Tore Frangsmyr, J.L. Heilron and Robin E. Rider (eds), *The Quantifying Spirit in the Eighteenth Century* (Berkeley, CA: University of California Press, 1990), 343–61.

Johnson, Samuel, *The Idler and The Adventurer*, vol. 2 of *The Yale Edition of the Works of Samuel Johnson*, ed. W.J. Bate, John M. Bullit and L.F. Powell (New Haven, CT: Yale University Press, 1963).

—— *The Rambler*, vols 3–5 of *The Yale Edition of the Works of Samuel Johnson*, ed. W.J. Bate and Albrecht B. Strauss (New Haven, CT: Yale University Press, 1969).

—— *Poems*, vol. 6 of *The Yale Edition of the Works of Samuel Johnson*, ed. E.L. McAdam Jr (New Haven: Yale University Press, 1964).

—— *Political Writings*, vol. 10 of *The Yale Edition of the Works of Samuel Johnson*, ed. Donald J. Greene (New Haven, CT: Yale University Press, 1977).

—— *Rasselas and Other Tales*, vol. 16 of *The Yale Edition of the Works of Samuel Johnson*, ed. Gwin J. Kolb (New Haven, CT: Yale University Press, 1990).

Kames, Henry Home, Lord, *Sketches of the history of Man*, 2 vols (Edinburgh, 1774).

Kaplan, Caren, *Questions of Travel: Postmodern Discourses of Displacement* (Durham, NC, and London: Duke University Press, 1996).

Kay, Carol, *Political Constructions: Defoe, Richardson and Sterne in Relation to Hobbes, Hume and Burke* (Ithaca, NY: Cornell University Press, 1988).

Kemp, P.K. and Christopher Lloyd, *The Brethren of the Coast: The British and French Buccaneers in the South Seas* (London: Heinemann, 1960).

Kennedy, Gavin, *Captain Bligh: The Man and his Mutinies* (London: Duckworth, 1989).

Kermode, Jenny, *Medieval Merchants: York, Beverley and Hull in the Later Middle Ages* (Cambridge: Cambridge University Press, 1998).

King, Geoff, *Mapping Reality: An Exploration of Cultural Geographies* (New York: St Martin's Press, 1996).

Kramnick, Isaac, *Republicanism and Bourgeois Radicalism: Political Ideology in Eighteenth-Century England and America* (Ithaca, NY: Cornell University Press, 1990)

Lahontan, Baron de, *New Voyages to North America*, 2 vols (London, 1703).

Lamb, Jonathan, 'Minute Particulars and the Representation of South Pacific Discovery', *Eighteenth-Century Studies*, 28:3 (1995), 281–294.

—— 'Eye-Witnessing in the South Seas', *The Eighteenth-Century: Theory and Interpretation*, 38:3 (Fall 1997), 201–212.

Langford, Paul. *A Polite and Commercial People: England 1727–1783* (Oxford: Clarendon Press, 1989).

—— *Englishness Identified: Manners and Character 1650–1850* (Oxford: Oxford University Press, 2000).

Lawrence, Karen, *Penelope Voyages: Women and Travel in the British Literary Tradition* (Ithaca, NY: Cornell University Press, 1994).

Leed, Eric J., *The Mind of the Traveller: From Gilgamesh to Global Tourism* (New York: Basic Books, 1991).

Lefebvre, Henri, *The Production of Space*, trans. Donald Nicolson Smith (Oxford: Basil Blackwell, 1991).

A Letter to a Member of Parliament Concerning the Present State of Affairs at Home and Abroad (London, 1740).

The Letters of Fletcher Christian, ed. Stephen Walters (Guildford: Genesis, 1984).

Linebaugh, Peter, *The London Hanged: Crime and Civil Society in the Eighteenth Century* (Cambridge: Cambridge University Press, 1992).

—— and Marcus Rediker. *The Many-Headed Hydra: Sailors, Slaves, Commoners and the Hidden History of the Revolutionary Atlantic* (Boston, MA: Beacon Press, 2000).

Livingstone, David N., *The Geographical Tradition: Episodes in the History of a Contested Enterprise* (Oxford: Basil Blackwell, 1993).

Lloyd, Christopher, *William Dampier* (Hamden, CT: Archon Books, 1966).

Locke, John, *Some Considerations Concerning Raising the Value of Money* (London, 1696).

—— *Two Treatises of Government*, ed. Peter Laslett (Cambridge: Cambridge University Press, 1988).

Lydon, James G., *Pirates, Privateers, and Profits* (NJ: The Gregg Press, 1970).

Lyttleton, Lord, *Considerations upon the Present State of Affairs at Home and Abroad* (London, 1739).

MacKay, David, *In the Wake of Cook: Exploration Science and Empire, 1780–1801* (London: Croom Helm, 1985).

Magnusson, Lars, *Mercantilism: The Shaping of an Economic Language* (London and New York: Routledge, 1994).

Mahoney, Robert, *Jonathan Swift: The Irish Identity* (New Haven, CT: Yale University Press, 1995).

Malynes, Gerald de., *The Maintenance of Free Trade* (London, 1622).

Mandeville, Bernard, *The Fable of the Bees; Or, Private Vices made Public Benefits*, 2 vols (London, 1724).

Marchant, Leslie, *An Island Unto Itself: William Dampier and New Holland* (Carlisle, Western Australia: Hesperian Press, 1988).

Marcus, George E. and Michael M. Fischer, *Anthropology as Cultural Critique: An Experimental Moment in the Human Sciences*, 2nd edn (Chicago, IL, and London: University of Chicago Press, 1999).

Marx, Karl, *Grundrisse: Foundations of the Critique of Political Economy*, trans. Martin Nicolaus (London: Allen Lane and New Left Review, 1973).

—— *Capital*, trans. Ben Fowkes. 3 vols (Harmondsworth: Penguin, 1990).

McClintock, Anne, *Imperial Leather: Race, Gender and Sexuality in the Colonial Conquest* (New York: Routledge, 1995).

McCorkle, Barbara, 'The Maps of Patrick Gordon's *Geography Anatomiz'd*: An Eighteenth-Century Success Story.' *The Map Collector* 66 (1994), 10–15.

McKeon, Michael, *The Origins of the English Novel 1600–1740* (Baltimore, MD: The Johns Hopkins University Press, 1987), 315–37.

McLeod, Bruce, *The Geography of Empire in English Literature, 1580–1745* (Cambridge: Cambridge University Press, 1999).

Meek, Ronald L., *Social Science and the Ignoble Savage* (Cambridge: Cambridge University Press, 1976).

Meier, Thomas Keith, *Defoe and the Defense of Commerce* (University of Victoria: English Literary Studies, 1987).

Mercator, Gerhardus, *A Geographical Description of the Whole World* [1636]. Facsimile edn (Amsterdam: Theatrum Orbis Terrarum, 1948).

Metscher, Thomas, 'The Radicalism of Swift: *Gulliver's Travels* and the Irish Point of View', in *Studies in Anglo-Irish Literature* (Bonn: Bouvier Verlag Herbert Grundmann, 1982), 13–22.

Millar, John, *Observations Concerning the Distinction of Ranks in Society* (London, 1771).

Miller, Christopher, 'The Postidentitarian Predicament in the Footnotes of *A Thousand Plateaus*: Nomadology, Anthropology and Authority', *Diacritics*, 23:3 (Fall 1993), 6–35.

Miller, Philip and Peter Hans Reill (eds), *Visions of Empire: Voyages, Botany and Representations of Nature* (Cambridge: Cambridge University Press, 1996).

Misselden, Edward. *Free Trade, or the Means to make Trade Florish* (London, 1622).

Moll, Herman, *Thesaurus Geographicus* (London, 1695).

—— *A System of Geography: or, a New and Accurate Description of the Earth in all its Empires, Kingdoms and States* (London, 1701).

—— *The Compleat Geographer: or, the Chorography and Topography of all the known Parts of the Earth* (London, 1709).

—— *A View of the Coasts, Countries and Islands within the Limits of the South Sea Company* (London, 1711).

—— *The World Described* (London, 1758).

Montesquieu, Charles de Secondat, Baron de., *The Spirit of the Laws*, trans. and ed. by Anne M. Cohler, Basia Carolyn Miller and Harold Samuel Stone (Cambridge: Cambridge University Press, 1989).

Moore, John Robert, 'The Geography of *Gulliver's Travels*', *Journal of English and Germanic Philology* 40 (1941), 214–28.

Morden, Robert, *Geography Rectified: Or a Description of the World* (London, 1688).

Morrison, James, *The Journals of James Morrison* (London: Golden Cockerel Press, 1935).

Mun, Thomas, *England's Treasure by Foreign Trade* (London, 1664).

—— *A Discourse of Trade from England unto the East-Indies* [1621] (New York: The Facsimile Text Society, 1930).

Munster, Sebastian, *Geographia* [1540]. Facsimile edn (Amsterdam: Theatrum Orbis Terrarum, 1946).

Neill, Anna, 'From Contact to Contract: Colonial Enclosure and Civil Identity in Eighteenth-Century Political Literature' (PhD, Cornell University, 1995).

Novak, Maximillian, *Economics and the Fiction of Daniel Defoe* (Berkeley, CA: University of California Press 1962).

Obeyesekere, Gananath, *The Apotheosis of Captain Cook: European Mythmaking in the Pacific* (Princeton, NJ: Princeton University Press, 1992).

—— 'British Cannibals': Contemplation of an Event in the Death and Resurrection of James Cook, Explorer,' in Kwame Anthony Appiah and Henry Louis Gates (eds), *Identities* (Chicago, IL and London: University of Chicago Press, 1995), 7–31.

Observations Arising from the Declaration of War against Spain (London, 1739).

Observations on the Present Convention with Spain (London, 1739).

Olson, Richard. *The Emergence of the Social Sciences 1642–1792* (New York: Twayne, 1993).

The Operations of the War for the first Twelve Months Examined and Accounted for (London, 1740).

Ortelius, Abraham, *Theatrum Orbis Terrarum* [1570]. Facsimile edn (Amsterdam: Meridian, 1964).

Pagden, Anthony, *Lords of all the World: Ideologies of Empire in Spain, Britain and France c.1500–c.1800* (New Haven, CT, and London: Yale University Press, 1995).

Petty, William, *Political Arithmetick* (London, 1791).

Pocock, J.G.A., *Virtue, Commerce and History* (Cambridge: Cambridge University Press, 1983).

Poovey, Mary, *A History of the Modern Fact: Problems of Knowledge in the Sciences of Wealth and Society* (Chicago, IL: University of Chicago Press, 1998).

Popular Prejudices against the Convention and Treaty with Spain examined and answered (London, 1739).

Porter, Roy, 'The Terraqueous Globe', in G. S. Rousseau and Roy Porter (eds), *The Ferment of Knowledge: Studies in the Historiography of Eighteenth-Century Science* (Cambridge: Cambridge University Press, 1980), 285–324.

Postlethwayt, Malachy, *Britain's Commercial Interest Explained and Improved* (London, 1757).

Pratt, Mary Louise, *Imperial Eyes: Travel Writing and Transculturation* (London and New York: Routledge, 1992).

Pufendorf, Samuel, *Of the Law of Nature and Nations*, trans. Basil Kennet, 3rd edn (London, 1717).

Purchas, Samuel, *Hakluytus Posthumus; Or, Purchas His Pilgrimes*, 20 vols (Glasgow: James MacLehose & Sons, 1905).

Ralegh, Walter, *The Discoverie of the large and bewtiful Empire of Guiana* (London: Argonaut Press, 1928).

Rawson, Claude, *Order from Confusion Sprung: Studies in Eighteenth-Century Literature from Swift to Cowper* (London: George Allen & Unwin, 1985).

—— '"Indians" and Irish: Montaigne, Swift and the Cannibal Question', *Modern Language Quarterly*, 53:3 (1992), 299–363.

Raynal, Abbé (Guillaume), *A Philosophical and Political History of the Settlements and Trade of the Europeans in the East and West Indies* [1798], trans. J.O. Justamond, 6 vols (New York: Negro Universities Press, 1969).

Rediker, Marcus, *Between the Devil and the Deep Blue Sea: Merchant Seamen, Pirates, and the Anglo-American Maritime World, 1700–1750* (Cambridge: Cambridge University Press, 1987).

Reed, Joel, 'Monstrous Knowledge: Representing the National Body in Eighteenth-Century Ireland', in Helen Deutsch and Felicity Nussbaum (eds), *Defects: Engendering the Modern Body* (Ann Arbor, MI: University of Michigan Press, 2000), 154–76.

Reflections on the Welfare and Prosperity of Great Britain in the Present Crisis (London, 1742).

Reinert, Thomas, *Regulating Confusion: Samuel Johnson and the Crowd* (Durham, NC, and London: Duke University Press, 1996).

Reinhartz, Dennis, *The Cartographer and the Literati – Herman Moll and his Intellectual Circle* (Edwin Mellen Press, 1977).

Rennie, Neil, *Far-Fetched Facts: The Literature of Travel and the Idea of the South Seas* (Oxford: Clarendon Press, 1995).

A Reply to the Pamphlet entitled Popular Prejudice against the Convention with Spain (London, 1740).

A Review of all that hath pass'd between the Courts of Great Britain and Spain (London, 1739).

Richetti, John, *Popular Fiction Before Richardson* (Oxford: Clarendon Press, 1969).

Rickman, John, *An Authentic Narrative of a Voyage Performed by Captian Cook and Captain Clerke inn his Majesty's Ships Resolution and Discovery*, 2 vols (Altenburg: Gottlob Emanuel Richter, 1788).

Rigby, Nigel, 'The Politics and Pragmatics of Seaborne Plant Transportation, 1769–1805', in Margarette Lincoln (ed), *European Voyages to the Southern Ocean in the Eighteenth Century* (London: Boydell Press, 1998), 183–98.

Ritchie, Robert C., *Captain Kidd and the War Against the Pirates* (Cambridge, MA: Harvard University Press, 1986).

Rolt, Richard, *A New Dictionary of Trade and Commerce*, 2nd edn (London, 1761).

Sahlins, Marshall. *How 'Natives' Think: About Captain Cook, For Example* (Chicago, IL, and London: University of Chicago Press, 1995).

Salmon, Thomas, *Modern History: Or the Present State of All Nations*, 3 vols (London, 1744–6).

Samwell, David, *A Narrative of the Death of Captain James Cook* (London: G.G.J. and J. Robinson, 1786), 27.

Schonhorn, Manuel, *Defoe's Politics: Parliament, Power, Kingship and* Robinson Crusoe *(*Cambridge: Cambridge University Press, 1991).

Sekora, John, *Luxury: The Concept in Western Thought, Eden to Smollett* (Baltimore, MD: The Johns Hopkins University Press, 1977).

Seidel, Michael, 'Defoe in Conrad's Africa', *Conradiana: A Journal of Joseph Conrad Studies*, 17:2 (1985), 145–6.

—— *Robinson Crusoe: Island Myths and the Novel* (Boston, MA: Twayne, 1991).

—— 'Strange Dispositions: Swift's *Gulliver's Travels*', in Frank Palmeri (ed.), *Critical Essays on Jonathan Swift* (New York: G.K. Hall, 1993), 75–89.

Senior, C.M., *A Nation of Pirates: English Piracy in its Heyday* (New York: Crane, Russak, 1976).

Senex, John, *A New General Atlas of the World* (London, 1721).

Senex, John, *A Map of North America Corrected from the Observations Communicated to the Royal Society at London and the Royal Academy at Paris* (London, 1710).

Seward, Anna, *Elegy on Captain Cook* (London: J. Dodsley, 1781).

Shaftesbury, Earl of (Anthony Ashley Cooper). *Characteristicks of Men, Manners, Opinions, Times*, 3rd edn, 3 vols (London, 1723).

Shipman, Joseph C., *William Dampier: Seaman-Scientist*, (Lawrence, KS: University of Kansas Libraries, 1962).

Sill, Geoffrey M., *Defoe and the Idea of Fiction 1713–1719* (Newark, DE: University of Delaware Press, 1983).

Sims, Norman, 'On the Fringes: Translation and Pseudo-Translation in Intercultural Encounters', in *Council on National Literatures: World Report*, New Series: 1 (1987), 13–27.

Sitwell, O.F.G., *Four Centuries of Special Geography: An annotated guide to books that purport to describe all the countries in the world published before 1888* (Vancouver: University of British Columbia Press, 1993).

Smart Christopher, Oliver Goldsmith and Samuel Johnson. *The World Displayed; Or a Curious Collection of Voyages and Travels, Selected and Compiled from the Writers of all Nations*, 8 vols (Philadelphia, PA: 1795).

Smith, Adam, *An Inquiry into the Nature and Causes of the Wealth of Nations*, ed. Edwin Cannan (Chicago, IL: University of Chicago Press, 1976).

—— *The Theory of Moral Sentiments*, ed. D. D. Raphael and A.L. MacFie (Oxford: Clarendon Press, 1976).

—— *Lectures on Jurisprudence*, ed. R.L. Meek, D.D. Raphael and P.G. Stein (Oxford: Clarendon Press, 1978), 5–140.

Smith, Alan K., *Creating a World Economy: Merchant Capital, Colonialism and World Trade* (Boulder, CO: Westview Press, 1991).

Smith, Bernard, *Imagining the Pacific: In the Wake of the Cook Voyages* (New Haven, CT, and London: Yale University Press, 1992).

Smollett, Tobias (ed.), *The Critical Review* (1756–62). 12 vols.

—— *The Complete History of England*, 11 vols (London, 1760).

—— *A Compendium of Authentic and Entertaining Voyages*, 7 vols (London, 1766).

—— *The Present State of All Nations*, 8 vols (London, 1768–9).

—— *Roderick Random* (London: J.M. Dent, 1964).

—— *The Briton*, in *Poems, Plays and* The Briton*: Tobias Smollett*, ed. O.M. Brack, Jr. and Byron Gassman (Athens and London: University of Georgia Press, 1993).

Solomon, Julie, *Objectivity in the Making: Francis Bacon and the Politics of Inquiry* (Baltimore, MD: The Johns Hopkins University Press, 1998).

Spector, Robert, *Political Controversy: A Study in Eighteenth-Century Propaganda* (New York: Greenwood Press, 1992).

Spiegel, Henry William, *The Growth of Economic Thought* (Durham, NC: Duke University Press, 1991).

Sprat, Thomas, *The History of the Royal Society of London for the Improving of Natural Knowledge* (London, 1702).

Stewart, Dugald, *Essays on Philosophical Subjects by the Late Adam Smith* (Dublin, 1795).

Stoddard, D.R., *On Geography and its History* (Oxford: Basil Blackwell, 1986).

Swift, Jonathan, *The Works of Jonathan Swift*, ed. Sir Walter Scott, 2nd edn, 19 vols (Edinburgh, 1824).

—— *Gulliver's Travels and Other Writings*, ed. Louis A. Landa (Boston, MA: Houghton Mifflin, 1960).

—— *Jonathan Swift: The Complete Poems*, ed. Pat Rogers (Harmondsworth, Penguin, 1983).

Nicholas Thomas, Harriet Guest and Michael Dettelbach (eds), *Observations Made During a Voyage Round the World* (Honolulu: University of Hawaii Press, 1996).

Thomson, Janice E., *Mercenaries, Pirates and Sovereigns: State Building and Extraterritorial Violence in Early Modern Europe* (Princeton, NJ: Princeton University Press, 1994).

Tooley, R.V., *Maps and Map-makers* (London: B.T. Batsford, 1987).

Tuck, Richard, *The Rights of War and Peace: Political Thought and the International Order from Grotius to Kant* (Oxford: Clarendon Press, 1999).

Tucker, Josiah, *A Brief Essay on the Advantages and Disadvantages which respectively attend France and Great Britain with regard to Trade*. 4th edn (Glasgow, 1756).

Tully, James, *An Approach to Political Philosophy: Locke in Contexts* (Cambridge: Cambridge University Press, 1993).

Trumpener, Katie, *Bardic Nationalism: The Romantic Novel and the British Empire* (Princeton, NJ: Princeton University Press, 1997).

The Tryal of Captain Thomas Green and his Crew before the High Court of Admiralty of Scotland and the Assessors Appointed by the Lords of the Privy Council for Piracy, Robbery and Murder (Edinburgh, 1705).

van Haren, Onno Zwier and John Campbell, *The Sentiments of a Dutch Patriot, Being the Speech of **** (London, 1746).

Vickers, Ilse, *Defoe and the New Sciences* (Cambridge: Cambridge University Press, 1996).

Wales, William, *Remarks on Mr. Forster's Account of Captain Cook's Last Voyage Round the World* (London: J. Nourse, 1778).

Wallerstein, Immanuel, *The Modern World System II: Mercantilism and the Consolidation of the European World Economy, 1600–1750* (New York: Academic Press, 1974).

Watt, Ian, *The Rise of the Novel* (Berkeley, CA: University of California Press, 1965).

Wiles, Richard C., 'Mercantilism and the Idea of Progress', *Eighteenth-Century Studies* 8:1, 56–74.

Wilkinson, Clennell, *William Dampier* (London: John Lane the Bodley Head, 1929).

Williams, Neville, *The Sea Dogs: Privateers, Plunder and Piracy in the Elizabethan Age* (New York: Macmillan, 1975).

Williams, Raymond, *Culture and Society 1780–1950* (London: Chatto & Windus, 1958).

Williams, William Appleman, *The Contours of American History* (New York: W.W. Norton, 1988).

Williamson, James A., 'Richard Hakluyt', in Edward Lynam (ed.), *Richard Hakluyt and his Successors* (London: The Hakluyt Society, 1946), 9–46.

Wilson, Kathleen, *The Sense of the People: Politics, Culture and Imperialism in England, 1715–1785* (Cambridge: Cambridge University Press, 1995).

Wiltshire, John, '"From China to Peru": Johnson in the Travelled World', in Greg Glingham (ed.), *The Cambridge Companion to Samuel Johnson* (Cambridge: Cambridge University Press, 1997), 209–23.

Wolf, Eric R., *Europe and the People without History* (Berkeley, CA: University of California Press, 1982).

Wollstonecraft, Mary, *A Vindication of the Rights of Woman* (Harmoundsworth: Penguin, 1992).

Young, Robert J.C., *Colonial Desire: Hybridity in Theory, Culture and Race* (London and New York: Routledge, 1995).

Zimmermann, Heinrich, *Zimmermann's Captain Cook: An Account of the 3rd Voyage of Captain Cook around the world, 1776–1780*, ed. F.W. Howay and trans. Elsa Michaels and Cecil French (Toronto: The Ryerson Press, 1930).

Index

Acapulco, port of, 93
Africa, 24–5, 47, 53, 77–81, 83, 97,
  124
  see also West Africa
Allen, Richard, 38
America
  conquest of, 10, 160, 167
  discovery of, 10, 42, 93
  and imperial wealth, 18, 37, 93
  Revolution, 149
  see also North America; South
    America
ancients, 107, 122
Anderson, George, 160
Anglo-Irish, 104–5
anthropology, 3
anti-conquest, 1
Arendt, Hannah, 13
assiento, 37
atlas, 87–8, 90–7, 99, 197 n15
Atlas Maritimus and Commercialis,
  95–7

Bacon, Francis, 7, 11, 35, 161, 190
  n6
Bakhtin, Mikhail, 85
balance of power, 6, 53
balance of trade, *see* mercantilism
Baldavia, Port of, 93
Bank of England, 36
Banks, Joseph, 150, 174, 175
Batavia, 169
Beaglehole, John, 158, 170
Berry, William, 86
Blaeu, Johan, 87
Bligh, William, 28, 149–50, 156,
  169–79, 183
  'Dispatch to the Admiralty', 173
  'Letter to Sir Joseph Banks', 174
  Log of HMS *Bounty*, 170, 173, 174–5
  A Narrative of the Mutiny, 172–3
  Voyage to the South Seas 173, 174–6
Bonnet, Stede, 38

Bounty, *see* Bligh
Bourdieu, Pierre, 29
Brando, Marlon, 172
Braudel, Fernand, 185 n7
Britnell, Richard, 186 n11
Brobdingnag, 107, 109, 110–15
Brown, John, 126
Bry, Theodor de, 6
buccaneer, 23, 31–51
  see also piracy; privateer
Burney, James, 175
Bute, Lord, 127, 138
Byng, John, 123–4, 138

Campbell, John, 122
cannibalism, 38–9, 49, 61–3, 68,
  70–2, 77, 81, 105, 166–7, 200
  n52
captains
  authority of, 28, 151, 172–3
  and discipline, 27, 149–50, 168,
    175–6
  foresight of, 28 173, 175, 179
  humanity of, 27, 149, 151, 156–69,
    172, 175–6, 178
  and moral spectator, 27, 150–2, 158
  and scientific observation, 150, 159
Caribs, 39
Caribbean, 24, 53, 57, 65, 135, 150,
  169
  see also West Indies; Jamaica
cartography, 25, 85–7, 103, 119, 196
  n8, 197 n12, n16
  see also geography
Charlevoix, Pierre de, 101
Child, Josiah, 19, 53
Chile, 93
China, 74, 100
Cicero, 122
chorography, 85
Churchill, Awnsham and John, 97
Christian, Fletcher, 170, 172–3, 176,
  178